THE FIRST CHRISTIAN CENTURY
IN JUDAISM AND CHRISTIANITY

Samuel Sandmel is Distinguished Service Professor of Bible and Hellenistic Literature at Hebrew Union College-Jewish Institute of Religion, in Cincinnati. He received his doctorate in New Testament Studies at Yale University. A past president of the Society of Biblical Literature, Dr. Sandmel was made Honorary Principal of Leo Baeck College in London for 1968-69. He is the author of *We Jews and Jesus*, *The Hebrew Scriptures*, and *Herod: Profile of a Tyrant*.

OTHER BOOKS BY SAMUEL SANDMEL

A Jewish Understanding of the New Testament

Philo's Place in Judaism

The Genius of Paul

The Hebrew Scriptures: An Introduction to Their
    Literature and Religious Ideas

We Jews and Jesus

Herod: Profile of a Tyrant

We Jews and You Christians: An Inquiry into Attitudes

Old Testament Issues (editor)

THE FIRST CHRISTIAN CENTURY
IN JUDAISM AND CHRISTIANITY:

Certainties and Uncertainties

SAMUEL SANDMEL

NEW YORK
Oxford University Press
1969

To CHARLES LILLEY HORN
Lay Scholar and Patron of Scholarship

Preface and Apologia

About three decades ago, I thought of some day trying to write a definitive study of the first Christian Century in Judaism and Christianity, on the supposition that, having been trained in both Judaism and Christianity, I might possess the means of creating some synthesis of the often difficult and elusive materials. Toward that objective I made frequent notations on matters of interest and of bibliography, and kept these notations in a box for the time when I might be ready to turn to the task. The box is now well filled, and my impulse toward creating a synthesis is still present, but I no longer feel an urge to write something "definitive." This is simply because I have come to recognize that it is no longer possible for any man in one lifetime to know all the sources intimately, to master or even control all the scholarly literature (how it increases!) minutely, and to be able to balance all the factors appropriately. Moreover, it dawned on me that some 85 to 95 per cent of what I would write would merely repeat what is already in the public domain, and the 5 to 15 per cent that would be my own would scarcely justify the toil which the mere repetition of the standard data would entail.

I had the desire, too, to write a commentary on the Gospel According to Mark, and to that end I even wrote an article, "Prolegomena to a Commentary on the Gospel According to Mark," which appeared in the *Journal of Bible and Religion* in October 1963. Though I still hope to write on Mark, I will not write a commentary, but rather a series of connected essays, for I now feel that that form of expression can serve better than one more repetitious commentary.

I also became aware of a feeling which I would describe as reactive rather than initiatory: a deepening exposure to and penetration into the liberal Protestant scholarship forced my encounter with the ways in which fundamental questions were constantly being raised. As I observed view clashing with view, I came to suspect that some, or much, of the difference and divergency in the illuminating scholarship was possibly due to the wish of the scholars to know more than could be known. This reactive feeling led me to try to clarify for myself, beyond what the scholarship asserts, what it is that scholarship does not know, or does not know for certain. Let me give three examples. First, the theory that the Prologue to the Gospel According to John is derived from a pre-Christian Gnostic source led me to inquire into what we know about Gnosticism in general and pre-Christian Gnosticism in particular. Second, out of my fascination with Paul, I began to consider the question of possible Jewish predecessors of a traveling missionary, and I felt the need to discover just how much we know about this. Third, I wondered, how much do we really know about Peter and Paul in Rome?

My abiding impulse to fashion a synthesis, plus my wish to try to distinguish between knowledge that is certain and that

which is not, shaped these Lectures, which, at the kind invitation of the Dubuque Theological Seminary, I gave in
February 1967. The lectures as given numbered three, not
four; as given, they were less extended than the present written form; and, naturally, they were not accompanied by the
notes which the printed version offers. They are, nevertheless,
substantially the same.

I must confess that in the Lectures and in the book a selec-
tivity has obtained. This does not rest on any philosophical
basis, but exclusively on my own bent. For good or ill, a synthesis is always to a large extent subjective, or even whimsical.
Furthermore, I have always felt handicapped in one regard. I
have done considerable work in Philo, and in Tanach, and in
Rabbinics, but New Testament is the area of my concentration. I teach a prescribed elementary course in Introduction;
occasionally I have had students in electives, in the Gospels
or in Paul. But only a small portion of my teaching has been
in New Testament, and I have often wished that the otherwise
admirable academic scene at Hebrew Union College could
provide for advanced seminars wherein a face-to-face confrontation by peers on moot issues could take place. Unhap-
pily, I am normally able to find such confrontation only
through the written word; the sharpened focus that comes
only through teaching has usually been denied me.

I think that there is a broad—and erroneous—assumption
among Christians that Jewish scholars are Rabbinists simply
by virtue of being Jewish. I should say a word about my com-
petency in Rabbinics. When a little boy, I was enrolled in an
after-school Hebrew school; at eight or nine I was able to speak
Modern Hebrew with a fluency almost equal to English; from
eleven to about sixteen I was immersed in Talmudic studies,
this in the traditional Jewish way. This is to say that neither
the language nor the idiom nor the context of Rabbinic Literature is alien to me. When a student at Hebrew Union Col-

lege, I learned the scientific method. I fall short, however, of being a Rabbinics specialist or expert. I have not devoted, and do not devote, to Rabbinics the intensive attention that I do to New Testament and Philonic studies; there simply is not time. I cannot describe myself as an expert Rabbinist; perhaps I can describe myself as a responsible one.

From time to time the question is put to me, how does it chance that I, a rabbi, have become a New Testament specialist? It is a quite natural question, for certainly it is still rare for this to happen. This was essentially the result of pure accident, though perhaps beyond that it was caused by the juncture of a favorable setting and the chance meeting of two people. In 1939 I was appointed to Hillel, at the University of North Carolina, where I served until I entered the U. S. Navy in 1942. Soon after settling at Hillel, I journeyed the ten miles to Duke University, with the specific objective of enrolling in a Ph.D. program in Old Testament. Harvie Branscomb was at that time the Chairman of Biblical Studies. He broached the prospect of my doing the Ph.D. in New Testament instead of Old; he invited, and even encouraged, me to do so. I willingly accepted his solicitous guidance. It was all that simple and all that unpremeditated. Dr. Branscomb left Duke in 1946 to become the Chancellor of Vanderbilt University. There he established a Chair of Jewish Studies, to which he appointed me when I completed my Ph.D. at Yale, after the war.

Dr. Branscomb often said that I interested him because I was neither an ex-Jew nor an indifferent Jew, but a practicing Jew. It is true that I was born to a world of traditional Judaism, and educated to that world. But perhaps it is also that, as a Jew in America, the contrast between my personal fate and the fate of my fellow Jews in Europe is written indelibly into my consciousness. For during the period between my first meeting with Dr. Branscomb and my later appointment at

Vanderbilt, European Jewry was destroyed. I could be no other than a practicing Jew.

Beyond the narrowly personal aspect, I can say that I have always tried to teach my students not only the substance of nineteenth- and twentieth-century scholarship, but also something of the *Zeitgeist* that shapes scholars. Neither a Wellhausen nor a Harnack can be fully understood except in terms of their age and background. In no sense am I of their stature; I have thought, however, that the reader ought to have some notion not alone of my opinions but also of my presuppositions. Perhaps in seeking to identify myself to the reader I have provided a superabundance. If so, this has been more inadvertent than deliberate, and also the consequence of difficult matters of delicacy and proportion.

I have had many hours of discomfort working on the notes, and I must own up to a change in direction midway that forces me to revise those notes I had already completed. The problem is this: all the pages of this volume would be insufficient to list the relevant bibliographical entries alone. Let me here be candid. I have not read everything. Knowing what I have read, I am able to state that there is more that I have not read than there is that I have. Should the notes display the tremendous scope of the scholarly literature? Or should I utilize them not so much for bibliographic prowess as for more extended discussions that, if put in the text, would unduly rupture the flow? It is the latter, primarily, that I have decided on.

I think that I have not fully cited, or even mentioned by name, certain predecessors who have made me feel uncertain about first-century matters because they expressed their own uncertainties. In part, I am not able to identify some particular influence on me; in part I can scarcely now go beyond attributing such an influence only to the general body of the free Protestant scholarship. That is to say, my uncertainties are not so much new or original as they are appropriated and now my own.

There are many to whom I owe thanks. I am grateful to the Faculty and Dean Calvin Schnucker of Dubuque University for the warmth of the hospitality they extended to me when I gave these Lectures. Harvie Branscomb was my teacher, and he remains my mentor and unreservedly cherished friend. Professor Irvin W. Batdorf, Professor of New Testament Literature at the Union Theological Seminary at Dayton, spent his sabbatical at Hebrew Union College during the past academic year, studying Rabbinic and Philonic Judaism. In this I was most fortunate: he read my manuscript at various stages of revision; he constantly pushed me to greater clarity by challenging some of my formulations; and out of his own deep learning he pressed me to consider his criticisms. I am deeply in his debt. Finally, I have been inordinately blessed in Mrs. Sam November, my secretary. Her solicitude and loyal attention cannot be exceeded; they fall short, indeed, only of her skill. Not only I, but my wife and sons as well, are perpetually in the debt of this remarkable woman.

S. S.

London, England
January 1969

Contents

THE FIRST CHRISTIAN CENTURY
IN JUDAISM AND CHRISTIANITY

Introduction

I have attended, and have given, enough lectures to observe in them an implied liberty—a pronounced stress on the subjective views of the lecturer, as if he has the license to stray from academic impartiality and neutrality and trespass into personal opinion or even idiosyncrasy. Sometimes a lecturer tries to disguise these trespasses, either by a feigned objectivity or a self-deceiving one, but I am not sure that such disguise remains concealed from his audience. At any rate, in these lectures on the first Christian century, I not only have no wish to withhold the subjective and the highly personal, but indeed, I wish to set forth openly and clearly my own responses to a rather long period of scholarly inquiry, and to a good many efforts, some inevitably cursory or desultory, others protracted and persistent, to grapple with a most formidable field of study.

My own particular bent in dealing with the first Christian century is as a historian of religious ideas and not as a the-

ologian, and especially not pre-eminently as an apologist for
some traditional viewpoint or even traditional religion.[1] Respecting the latter, I can possibly be guilty of deceit, especially of deceiving myself. There is and has been no secret
of my Jewish affiliation or my Jewish loyalty, for the titles
of books I have written are clear on this. Yet as a professional
student, I hope I have been, and am, able to rise above a certain partisanship that afflicts research on the first Christian
century, a partisanship that has seemed to make it obligatory
for a Jew or a Christian in our day to apologize for and
defend one side of the opposing Jewish-Christian partisan-
ships which manifested themselves in that century and later.
I want to steer clear of such special pleading, but it is very
difficult to do so. I shall try, however, even at the risk of
being misunderstood. An example of the difficulty is this. I
would allege that there exists a recurring denigration of first-
century Judaism on the part of some or even many Christian
scholars. Yet insofar as I am aware of my intent in regard
to this, it is not to retort in pique, but rather to set the record
straight in terms of responsible and tenable scholarship.

I abstain from describing myself as a theologian because a
frequent definition of theology, especially since the days of
Schleiermacher, demands that theology as a discipline must
go beyond the mere analysis and classification of religious
ideas and tenets and must proceed to set forth their continued
relevancy. Such a definition of theology rules me out as a
theologian, for there is in the legacy from the first Christian
century very much that commands my interest as a student
but not my loyalty as a person. Indeed, more than one religious idea that I find fascinating to study I find personally
uncongenial, and some of the first-century ideas are even
markedly distasteful to me. (I have in mind here some facets
of material in Philo of Alexandria.)[2]

I do not suppose that a statement of self-description can

omit an admission, or proclamation, that I belong in the framework of free scholars, and therein should be classified with the liberals or the modernists, and not with the conservatives or with the orthodox. The Jewish legalism which I shall give some attention in Lecture II has historical interest for me, but I do not accept its literal binding authority, any more than would a free Christian scholar feel himself bound to accept the literal authority of doctrines explicit in the variegated Christian writings of the same period. It is a fact, of course, that there are scholars, and fine ones, who do accept the binding authority of major documents of that century. My self-description is not intended to asperse such scholars, but only to identify myself.

PIETY AND SCHOLARSHIP

I must own up to this, too. I have felt the impulse from time to time to flee from the study of the first Christian century for two quite unrelated reasons. The first of these is that I have often found myself out of tune with an intermixing of piety and scholarship which I encounter. It has seemed to me very often that piety has served as an obstacle to comprehension rather than a channel for it. This has been the case, for example, in certain Jewish works that represent the swing of the pendulum from the excessive denunciation of the Pharisees in the Gospels into responsive yet excessive adulation of them. In the same way, some of the scholarship on the Dead Sea Scrolls has resulted in opinions that these scrolls, far from being valuable only in themselves, have the additional special value of confirming, or refuting, Christian claims or Christian history.[3] I feel this also when I read that only a believing Christian can understand the Christian documents, on the basis that faith speaks only to faith;[4] I do not understand what there can be about the Christian ideas that render them so esoteric as to be beyond the comprehension of a diligent student of whatever background, or beyond the potential grasp of them by a non-Christian mind, if it is only nearly equal in capacity to a Christian mind. Moreover, if only a Christian can understand the Christian documents, it would seem to me reasonable that Christians would be automatically disbarred from understanding the non-Christian religions, both of the ancient world and of the modern world. Again, some of the recent New Testament scholarship has so eluded me on a very elementary level that I simply cannot grasp what the author is saying, as if the obligation to communicate is solely the reader's, and not the writer's.[5] For these reasons I find myself at odds with the tone of a substantial quantity of recent scholarly research, and, hence I have had, from time to time, the impulse to flee from it as essentially alien to my own person.

THE NATURE OF THE SCHOLARLY CHORE

But by far the greatest difficulty that I have is the sheer volume of the scholarship. It is as true to say that I have mastered much of it as it is to say that there is more of it that I have not mastered. It is also true to say that there is so much material that no one person can be the master of it all, but must own up to his lack of knowledge; there are areas in which he has a mere surface acquaintance of the materials, or here and there he has enough knowledge to control the data, yet only to a limited extent can he boast of genuine mastery. The language tools that need to be taken for granted necessarily include Hebrew, Aramaic, and Greek. Syriac, Latin, and even Coptic Ethiopic are highly desirable. French and German and Modern Hebrew are inescapable tools. Italian, Dutch, and the Scandinavian tongues have a relevancy and cannot remain totally unconsidered.

Furthermore, let me enumerate the types of literature one must know: Apocrypha and Pseudepigrapha, the Hellenistic Jewish literature, the Rabbinic Literature, the New Testament, the Apostolic Fathers, and the Apocryphal New Testament, and the works of the Greek and Roman pagan writers. It is also important to have some knowledge of such matters as the ways and manners of Roman colonial rule, the pagan religions and especially the mysteries, and the types of syncretism that mark the age. This totality is staggering enough to be discouraging. Then there are certain specific topics that demand attention: for example, institutions such as the local synagogue and the local church, the arrays of officials, the liturgy, the proposed solutions of the problems of theodicy, the division of time into the eras of this age and the coming age, and the import of the forms of interpretation of Sacred Scripture. All these constitute data for ingestion and digestion beyond human capacity.

THE LIMITS TO SCHOLARSHIP

Yet beyond this staggering bulk, especially if one is to know the secondary scholarly literature, there is another difficulty for me. It is this. Though I have on a number of occasions expressed my admiration for the quality of the scholarship that exists on the first Christian century, at the same time, the more I work in that century, the more persuaded I become that scholars have in significant part deceived themselves about the possibilities of exact and responsible conclusions. The bent among scholars seems to me that of knowing more than can be known; they seem to be certain—where I find myself tantalized by uncertainties. Scholars very often seem to consider themselves able to solve problems which, perversely, remain continuing enigmas to me. The paradox is that I believe wholeheartedly in the responsibility of scholarship to press on to ultimates, and at the same time I am oppressed by the conviction that the accumulated scholarship has tended to go farther than it can reasonably penetrate.

It is precisely this paradox of unlimited faith in scholarship, and inescapable reservations about it, that provides the theme for these lectures. Even while conscious of my own personal limitations and of my awareness that in some areas I must own up to the attenuated acquaintance virtually equal to ignorance, I have thought that there might be some utility in my setting forth some aspects of my quandaries—what I think I know and what I think I do not know, what I am unsure about, and points at which I find myself necessarily undecided. To use an absurd mathematical formula, I have a conviction that for every fact about the first Christian century that I can be sure about, there are nine pseudo-facts that I am unsure of; and great as is the collective knowledge in modern scholarship, the areas where we lack knowledge are immensely greater. If this contention is right, as I believe it is, it will also follow that much of the effort of scholars to provide correlations, and to make inferences from such alleged correlations, and to trace supposed developments, is at the minimum subject to substantial challenge, and at the maximum must necessarily be characterized as imaginative and ingenious and, at the same time, at least a little bit unsubstantial.

One reads that the passage, Galatians 3:19, "The Laws were ordained by angels," has yielded no less than 300 different explanations.[6] This multiplicity of explanations can be accounted for only by recourse to a rule-of-thumb: where the explanations are multiple, the evidence is necessarily minimal. The parallel is, of course, also true: where the evidence is minimal, the explanations will be multiple. But now to proceed.

Lecture I

The Significance of
the First Century

Certain startling developments took place during the first Christian century. At its start, the sons of Herod were allowed by the Romans to have certain royal prerogatives, and in a sense one might say, at least respecting Archelaus of Judea, that kingship existed; at the end of the first Christian century, kingship had disappeared from Judea for all time. At the beginning of the first Christian century, the Temple in Jerusalem was still operative, under the leadership of priests descended, at least in theory,[7] from Aaron; at the end of the first Christian century, the Temple lay in ruins and the sacrificial cult was at an end.[8] At the beginning of the first Christian century, the title of rabbi[9] was still unknown; at the end of the first Christian century, the Rabbinate was a flourishing institution. At the beginning of the first Christian century, there was as yet no final canon of the Hagiographa; possibly by the end of the first Christian century there was such a canon.[10] At the beginning of the first Christian century, Christianity had not come into existence; by the end of the first Christian century, not only had it come into existence, but it had come to be marked by internal differentiation and diversity; moreover, it had created substantial portions of that literature which in the second Christian century was destined to become virtually canonical. One must not make too many claims for the uniqueness of the first Christian century as contrasted with other centuries, but surely this tabulation indicates the broad range of highly significant developments and transitions which would be noteworthy even if there had been no lasting effect from what took place. But the fact is that the first Christian century witnessed developments whose influence is still to be felt with some full and tremendous force, even in our own time.

It is this latter circumstance which undoubtedly accounts for the desperate desire on the part of scholars to see the first Christian century in the greatest possible clarity and with the fullest possible security. But when I contemplate whether the desired clarity is attainable, I find myself troubled by a good many considerations. For example, I have wondered just how feasible it is for a modern citizen of the West, whether of Europe or of the Western Hemisphere, to project himself backward into the first Christian century and grasp its import and absorb its flavor and comprehend its essence.[11] Are we scholars possibly guilty of reading back into the first Christian century the dominant motifs from the second or third century?[12] Is it possible that data we possess about the first century has come down to us in distorted perspective, and that we attribute undue importance to some secondary items and render secondary some items which were, in the first century, no less than dominant?[13] It is to my mind quite possible that, consciously or unconsciously, scholars have tended anachronistically to attribute to first-century doctrines an overheightened emphasis, which such doctrines acquired only in our modern era—as, for example, seems to me the case with eschatology.[14] All too often, it seems to me, scholars have been unwilling to rest their hypotheses on the basis of what *may* have been so, and instead have insisted on what *must* have been so.

AREAS OF UNCLARITY
Literature

It must remain clear that I approve most strongly of the efforts of scholars to press ceaselessly toward the goal of fullest knowledge, and I do not lament at all that scholars in so many instances went beyond the reasonable evidence into unreasonable conclusions. Scholarship is at its best when it is self-critical, for at its best it contains within itself the best means of self-correction. My reservations might be stated in this way: there have emerged into the arena of public notice, scholarly assertions, made in good faith, which seem to me not so much wrong as unsubstantial and unsubstantiated. I think, for example, of various portrayals of so-called intertestamental Judaism[15] which are based on Apocrypha and Pseudepigrapha. That literature was thoroughly combed for its contents, and the attendant doctrines carefully sorted out and analyzed and then synthesized, and implicit or explicit weight was given to this or that item. I would allege that, in the process, we have been asked to believe that the individual author of some particular book—as for example, Tobit or Judith—represented both the author and his audience, and that the author's attitude was simultaneously a reflection of a broadly held antecedent position, and on the other hand, that the particular attitude permeated virtually the entire community. Now it is quite possible that there was such a thing as a mass-mind, or an aggregate of mass-

minds, but I am by no means persuaded that we are in position to be certain that individual formulation and group
acquiescence were so simple and ready at hand. In particular
I feel this most acutely in the case of the apocalyptic literature and the apocalyptic tendency, for I have a recurring
suspicion that even at the time this literature was being produced it elicited resistance as well as acquiescence.[16] That
such literature was copied and much of it translated into
Greek and into other languages necessarily implies that there
was some audience favorable to the literature, and, at least
in this sense, the author and some part of the audience which
read him were in tolerably good accord. To my mind, however, it is equally possible that individual apocalyptic books
represent acceptance by what I might call a limited coterie[17]
of the people, and I am quite in the dark as to whether the
influence extended beyond the coterie or was strictly limited
to it. Moreover, within the apocalyptic literature, there are
discernible some particulars which represent clash and conflict, as between the views expressed in one writing and views
expressed in another, and I am unable to decide for myself
whether these were direct head-on clashes, and reflect expression and prompt response, or whether the diversity of
formulations represent quite separate and separated viewpoints which never chanced to encounter each other, but
simply emerged from individual minds or from limited groups
that never encountered other minds or other groups which
held divergent viewpoints on the particular topics. I am
quite uncertain whether IV Ezra, with its remarkable inquiry into the origin of evil, reflects an antecedent mass-mind
and expresses its substance, or, on the other hand, is only a
remarkable creation by one mind which ultimately influenced
many minds.

We need to consider the possibility of a diversity of experience, in that one writing may have called forth immediate active response, and another may have gone relatively unnoticed. In dealing with Apocrypha and Pseudepigrapha, scholars have tried to tell us in the most precise terms where and when and in what language particular books were written,[18] and sometimes the scholars have seemed able to tell us whether the writer wrote with an ordinary pen or with a ballpoint. And even if we were prone to accept some one explanation of the diversity offered about the authorship of a given piece of writing, we would necessarily remain in the dark as to its readership, both in extent and in scope. Knowing when a particular work was written in no way enables us to know what the immediate or long-range effect of that writing was, even when we find it quoted at a later stage. Not only must we reckon with diverse elements in the Judean population—such groups as Pharisees, Sadducees, and Essenes, to whom we shall advert later—but, more broadly, it seems reasonable to me to suppose that the total population encompassed both the literate and the illiterate,[19] and also the avid readers of books and those who disdained reading.[20] (Even in our age of almost universal literacy, a very substantial portion of the population willingly abstains from reading anything—an impressive observation. I myself have had a fair amount of work published, and scarcely a week goes by that I do not receive a letter from someone with what I must describe as a remarkable flair for either misunderstanding or for pursuing idiosyncratic irrelevancies; indeed, from time to time I get a letter which begins: "I have not read your book but permit me to say. . . .")

I am by no means the first person to suggest that it is not feasible to generalize about the populace on the basis of the literary documents alone, for manifestly there are the nonliterary papyri that yield surprises,[21] and certainly our contemporary experience with popular religion should inhibit us from assuming that all minds work on the same level, and that all religious suppositions operated on a single dimension.

Judea and the Dispersion

There are two related phenomena that again confront me with a series of perplexities. Not only was there Judea, there were also Jews throughout the settled world, and, of course, Jews throughout the Graeco-Roman civilization. Indeed, the various studies of the spread of Jews in the Graeco-Roman world constitutes a problem; however much the statistical guesses[22] vary from each other, they all attribute to the Graeco-Roman Dispersion a Jewish population far in excess of that of Judea. Nevertheless, though it is the Judean scene that claims the major attention of modern scholars— as perhaps it should, for both Jesus and Rabbinic Judaism were Judean manifestations—what is most surprising is the almost total disinterest in Graeco-Roman Jewry that modern scholars seem to me to exhibit.[23] To my mind there is no question but that the Hellenistic experience of Jews, which began in the fourth pre-Christian century, is of signal importance, but I have not seen in the usual scholarly approach any effort to distinguish between the Jewish experience of the Hellenistic encounter as a totality[24] and the Diaspora experience of it as an important particular. If this phenomenon, of a lack of scholarly notice and interest, is at all to be explained, the explanation may conceivably go along this line, that the formative period in both Judaism and Christianity are Judean, and the Hellenistic Judaism was in the long run a *cul de sac*, so that Hellenistic Judaism can afford to be dealt with lightly, or ignored by both Jewish and Christian scholarship.[25]

Hellenization

I have elected to deal with Hellenistic, Dispersion Judaism in Lecture III; here I must abstain from entering into questions of substance. Yet, reverting to the mere statistical, there were Jews spread throughout the Graeco-Roman world, and these Jews lost their ancestral tongue and absorbed the Greek language; at least in this regard we can speak of Hellenization as a process. On the other hand, from the time of Alexander the Great, the Greek language came to be spoken in Judea itself and an abundance of Greek words made their way into the native Aramaic. If by Hellenization we mean only the phenomenon of the adoption of language, either in totality, as seems to have been the case of the Jews in Alexandria, or partially, as in the case of certain common words in Judea, then noticeable as such Hellenization was, it was still something of no great consequence. All too often, Hellenization has been conceived of in the scholarship as primarily a matter of geography, with the consequence that an Apocryphal or Pseudepigraphic work that appears to have been composed in Greek rather than Hebrew would necessarily represent an origin in the Diaspora, whereas if it appears to have been originally written in Hebrew or Aramaic, then it would have originated either in Judea or in the surrounding area. While I am prepared to assume that *in all probability* Jewish works written in Greek came from the Dispersion and Jewish works in Aramaic or Hebrew from Judea, I am by no means persuaded that this was *necessarily* so, for to my mind it is quite possible that works in Greek were composed in Judea[26] and works in Aramaic were composed in the Graeco-Roman Empire.

There are, however, aspects of Hellenization that go far

beyond language and that involve both religious ideas and institutions. What I think that I have missed in some of the acute discussions of Hellenization is the distinction which I would here draw between adaptation and apostasy. That apostasy from Judaism did occur is illuminated in the instance of Tiberius Julius Alexander, the nephew of Philo of Alexandria, who was made the general of the armies by Titus. Yet Philo himself has scarcely been exceeded in Jewish loyalty in the long history of Judaism, and still it is scarcely possible to imagine a figure in whom Hellenistic modes of thinking, and the substance of Hellenistic philosophy, could be more fully represented than Philo. How much of this "Hellenization" in Philo was conscious, and deliberately aimed for, and how much unconscious, we are quite unable to say. What is manifest is that even advanced Hellenization such as Philo's was not an instance of deliberate and chosen apostasy, but only a reflection of the impact of an environment upon a person. The Jewish Hellenizers, in the Maccabean period, including those who did away with the signs of circumcision, were unquestionably trespassing Jews, but nothing in the documents as I read them leads me to believe that they went to the extremity of conscious, deliberate apostasy.[27] At the risk of anachronizing, if I understand apostasy, especially when it is either Judaism or Christianity that one abandons, there is involved a conscious rejection of one tradition and the choice of another, and this is quite different from an unconscious syncretism wherein there is no conscious break at all with the inherited tradition but only the absorption of themes, motifs, or practices from an outside tradition.

Aspects of Syncretizing

It was George Foot Moore who pointed out what has been characteristic of Christian and Jewish syncretism: these traditions have borrowed only those values which they considered that antecedently they already had. The relevance of these observations seems to me to be this: Hellenization in the sense of unconscious adaptation was inevitable in the entire Graeco-Roman period and it was also inevitable in the first Christian century. That which was palpably alien, or which was not subject to rationalization as native and appropriate, was not absorbed; that which was absorbed was rapidly adopted and adapted. It seems to me that one might distinguish among three types of possible Hellenization,[28] which represent in part different degrees, but also in part different types: first, Hellenization in language, that is, the adoption of Greek, either with or without the abandonment of the Hebrew; second, the adoption of Greek modes of thought and even the content of Greek philosophy; and, third, the adoption of Greek ways of doing things. There is no dispute that there was a Hellenization in language; Greek words made their way into Palestine and are reflected in Rabbinic Literature.[29] As to philosophy, there are some echoes of Platonic and Stoic ideas in Rabbinic Literature[30] and recapitulations of Pythagorianism, Platonism, and Stoicism[31] in Philo, which I shall discuss in Lecture III. Yet there are issues one might raise at this point, particularly the possibility of the adoption and adaptation of limited facets of Greek religious practices, even within Judea. Thus, the sudden, ubiquitous use of wine[32] among Jews, in the *kiddush* welcome of the Sabbath, in the rite of circumcision, in the *Havdalah*,[33] in the marriage ceremony, in the Passover *seder*, must have had some kind of origin. No adequate basis seems to be discoverable from the Tanach. One theory, that of Erwin R. Goodenough,[34] that the broad use of wine was borrowed from a contact with the mysteries,[35] especially those of Dionysus, is not unreasonable, but it is disputed by some interpreters on the ground that Jews would not have borrowed anything at all from the

Greek mysteries. If this is the case, we are left with scarcely any means of explaining the abrupt flourishing of wine in Jewish ceremonies. On the one hand, we have no literary evidence by which we can assert that this particular borrowing took place; on the other, are we adequately setting ourselves into the Graeco-Roman period when we conclude in advance that Jews would find the borrowing of the broad use of wine inconsistent with their loyalty[36] to Judaism? I would imagine that the resistance to believing that Jews would do such borrowing would be less if it were not assumed by scholars that any such borrowing was necessarily total, and not merely selective. The argument seems to be that since Palestinian Jews remained monists and deliberately rejected dualism, then manifestly they would scarcely have borrowed the use of wine from the dualistic mystery religions. It does not seem to me that we possess the controls by which we can settle this particular issue of the wine, and just as I would not urge that it is true that such borrowing took place, I would at the same time not deny borrowing as a possibility. Indeed, in our own day I observe some types of Jewish borrowing—the Christmas tree becomes in some Jewish families a Chanukah "bush," and fancy wrapping paper and fancy string have made their way into Chanukah from the Christmas usages. I would also comment that I have been present when some Jews have been chided, openly or implicitly, for such borrowing, and they have asserted that they are borrowing an external, and in no way making any theological capitulation. Rather strangely, Jews can find among other Jews an incongruity in borrowing the Christmas tree, but no incongruity in borrowing Christmas wrappings for Chanukah gifts. I would denominate this as selective syncretism and I would therefore regard such selective syncretism as a broad possibility in the Graeco-Roman period.

In the same sense I would *not* deem it reasonable to assume that Jews would borrow emperor worship. The well-known story found in II Maccabees and IV Maccabees, which commends the woman Hannah and her seven children for preferring martyrdom rather than this capitulation, must imply that Jews saw a limit beyond which they could not go in the overt acceptance of Greek ways. I must note a difference between the two versions. In II Maccabees we are given a laconic narration of the martyrdom; in IV Maccabees the Stoic framework[37] into which the account is set is primary and the narration completely secondary, for it is now a sermon on how pious reason leads to the possession of the four cardinal virtues, enabling the woman and her children to be immune to the pain and destruction in the consuming fire. I suppose the issue to my mind is that I would define the rejection of emperor worship as falling within that area where Jews saw what they deemed reprehensible, yet where they did not recognize an item as inherently alien, they might readily absorb it. Accordingly, they would reject emperor worship, but not their understanding of Stoicism.

Palpable idolatry, it would seem to me, would be unmistakably recognizable as alien. But unconscious syncretism would work in a most subtle way; for example, the syncretism which might outrage one generation, as clearly embodying a disloyalty, might have seemed quite congenial to another generation, which could be unaware that it was borrowing what a preceding generation had regarded as something impossible to borrow. To introduce still another factor, it is to my mind quite conceivable that what Jews in one particular place would find distasteful to borrow, Jews in another place would have no reluctance about borrowing. The account in Josephus of the effort to assassinate Herod in his detested theater at Jerusalem, this approximately 10 B.C., would reflect not only an antipathy to Herod but the recorded antipathy to theater; on the other hand, how shall we understand Ezekiel,[38] the tragic playwright from whom a fragment of the great drama called "The Exodus" has been preserved?

If all these comments are in order, then the reasonable conclusion is this: the modern scholar is quite unable to be precise about what there was in Hellenism that Jews would necessarily reject. He could be certain only in extreme cases, such as the refusal to bow down to idols or to bow down to the emperor. But short of these extremes, there is the possibility that Jews might have borrowed almost anything, from language through ideas and even forms or rites.

Indeed, what seems to me most striking about the first Christian century and the matter of Hellenization is that we must reckon with the antecedent aggregation of an advanced measure of Jewish-Greek syncretism already considered traditional by that time. Jews inherited from the third, second, and first pre-Christian centuries aspects of Hellenized Judaism which by the first Christian century they took to be normal Judaism. It was in the third pre-Christian century that the encounter with Hellenism was the sharpest, when the rejection was the most acute.[39] But, conceivably, what might well have been shocking in the third pre-Christian century was quite likely to have been stabilized and acceptable by the first Christian century,[40] especially in matters that would not involve overt forms. Thus, if as early as the sixth pre-Christian century, as I believe was the case, *hochmah*, wisdom, and *torah*, revelation, were already identified, and if in succeeding centuries *hochmah* came to be personified and then hypostasized, and if in the third pre-Christian century *hochmah* came to be equated with *sophia* and with *logos*, then by the first Christian century, the identification of *torah* and *logos*[41] would already have been traditional. If this is so, neither John nor Philo was innovating anything in describing their religious outlooks in terms of the *logos;* by their time this was a normal form of expression for them.

If only we knew more about the kind of communication[42] that went on between Dispersion Jews and the religious leadership in Judea, we would be able to see more clearly to what extent there was a substantial difference in the acuteness and extent of Hellenization in Judea and the Dispersion. In theory, there was more likelihood of more advanced, yet innocuous, Hellenization in the Dispersion than in Palestine; but while that theory helps us to understand the developments, we should abstain from being bound by it, and avoid some modern anachronistic preconceptions which would dictate that Jewish Palestine rejected every kind of Hellenization and that Dispersion Judaism accepted it only in externals.[43]

The Missionary Impulse

If Hellenization represents a certain inroad from the outside into Judaism, then the reverse of the process, the Judaization of the outside, or at least some portion of it, demands consideration. It is perhaps a viable distinction to differentiate between welcoming into a community an outsider who volunteers to enter, as was the case with Ruth, and pursuing an active, aggressive movement designed to persuade outsiders to enter. By a missionary movement I believe that we would mean something different from the mere passive reception of would-be proselytes.[44] Virtually all the evidence available concerning outsiders joining themselves to Judaism deals with passive reception, as exemplified in the case of the kingdom of Adiebene[45] and also the "God-fearers," [46] or half-proselytes, mentioned from time to time. Significantly, the Rabbinic Literature not only ascribes to some of the most eminent of the rabbis an extraction from converts to Judaism, but even makes converts of the descendants of the wicked Haman.[47] What remains elusive, however, is the question of a Jewish missionary movement. The testimony of Matthew 23:15 need not be set aside; it should rather persuade us that at least the Pharisees maintained or countenanced something of a missionary movement. The figure of Paul, however, seems to be without any direct forerunner,[48] and it is difficult to know whether it was his newly found convictions, especially the eschatological, that propelled him into his missionary labors, or whether there was ample precedent before his time to account for the phenomenon. Was Paul unique in Jewish history in being an active, traveling missionary, or does his uniqueness lie in the kind of missionary that he was? We do not know. The Didache and the Didascalia are not so much missionary handbooks as they are manuals for would-be proselytes. Curiously enough, the Rabbinic Literature conceives of Abraham, and of Sarah, as master missionaries, dedicated to converting Gentiles, and it attributes to the Haran episode (based on the wording of Genesis 12:5) a great moment of mass proselyting.[49] Yet the sources do not inform us in any rounded way about active missionary movements, and we do not know of even one Jewish missionary who might be mentioned in some analogy to Paul.

Contacts with Gentiles

We are in the dark with respect to how facets of the Judean population, ranging from the lofty upper classes, through the middle class, to the lower classes, would have had sufficient contact with the Greeks to explain the diverse forms or extents of Hellenization. Though Josephus makes it plain that Judea was dotted with Gentile cities, some of which were Grecian cities and not simply Syrian or Phoenician, I do not recall anything that he tells us that would throw full light on this matter of daily contacts.[50] Indeed, we have a comparable paucity of information about contact between Judeans and Samaritans[51] and are unable to go beyond an impression of a general hostility into any comprehension of what day-to-day contacts might have existed. I am by no means sure that the animosity between Judeans and Samaritans was duplicated between Jews and Greeks. To my mind it is not necessary to attribute to Jew and Greek the same type or profundity of animosity which marked Jew and Samaritan, for animosities in religion are deepest where there is overlap and rivalry, and they can be inconsequential where the difference is almost total. That some of the so-called Jewish fragments preserved in Eusebius and in Josephus represented Samaritans indicates that the Samaritans, too, spread beyond Judea and engaged in literary activity, and we must therefore keep in mind the probability that the Samaritans to some extent too were Hellenized. In the court of Herod, just prior to the first Christian century, we find the Syrian Greek Nicolaus[52] of Damascus serving in a high capacity as counsellor, and the Spartan charlatan Eurycles[53] well received, but I know of nothing in Josephus to suggest that a gifted Samaritan would have found any such opportunity in Herod's court.

THE SIGNIFICANCE OF THE PLURAL SECTS

When I speak of Sadducees, Pharisees, Essenes, Therapeutae, and the like,[54] and, in this context, Christians also for at least part of the century, I find it essential to keep reminding myself that all these groups or sectaries or sectarians were Jewish. Granted that they differed from each other in certain ways, and that some of the ways can be classified as antithetical, as for example, the Pharisees and the Sadducees on the oral law, still it is essential to note that, since they were all Jews, what they had in common was overwhelmingly greater than what it was that separated them. To put this in another way, we must conceive of them as differing profoundly, indeed most profoundly, on only limited aspects of their common Judaism. Indeed, we must make provision in our thinking for the possibility of differences within a relatively homogeneous grouping being quite as significant as the differences between heterogeneous groups. For example, the disputes recorded in Rabbinic Literature between the academy of Hillel and the academy of Shammai[55] might possibly be classified as intra-Rabbinic disputes or an intra-Pharisaic series of disputes, yet they took place in the framework of common presuppositions.

If there is danger in assuming a certainty of knowledge about the divisions and subdivisions in the populace and about the hypothetical values that they invested in their religious ideas, how much the more formidable becomes the problem of equating the Apocryphal and Pseudepigraphic literature not only with specific times, but also with segments of the population, as has been done so often? It is quite customary to equate IV Ezra with the Pharisees, and, perhaps, this is an identification with which we need not quarrel. But in another sense, we must ask ourselves the question, what have we gained when we have made the identification? Do we understand IV Ezra any better when we label it Pharisaic?

My reason for stressing the heterogeneity of the population and the impossibility of allocating "intertestamental" literature to particular groups is to suggest that in the developments in the first Christian century we simply do not deal with straight-line trends and tendencies susceptible of neat separation from each other. Rather, we deal with currents and cross-currents, with competing views on many levels and in many dimensions.

RABBINIC JUDAISM

Out of the flux and out of the flow and out of the conflicts and out of the differences emerged the two surviving facets of first-century Judaism, namely, Rabbinic Judaism and Christianity. We must not delude ourselves into believing that what emerged necessarily had to emerge, or that we are able to specify the exact causes which led to the precise effects, whether in the case of Rabbinic Judaism or in the case of Christianity. True, in the case of one event, the destruction of the Temple in A.D. 70, we can see clearly many aspects of cause and effect. Manifestly, Rabbinic Judaism would probably not have emerged to its uncontested leadership in the first century had the Temple not been destroyed. Yet possibly Rabbinic Judaism was only propelled forward by this single event. Its roots are multiple and they developed before the first century. Its shoots arose in a variety of directions before A.D. 70; possibly the events of 66–70 forced a kind of consolidation of divergent elements. In this sense, the events of 70 hastened a development which I am persuaded would have come about without the destruction of the Temple, but the *de facto* end of the sacrificial cult and of the priesthood necessitated the development of Rabbinic Judaism. Indeed, the Rabbinic Literature, which is characterized by the relative absence of any historical sense, has its clearest reflection of *some* knowledge of history in its frequent allusions to the incident of the destruction of the Temple. Apart from this event, the Rabbinic Literature gives the over-all impression of something static, not that of historic movement or of historic self-understanding. That series of events, such as the deposing of Archelaus in A.D. 6, the list of Roman procurators from 6 to 41, the rise of the Sicarii and the agitations which culminated in a revolt that began in

66—all this material is virtually lacking in the Rabbinic Literature. The stray data that are present do not lend themselves to being arrayed into any intelligible sequence of events or into a clear depiction of what was happening and why and how. The destruction in 70, accordingly, is in this sense the single item of historical occurrence that commands the attention of the rabbis and seems fixed in their memory. We must, of course, observe that caution to which responsible scholars have alerted us, of not detaching 70 from the subsequent Jewish history, especially the Bar Kochba rebellion. We should, accordingly, interpret 70 as a symbol of multiple changes, and not simply as a date. With this qualification, there can be no question that 70 is the key event in the history of Judaism in the first Christian century. Perhaps one can even say that it is the key date in the history of postbiblical Judaism.

The event of A.D. 70, however, must not blot out from our vision the wide range of a variety of Jewish thinking and of Jewish experience not directly related to it. Indeed, the various messianic movements, apart from that with which the name Jesus is associated, imply the birth and the growth of a whole garden of religious ideas and religious sentiments and of religious pre occupations. At least one of these might here be mentioned, namely the emergence of an association of ideas, a joining of the concept of the messiah with that of universal judgment on mankind and with that of the resurrection of the dead. The idea of the messiah is older; the idea of the universal judgment is older; the idea of the resurrection is older. In the first century these ideas have already become intertwined. Yet still other religious ideas besides these were to be found in the populace, even though we can see them only dimly and cannot always see their relationship to each other. Those tendencies that flowered into that vague business, Jewish gnosticism, or into practical mysticism, or, indeed, into mysticism itself, cannot be excluded from our vision, even though we encounter acute problems about these movements in general and even more acute problems when we try to array them into some orderly place in the first Christian century.

AUTHORITY

I wish that we could see clearly the role of monarchy in first-century Judea, and, indeed, the role of the authority of the person, whether of the monarch or the high priest. The last king, Agrippa II, is most indistinct, even in the pages of Josephus; like old soldiers, he simply fades away.[56] Can we assume that whereas a Hyrcanus prompted the farcical trial of Herod by the Sanhedrin, Herod himself, when king, could virtually liquidate it? After the deposing of Archelaus in A.D. 6, did the procurators regard the Sanhedrin in some way as their surrogates? Did high priests truly have that authority which Acts 9:1-2 describes, of extraditing dissident persons, as from Damascus?[57] When Agrippa I assumed the limited throne in 38-39, where did authority lie? In what sense was some of the royal authority transmitted, or acquired by the rabbis after 70, culminating in the patriarchate[58] of the second Christian century? In a general way, I think that a pattern is discernible; what troubles me is my inability to see the precise steps, and to feel on secure ground respecting specific periods and specific persons and genetic developments.

Moreover, I fail to see a clear relationship between this question of the authority of persons and the more significant question, the authority of the tradition. Indeed, I feel that Jewish scholars, fully cognizant of the authority of the tradition, all too often abstain from inquiring into the question of the authority of persons, and Christian scholars seem to confront this question of the authority of persons primarily in relationship to the Sanhedrin and Jesus.

THE RELIGION OF A BOOK

What seems to me even more serious is the failure adequately to note the key to the century, both of the development of Judaism and also of Christianity, namely the import of a religion of a Book. I see no reason to doubt that, even prior to the first Christian century, the Torah and the prophets had already come to be "canonical," and I suspect that Psalms was equally so regarded. I am by no means sure that the canon of the Hagiographa was completely fixed by the end of the first Christian century, even though I am one of those who is willing to use the Council of Jamnia in A.D. 90 as a convenient date and place for the final fixing of the canon. The ignoring of Daniel as a prooftext for resurrection, with Daniel the only one of the thirty-nine books that has an explicit statement of resurrection, may be significant or it may not be; both the Gospels and the Rabbinic Literature "prove" resurrection from the Pentateuch.[59] It is quite likely that the Pentateuch was the authoritative book and hence it is possible that resurrection had to be proved from it. But I am puzzled as to why the last verses of Daniel were not cited, either in the Rabbinic Literature or in the Gospels, as the prooftext for resurrection. Could it be that Daniel, while sacred to some Jews, had as yet not achieved that consensus of sacredness to all Jews which canon implies?

But the bare circumstance that the Pentateuch was appealed to to prove resurrection is in itself an example of what may be subsumed under the rubrics of a Book religion. Not only was Scripture studied, but Scripture was necessarily interpreted—on one level in the literal sense, in that it was translated from the Hebrew into the Aramaic Targum, so as to be intelligible to the populace. Beyond that level, the process of more advanced forms of interpretation represents a type of religious experience which seems to me quite different from the religious experience of merely worshiping at the Temple under the direction of hereditary priests. Here two different items command some attention. The first is the growth of "oral" law, under a theory which supposed that, along with the written revelation of the Pentateuch to Moses, there was an accompanying oral revelation, equally authoritative and equally binding. The attitude found in the Gospels (Mark 7:8; Matthew 15:3,6) that the "tradition of the elders" was a human achievement,[60] not a divine one, is totally at variance with the attitude of the Pharisees, and of others who believed in the oral law. There can be no question that the concept of an oral revelation was the device by means of which divine authority could be invoked for attitudes and doctrines and legal inferences that are not explicit in Scripture. To put this more precisely, divine authority could be invoked for innovations, and the innovations regarded as not really innovations, but only as a later articulation of something already contained in the pristine revelation to Moses.

The Jewish process of deriving innovations from the scriptural text by types of exegesis, however artificial they may seem to our age, is not so much Jewish as it is a natural concomitant to any religious tradition which enshrines a body of ancient writing as its sacred scripture. When once the idea is set forth that an innovation can acquire divine authority, and implicit antiquity, this through being part of an oral revelation, and when judicious prooftexting can guarantee the acquired authority, then promptly the possibility of abuse can arise.

When once interpretation in general is sanctioned, the question is this: are there legitimate ways and also untenable ways in which Scripture may be interpreted? To Hillel, whose dates are guessed at as encompassing a public career from 30 B.C. to A.D. 10, there are attributed a series of seven norms of interpretation, the so-called Seven Rules of Hillel, which rules were expanded to thirteen by Rabbi Ishmael ben Elisha, who flourished at the end of the first Christian century and the beginning of the second century.[61] If these norms or rules of interpretation were designed to legitimize certain forms of exegetical reasoning and hermeneutics, then it is equally likely, or even more so, that the same norms were also intended to delimit or to prohibit. Passing allusions in Rabbinic Literature to two types of ancient interpreters, the *dorshe reshumot* and the *dorshe hamurot*[62] ("interpreters of signs" and "interpreters of parables"), are both ordinarily taken to be allusions to allegorical modes of interpretation. In context, at one stage these appear to be regarded as an archaic and no longer valid type of interpretation.

The allegories that abound in Philo show absolutely no relationship to the rules laid down by Hillel and Ishmael, and quite conceivably Philo's allegories[63] would have been ruled improper had they come to the notice of the tradition which espoused the seven or the thirteen rules of interpretation. We do not see in fullest clarity what the implication of the rules was, but when we notice the kinds of interpretation found in the Qumran Scrolls—for example, in the Commentary on the Book of Habakkuk—then we are aware of what we might define as unrestrained fancy, if we were to speak from the perspective of the Hillel-Ishmael chain. At the minimum, despite our inability to be precise in fixing the types of differing interpretation, we can be aware that there were variant modes of interpretation in differing parts of the populace. Most important, we glimpse the experience of a Book religion becoming heterogeneous and perhaps even fragmented.

From time to time, various theories or variations of the same theory have arisen which suppose that scriptural interpretation began in Alexandria,[64] and then moved to Judea. I have remained unpersuaded by the arguments, and I have seen no reason to suppose that a native Judean series of types of hermeneutical principles could not have arisen. To my mind it seems quite logical that, in the growing centrality of Scripture, interpretation and exegesis inevitably were born, and within Judea. Out of the differing modes of exegesis, there arose the effort to set norms and limits so as to exclude what to some seemed to be farfetched and excessively imaginative and also irresponsible. One does not need Alexandria to understand scriptural interpretation in Judea.

Yet the very notion of the development of rules of interpretation and the suggestion that such rules arose to delimit, to rule out other types, should alert us to the varieties, and should make intelligible to us the presence of the diverse modes of interpretation, and the diverse results of it, as among the Qumran community, Philo, Paul, and the Epistle to the Hebrews.

In all such interpretation, the basic process has seemed to me to be primarily, though not exclusively, this: that an innovator had his idea or his prepossession to begin with, and thereafter he justified it by recourse to Scripture. I am aware, of course, that those who pored over Scripture were prompted by Scripture to create their innovations. Yet prooftexting as such, the seeking of a scriptural sanction for an innovation, would imply to my mind that first came the conclusion and then only thereafter the prooftext.

So broadly did Scripture and interpretation come to characterize Jews, wherever they were, that interpretation, whether within the Hillel-Ishmael norm or outside of it, was inescapable. What here deserves notice is a recurrent tendency on the part of scholars to ascribe to Paul the methods of the rabbis, as if interpretation were limited to this one aspect of first-century Jewish life. There is scarcely any doubt that the conclusions Paul drew from his citations of Scripture are the reverse of the Rabbinic, and the convenient summary that has been made that Paul argues like a rabbi for non-Rabbinic purposes[65] represents an inadequate comprehension of the broad extent of the interpretive processes. The conclusion seems to me inevitable that one need not suppose some Rabbinic influence on Philo and Paul, simply on the basis that they both engaged in scriptural prooftexting.

Yet perhaps it might be put in a somewhat different way; the religion of a Book not only sets up the Book as the authority, with the result that innovations needed to be squared with it, but also the Book itself begets innovations, insights, doctrines, perceptions, perspectives, all of which open new horizons of religious speculation and religious dedication. Those portions of the Dead Sea Scrolls which seem clearly to reflect a disillusionment with the Temple cult,[66] and an abandonment of it, could have taken place only when, by implication, the Book rivaled or supplanted the Temple cult in the minds of those willing to abandon the cult. Had there been no Bible, there would have been no such defection from the cult. That there was defection, even prior to the termination of the cult in A.D. 70, attests to the force and influence of Scripture.

Such a conclusion would in no way surprise us respecting the Dispersion, for while Jews could not carry the Temple with them, they could carry Scripture. We need to reckon with loyalty to Judaism, accompanied by the willing contributions to maintain the Temple through the tax of a half-shekel, and the later *fiscus judaicus;* and even if we can concede that adherence to the Jewish group was a matter primarily of *ethnic*[67] loyalty, Scripture in turn was the rock on which ethnic loyalty was built; it was the scriptural laws that were the Jewish laws the Romans recognized as a privilege of Jews to maintain in their Dispersion. While the influence of Scripture in this sense of the unifying force is readily understandable in the Dispersion, perhaps it is not quite as understandable in Judea, where there was geographical proximity to the Temple. The very quantity of biblical interpretation produced in Judea, and the depth of this interpretation, would to my mind attest to the permeation of Jewish communities within Judea by Scripture, and by a deep devotion to it, and by the desire to know it, and by the impulse to interpret it. Indeed, the Pseudepigraphic literature, in attributing the authorship of late books to the ancient characters of Scripture, is, in this very process, an attestation of the peoples' intense concern with Scripture.

EDUCATION

The assumption that Scripture permeated the Jewish awareness necessarily implies a broad spread of knowledge, whether by oral or written instruction. Obviously, the academic tradition in the *yeshivot*[68] ("academies") implies a type of learning and education that one would scarcely attribute to the ordinary Jew; it is quite likely that formal illiteracy was widespread. What must be inferred, however, is that the ordinary Jew did have relatively broad knowledge and relatively high education. The saying in Rabbinic Literature that an *am ha-aretz*[69] ("a person of the land") cannot be pious has often been taken to imply an arrogance on the part of the educated as over against the uneducated, and, naturally, if it reflected arrogance, we would all set ourselves against arrogance. It is more likely, however, that this sentiment is not so much arrogance as merely a statement of fact—that a person who adheres to a Book religion can scarcely be pious if he does not know the Book. One is here reminded of the incident of the Ethiopian eunuch in Acts of the Apostles 8:26–40, who reads Isaiah, and who asks the question, "How can I [understand], unless some one guides me?" Whether the incident is historical or not is irrelevant, for clearly its point is that one can be influenced by the Bible only if he knows and comprehends its contents.

That there were ignorant people is, of course, self-evident, but that one could be an authentic Jew, or authentic Christian, and totally ignorant of Scripture (this in the age prior to the growth of the Church into its elaborate medieval form) is to my mind unthinkable. While I would be willing to concede that Paul on occasion expounded Scripture to those who did not yet know it, I would insist that those who responded to Paul inevitably became acquainted with Scripture. Scripture necessarily permeated the Christian community, and we can never understand the way in which Old Testament reappears in paraphrase or quotation throughout the Gospels except on the basis of the permeation of Christians by Scripture. Parenthetically, the supposition that because Matthew gave elaborate citations of Scripture he must have been Jewish by birth is quite unnecessary; he may have been Jewish by birth, but this is in no way indicated simply by the fact that the Gospel According to Matthew abounds in scriptural quotations.[70]

Not only is the question of authority insufficiently raised respecting Rabbinic tradition, but its two aspects, that of persons and that of a literary corpus of a tradition, are insufficiently confronted respecting Christianity. The key word here is *insufficiently;* the pericope (especially Mark 1:22 and parallels) that describes Jesus as differentiated from the scribes as teaching "with authority" seems to me to have tremendous import and significance for subsequent times, as I shall suggest in Lecture IV.

POPULAR SUPERSTITION

It is always difficult to distinguish between religion and superstition, and certainly even more difficult to distinguish between popular religion and superstition. All too often the distinction has been that if it is mine, it is religion; if it is yours, it is a superstition. It is also necessary to note that in our time there is a significant difference between the intellectuals within a religious tradition and the ordinary practitioners of it, and that what seems to some practitioners to be the essence of religion is to the intellectuals nothing other than superstition. If we were to assume for the moment that the knowledge of Scripture and depth in that knowledge constituted a level of religion different from superstition, then we must be willing to understand that, in lower levels of the populace, superstitions and aspects of folk religion abided. What we must not do, however, is to assume that intellectuals, whether then or now, are completely free of superstition or of reflections of popular religion. What I am pointing to is that in addition to being permeated by Scripture, the populace also had an elaborate angelology and, related to it, a demonology. I rather suspect that since angels are mentioned in the Old Testament as ordinary divine messengers, we have a greater reflection of experience with angels than we do of demons; yet I imagine that to the ordinary person, the situation was reversed and he had more experience with demons than with angels. As early as the days of the composition of the Book of Daniel, the angels had come to be individualized and were endowed with specific names and specific titles.[71] As to demons, scholars have noted that Rabbinic Literature gives us three classes of them, and Johanan ben Zakkai, the first-century rabbi, is said to have known 300 kinds (Gittin 68A).

I suppose that the essential difference between an angel and a demon is that an angel is one who does good and a demon one who does evil. Yet one must be on guard making such a distinction, for it may well be a modern one, and there is some evidence that the words angel and demon had at times an interchangeable connotation.[72] Just as there was not necessarily an evil connotation in the word demon, so there was not necessarily a benevolent connotation in the word angel. Accordingly, when Paul speaks (Galatians 3:19) of the law as being mediated by angels, it is as legitimate on the face of things to interpret these angels as malevolent ones as benevolent ones, and it is only the full context in Paul that would tend to establish what his intention was. The passage, I Corinthians 11:10, that women should have their hair covered because of the angels, readily lends itself to the suggestion that has often been made that Paul here means what we would call demons; the same suggestion does not appear to be made as strongly, though probably it should, respecting the angels mentioned in Galatians 3:19.

Yet the question that one must raise is not whether there are sufficient scholarly studies of demonology and angelology respecting Old Testament, intertestamental literature, New Testament, and Rabbinic Literature, for this material has been worked over again and again. What is more to the point is, first, the manner in which modern scholarship finds it quite convenient to de-emphasize demonology and angelology, probably on the principle that it is primarily the matters of ongoing relevancy which should claim scholarly attention, and second, the circumstance that, beginning with the Protestant Reformation, the belief in literal angels and demons began to disappear, and this supposedly justifies the diminution of modern attention to the angels and demons of first-century Christianity[73] and of Judaism. What I am protesting is a present-day disposition; angels and demons loom much larger in the first-century literature than they do in the modern interpretation of it, and, anachronistically, scholars quite normally depict Paul, Jesus, and the rabbis as if they lived in our own modern, naturalistic, demonless world. Yet to what exact extent the people of the first century believed their lives to be influenced or controlled by demons eludes me.

In the foregoing, what I have stressed is the limitation on our knowledge, or rather, the limitation on our precise knowledge. The amount that we know is overbalanced by the greater amount that we do not know. Much of what we do know, we know only inexactly. The first Christian century is a congeries of uncertainties, of reasons for scholarly doubts, and reasons for scholarly insecurities.

Notes

1. I wrote in "The Jewish Scholar and Early Christianity" (*Jewish Quarterly Review*, 1967, Seventy-Fifth Anniversary Volume, pp. 473–81), that I regard my obligation not to the Pharisees but to the truth.

2. I cannot share in the repeated themes of an ascetic bent which almost equal a deliberate mortification of the flesh. At such points Philo seems to me unhealthy-minded. I am amused by his denunciation of the Sodomites for their Roman meals (*The Contemplative Life*, 60–62; see also *On Abraham*, 135–6), in that at the Jewish Passover *seder* as observed in my parents' home there was retained at least one vestige of the Roman meal, the "reclining," by the father on a pillow on his chair. This reclining appears even in the "four questions" that the youngest child asks: "Why do we, this night, recline?"

3. I have in mind recurrent articles in various media by John Allegro who uses the Scrolls to assert the absence of any originality on the part of Christianity.

4. Some eighteen years ago this motif that "faith speaks only to

faith" was rather frequent among interpreters. I encountered one formulation of it, which I have recently searched for in vain, that went on to imply, or even to state, that a non-Christian cannot understand Christianity. At the time I was reading this, Rudolf Bultmann was lecturing at Vanderbilt University, where I was then teaching. I showed him the passage. As I recall, his comment was that the statement was incorrect respecting the externals, such as events and doctrines, but correct respecting the internal act of faith. I was, and remain, unconvinced; indeed if it is true that a non-Christian cannot understand Christianity, then I have been engaged in a fruitless occupation. Moreover, at what stage does a convert to Christianity come to understand it? If only after his conversion, then can his conversion be authentic? If before his conversion, then is it true that a non-Christian cannot understand Christianity?

5. I do not have in mind a work such as Karl Barth's *Commentary on Romans*, which I found incomprehensible, for I take the work to be more parenetic than academic, and poetic exhortation kindred to the manner of Martin Buber, in *The Prophet*. Rather, I am thinking of strictly academic works such as James Robinson, *The New Quest for the Historical Jesus*. I did not, and do not, find such obscurity in the older scholarship; in fact, the older scholarship seems dedicated to clarity.

6. See J. R. Cohu, *S. Paul in the Light of Modern Research*, p. 46n.

7. The capricious deposing and appointing of high priests by Herod (see my *Herod: Profile of a Tyrant*, pp. 121, 177) and by Valerius Gratus (see Josephus, *Antiquities of the Jews*, XVIII, 34–5; Gratus deposed no less than five high priests) scarcely lends credence to the *de facto* retention of Aaronide descent as a prerequisite; so too, E. G. Hirsch, *Jewish Encyclopedia*, "High Priest," VI, esp. p. 393.

8. See Kenneth Clark, "Worship in the Jerusalem Temple after A.D. 70," in *New Testament Studies*, VI (1960), pp. 269–80, and Alexander Guttmann, "The End of the Jewish Sacrificial Cult," *Hebrew Union College Annual*, XXXVIII, pp. 137–48.

9. See *Jewish Encyclopedia* and *Interpreter's Dictionary of*

the Bible, "Rabbi." In the former, the ending *iy* is interpreted as a possessive pronominal afformative which lost its
possessive sense. Albright, on the other hand, has called the
form a "caritive"; I see no gain in this dubious terminological
crotchet. One notes the total vagueness about "rabbi" in the
circumstance that *Interpreter's Dictionary of the Bible* has
various entries: "Doctor," "Master," "Rabbi," and "Teacher."

10. I would stress that the information respecting the Hebrew
canon is so sparse as to reveal almost nothing about the
process of canonization and its time and place, and that
"Jamnia 90" is a harmless convention, and not a known fact.
Respecting the Alexandrian canon and the process, we know
absolutely nothing. The article "Canon," by R. H. Pfeiffer,
Interpreter's Dictionary of the Bible moves from the cautious
statement, ". . . we may fix the closing of canon by the
canonization of the Writings, *ca.* A.D. 90," (p. 509) into the
statement (p. 510): "Under the leadership of Johanan ben
Zakkai, the Council of Jamnia (*ca.* A.D. 90) closed the third
canon." Pfeiffer provides a good bibliography; I would
commend especially P. Katz, "The O T Canon in Palestine
and Alexandria," *ZNW* (1956), Vol. 47, pp. 191–217. See
page 94, note 2.

11. The issue here is not so much that of how full and reliable
is our accumulation of fact, but the import, and the weight,
of those facts in the ancient setting. Can we ever completely
shed our innate disposition to recreate the past in terms of
the present? Granted that, with Henry Cadbury, *What
Manner of Man,* we must see Jesus as a first-century Jew,
and not as a nineteenth-century one, can we move beyond
rejecting palpable anachronisms, and arrive at verisimilitude
in the re-creation of the ancient setting? Will there not
always, inevitably, be a gap between our most prudent efforts
and the elusive reality?

Studies of particular words such as faith, grace, righteousness, and the like, also concern me; our ability to define
them falls short of knowing the force of these words, force
as distinct from meaning.

12. The issue is in part the question of the dating of documents
and in part that of understanding the Gospel process. Beyond that, I have in mind the question of how burning some

particular issue was at diverse times. Were docetism, encratism, and gnosticism, for example, of the same divisive character at all times, or were there periods and geographical areas where different measures of "toleration" existed?

13. As one example, I would cite the problem of "Judaizing," which is sometimes in the forefront in the Epistle to the Galatians (2:14). Is the issue of the same magnitude in Ignatius (Magn. 8:1 and 10:3)? Filson, in *Interpreter's Dictionary of the Bible* "Judaizing," is entirely correct in noting that the modern use of the word is quite out of accord with the old Christian use.

Beyond this one term, I find myself very much in the dark respecting the weight, extent, and distribution of Jewish and Christian heretical tendencies and movements. (In the article—an unsatisfactory one—"Heresy" in *IDB*, read *mīn* in place of the erroneous *mīw*, and for *gdbh* (?) possibly read *aguda*.) The shift from a relatively tolerable diversity into a direct or indirect opposition to the divergent is very clouded for me, especially respecting early Christianity. It seems to me that the rapid geographical spread of Christianity necessarily entailed diversity, and only as the concurrent diversities directly encountered each other in particular localities could diversity prompt the distinction between orthodoxy and heresy. Moreover, heresy, as something beyond mere ugly name-calling applied by one man or one group to a peer man or group, would imply the emergence of both a broad consensus on doctrine, and also accepted officials whose views were more authoritative than simply individual opinions. True heresy can arise only when a true orthodoxy has arisen. The key problem to me in early Christian heresy is my conviction that early Christianity promptly and naturally became extensively diversified. See Walter Bauer, *Rechtglaubigkeit und Ketzerei im ältesten Christentum*.

14. I am saying, of course, that in addition to the eschatology truly present in the Christian documents, modern theologians (not always versed in New Testament) have extended it in scope, and to my mind, have often altered its import, or even betrayed it. Stephen Neill (*The Interpretation of the New Testament, 1861–1961*, pp. 195–6), in discussing "eschato-

logical," notes correctly that the word "is used by scholars
in half a dozen senses, often without definition, and the
confusions are endless." I get the impression that "eschatology" is often only a slogan word in some modern
Protestant and, now, some Jewish writers. I attribute this
development to what seems to me to be Schweitzer's way of
handling a genuine dilemma—that passages in Paul, and in
the Gospels in words attributed to Jesus, expect the early
End, an End which did not ensue; the Church, however, has
nevertheless abided. Schweitzer handled the issue of the
failure of the End to materialize by conceiving of Jesus not
so much as predicting the End, but as being himself possessed by the conviction that it was through him that the
eschatological events would take place; Jesus believed that
he must die, and hence went to Jerusalem with the expectation that at his death the End was to arrive. Perhaps it does
not do violence to Schweitzer to say that he substitutes
Jesus' acts for Jesus' prediction, and assumes by this substitution that, on the one hand, he has eliminated the problem of a prediction which did not come true, and on the
other, he has discovered a motif which to him has ongoing
relevancy.

The other way of handling the dilemma is that of C. H.
Dodd in *The Parables of the Kingdom;* that is to say, abiding
Christianity slowly reversed the time-factor in eschatology,
depriving it of futurity, and allocating the climactic moment to the appearance of Jesus in the past. Certainly there
are passages, especially in Matthew, which bear out Dodd,
and certainly "realized Eschatology" is present, or inferable,
from John. With such sanction in the New Testament, it is
not to be wondered at that additional interpreters, such as
Hans Conzelmann, *The Theology of St. Luke (Die Mitte
der Zeit)* have proceeded to stress the motifs in the Gospels
in which salvation is deemed to have come already in the
past. (Perhaps, in interests of accuracy, one should quote
Conzelmann, p. 27: "The time of the End did not break in
with Jesus. Rather, the future time of salvation was portrayed in advance . . . in the life of Jesus. . . . Not that
the kingdom of God has come, but that through the life of
Jesus the hope of the coming kingdom has been established.

Its nearness thus becomes a secondary factor.") Still other approaches to the problem of unrealized predictions may be cited, as for example, Martin Werner, *The Formation of Christian Dogma,* who argues that as eschatology faded in the early Church, dogma arose to replace it; also, Wilhelm Bousset, *Kyrios Christos,* who sees a shift from the future eschatology bound up in the Son of Man of primitive Christianity, and the kyrios-worship of the Hellenistic community which transforms the future into the present. There is no doubt in my mind that the documents reflect a shift. What perturbs me is the way in which the term "eschatological" has at times been altered in meaning, and the alteration superimposed on the documents, and also the way in which a theme of restricted scope emerges in some interpreters as ubiquitously present. I find this especially in Rudolf Bultmann, *Theology of the New Testament,* in connection with the Christian community in Paul, which, to my mind, fully believed in eschatology, but ought not to be described as the eschatological community.

15. See Lecture II, pp. 63–66. The general statement can be made that synthetic studies, such as R. H. Charles, *Religious Development Between the Old and the New Testaments,* regard the intertestamental period as that of a direct bridge from Old Testament to New Testament. Such studies synthesize the materials (truly so diverse as to preclude any reliable amalgamation) in the interest of this particular bridge. They represent modern versions of Eusebius' *Preparation for the Gospel.* These syntheses, then, do not emerge from the material itself, but from the use to which the material is put.

16. When I read in Josephus, *The Life,* 415, 426–7, the attack on the history by Justus, who had attacked Josephus, I become aware of the ancient equivalent of some of our modern feuds, as among the British historians. The prepossession seems to me to exist that ancient writings were uniformly and universally accepted and praised. This, of course, was not the case. Does Philo's scorn of "the literalists" (see Montgomery Shroyer, *Alexandrian Jewish Literalists*) represent his reaction to reactions to his writings?

We cannot, of course, weigh the measure of resistance

that particular apocalyptic books aroused; we can only note the relative disdain in the Rabbinic Literature for the apocalyptic tendency, and the large failure of Jews to preserve this literature. Was this failure an accident, or deliberate?

At any rate, the appearance of some doctrine in some apocalyptic book may reflect an idiosyncrasy, not a mass judgment.

17. I am not happy about this word, but I know of none better. I use it in place of a frequently used phrase that I object to, "apocalyptic Judaism." I cannot acquiesce in a judgment, or a view, that the apocalyptic was broad and encompassing, and distinct from the groupings such as Pharisees or Essenes; rather, there existed this tendency among individuals within or without the groupings.

18. The handbooks, when culled, bear out my contention of overprecision, for often not only do the scholars suggest an era, but they give a specific year and sometimes even what portion of a year.

19. The handful of allusions in the Apocrypha and Talmudic literature throws very little light on the substance of the educational system among Jews. See *Jewish Encyclopedia*, "Education," V, p. 43, and "Bet Ha-Midrash," III, pp. 116–18. The more recent literature is given by Kaster in *Interpreter's Dictionary of the Bible*, "Education," II, p. 34. The *Bet Sefer* was the elementary school, and the *Bet Ha-Midrash* the advanced. Similarly, we know very little about education in early Christianity; see Krister Stendahl, *The School of St. Matthew*, pp. 33–5. Respecting literacy, the possibly oral character of much of the instruction suggests the likely need to distinguish between schooling and literacy. Kaster infers from I Macc. 1:56ff. that "literacy was quite widespread," a tenable statement respecting Scripture, but still a vague one.

The permission for children to read on the Sabbath (Sabbath I:3) and for the preceptor (*hazzan*) to check on them without himself reading shows clearly that reading was part of the instructional system. Piquantly, the Jerusalem Talmud comments that youngsters, reading by candlelight, required the supervision of the *hazzan* to deter them from violating the Sabbath through extinguishing the candle—

so as to escape from the chore of learning (Albeck, *Shisha Sidre Mishnah, Seder Mo'ed*, p. 18).

20. I have been able to find no information of any substance regarding the circulation or readership of non-biblical books. The issue is not the fact of circulation, which is undeniable, but the extent of it, which is most uncertain. The prohibition against the free circulation of non-canonical books (IV Ezra 14:44–48), as well as the prohibition against reading Homer (although Saul Lieberman, *Hellenism in Jewish Palestine*, 105–14, distinguishes between study and mere reading, with only the former prohibited) are intelligible only if the circulation was broad enough to occasion the prohibition.

21. See Viktor Tcherikover, *Hellenistic Civilization and the Jews*, pp. 346–54, and Stübe, *Jüdisch-Babylonische Zaubertexte*.

22. See the sober judgment of Tcherikover, *Hellenistic Civilization*, pp. 292–5. The various estimates were assembled by Rosenthall in *American Jewish Year Book* (1949), pp. 319ff.; Tcherikover reproduces them (pp. 504–55, n. 86): Baron: eight million, three in Palestine and five in the Dispersion; Beloch: six million, two in Palestine and four outside; Juster: seven million, five in Palestine, two outside; Harnack, four million plus, 700,000 in Palestine. Baron's discussion is found in *A Social and Religious History of the Jews*, 2nd ed., Vol. I, p. 170 and note 7, pp. 370–72.

23. More specifically, it is almost the Graeco-Jewish literature alone, and not the history, that claims attention. Jean Juster, *Les juifs dans l'empire romain*, published in 1914, remains the standard work. Tcherikover is the greatest scholar since Juster on Dispersion Jews, but in general confines his studies to the period up to Pompey's conquest in 63 B.C. One should not read Juster without Tcherikover. We could wish that Elias Bickermann would supplement his excellent sporadic writings with his synthesis; I have found him extraordinarily illuminating, even while I occasionally disagree with him. We await with interest the bibliographical project on Hellenistic Judaism undertaken by Professor G. Delling of Halle.

24. See, though, for contrast, Marcel Simon, *Verus Israel*, pp.

52–86. More recently, Tcherikover has significantly divided his book, *Hellenistic Civilization and the Jews*, into two parts, "Hellenistic Civilization in Palestine" and "Hellenistic Civilization in the Diaspora." The chore of synthesis, especially of reaching back beyond 63 B.C., remains urgent.

25. In general, Jews have neglected Hellenistic Judaism because the sources are not in Hebrew and were not preserved by Jews, and Christians have neglected it because the direct nexus Christians usually see is from Jesus to the Judean apostles and then to the Pharisaic Paul, and only thereafter to expanding Dispersion Christianity. In my judgment, if we distinguish between the Gospels, which are Greek documents, and the Judean scene that they depict, more light is thrown on the Gospels by Hellenistic Judaism than by the Rabbinic sources. See my "Judaism, Jesus, and Paul: Some Problems of Method in Scholarly Research," *Vanderbilt Studies in the Humanities*, I, pp. 220–50. To the judgment there expressed on Strack-Billerbeck, I would here add that that enterprise, despite its formidable mass, does more to mislead than to enlighten. The fault, though, is less with Billerbeck than with many who use him.

26. Admiring as I do Saul Lieberman, *Greek in Jewish Palestine* (1942), and *Hellenism in Jewish Palestine* (1957), especially for their corrective effect, I occasionally have felt anxious about what have seemed to me to be too ready generalizations from too little data. Perhaps, though, what troubles me is not Lieberman's work, but what have seemed to me to be frequent conclusions made by other scholars, who base their ideas on extensions of what Lieberman is presumed to have said but has not (as he himself comments respecting G. Allon). Such scholars get the impression from Lieberman of extensive and deep Hellenization, whereas his books seem to me to portray a restricted Hellenization. To take one item, there is significance to my mind in Lieberman's pointing out that of all the hundreds of Greek authors only Homer is mentioned by name in the Talmud.

27. Tcherikover, *Hellenistic Civilization and the Jews*, pp. 212–24, correctly sees the Hellenizers as a *Jewish* party, not as an aggregate of apostates as they often appear to be in parochial rewritings.

28. On degrees of Hellenization, see my *Philo's Place in Judaism*, pp. 3–13, and opinions there cited.

29. The standard work is Samuel Krauss, *Griechische und lateinische Lehnwörter im Talmud, Midrasch, und Targum*, 2 vols. This book is supplemented, and at points corrected, in Saul Lieberman; see note 26 above.

30. I know of no encompassing study; I can cite only Bergmann, "Stoische Philosophie und die jüdische Frömmigkeit," *Judaica: Festschrift zu Hermann Cohens Siebzigstem Geburtstage*, pp. 145–66. What is present in Rabbinic Literature is almost exclusively conclusion, rather than the dialectic process itself, with the result that we deal with echoes, of varying shades of dimness, rather than with substantial knowledge. The most prominent reflection of Plato is his theory of ideas, that is, of archetypes and imitations. In general, these are transformed from a static, vertical relationship, into a horizontal, chronological relationship, usually relating to archetypal forms, deemed to have been in existence at the point of the Creation, and providing the patterns for the subsequent created entities. The problem of the relation of Abraham to the later laws of Moses (a problem later aggravated for the rabbis on their encountering the argument of Paul) becomes "solved" by assuming that pre-existent, archetypal laws were available from Creation on, with the result that Abraham was a pre-Mosaic observer of the Mosaic (and even the Rabbinic) Laws. This shift to the chronological enters in its own way into Christian writings as diverse as The Epistle to the Hebrews and Eusebius, *Preparation for the Gospel*.

31. On the presence of these elements in Philo, there is no disagreement at all among the scholars.

32. It is somewhat startling to note in the Tanach the paucity of allusion to wine in religious ceremonies. (Wine appears, for example, as a libation in Numbers 28:14, there accompanying the new-moon sacrifice.) The Rabbinic Literature does not initiate the ceremonial use of wine, but treats it, rather, as though its use is already the ordinary, accepted procedure, even being part of the postprandial grace. The article "Wine" in *The Jewish Encyclopedia* abstains completely from raising the problem. A good bibliography is found under

"Wine" in *Interpreter's Dictionary of the Bible,* but there
too the problem is not raised. George Foot Moore, *Judaism,*
has no entry on wine in his index; he comments (Vol. III,
pp. vii–viii): ". . . I have not meant to become involved in
. . . the question when, where, and how the Jews got some
of the notions which others seem to have entertained before
them. . . ."

33. The ceremony that "separates" the end of the Sabbath from
the ensuing day.

34. See Erwin R. Goodenough, *Jewish Symbols in the Greco-
Roman Period,* V–VI. See especially VI, pp. 126–8.

35. I am tantalized by a reservation in Moore's wise comment
(*Judaism,* II, pp. 394–5): "Borrowings in religion, however,
at least in the field of ideas, are usually in the nature of the
appropriation of things in the possession of another which
the borrower recognizes in all good faith as belonging to
himself, ideas which, when once they become known to him,
are seen to be the necessary implications or complements of
his own." To this word "ideas," Moore appends the footnote: "The adoption of foreign rites and adaptation of
myths are a different matter." I could wish Moore had not
been so laconic. Does he mean that rites and myths, by virtue of being concrete, are less readily borrowed? If so,
the difference would seem to me to be one only of degree.

I would add to the reservations which Moore makes about
rites and myths the item of specific theological beliefs,
distinguishing between central and crucial items that seem
palpably alien to a borrower, and less central matters that
do not.

36. Presuppositions among scholars seem to follow the form of
stating a term (for example, a Jew), predicating loyalty, and
of implying that such loyalty has inescapable consequences.
Loyalty seems to me a multifaceted term. A tiny Jewish
congregation in a small Southern city appealed to my office
at Hebrew Union College for prayerbooks, advising me
that until these arrived, the Sabbath evening service would
need to remain what it was: the recitation of the Lord's
Prayer. Loyalty and its connotations lack inescapable consequences, for men are most subjective in their interpretations.

37. A similar framework, of piety on the one hand, and the acquisition of the four virtues on the other, is found in Philo's *De Decalogo*. See my "The Confrontation of Greek and Jewish Ethics: Philo, De Decalogo," CCAR *Journal*, January 1968. In IV Maccabees, the control of the senses and passions leads to immunity from the pain of the fire.

38. Four fragments of his drama on the Exodus are preserved in Clement of Alexander (*Stromata*, 1, 23, 155) and Eusebius, *Preparation for the Gospel*, IX, 29, 14. Ezekiel is usually taken to be an Alexandrian of the second pre-Christian century. The fragments are reprinted in Wallace H. Stearns, *Fragments from Graeco-Jewish Writers* (1908); among other literature see K. Kuiper, "Le poète juif Ezéchiel," *Révue des Études Juives* (Old Series), XLVI (1903), 48–73 and 161–77; see also J. Gutmann, *Ha-sifrut ha-yehudit ha-hellenistit*. On Herod and the theater in Jerusalem, see *Antiquities of the Jews*, XV, 268–89; it should perhaps be noticed that Josephus focuses on the popular displeasure with the ornaments in the theater, rather than the theater itself. But displeasure with theaters is frequent in Rabbinic Literature.

39. That is to say, the Maccabean revolt was the sharpest rejection of Hellenism. To what extent was it religious and to what extent quasi-nationalistic—assuming these elements are separable? Had Antiochus Epiphanes IV abstained from his ill-advised religious interference, would the rejection of Hellenism have been so acute? See the very perceptive paragraph in Elias J. Bickerman, "The Historical Foundations of Postbiblical Judaism," Louis Finkelstein, ed., *The Jews: Their History, Culture, and Religion*, I, pp. 107–10, and also Bickerman's *The Maccabees*.

40. The growing incidence of Greek names is unmistakable. Nevertheless, the rabbis in the post-first-century period attribute (in Genesis Rabba to Genesis 46:6) the redemption of the ancient Hebrews from Egypt to four virtues, one of which was the abstinence from taking on Greek names: Judah did not become Rufa, nor Reuben Julian, nor Joseph "Lestum," nor Benjamin Alexander!

41. See the good discussion in Charles Guignebert, *The Jewish World in the Time of Jesus*, pp. 89–95. The novelty in

John 1 is, of course, not the use of *logos,* but rather its identification of the *logos* with Jesus.

42. How little we know can be discerned from the paucity of materials assembled in Juster, *Les juifs,* I, 388ff.

43. See, for an example of what I hold as untenable, the conclusion in Samuel Belkin, *Philo and the Oral Law,* pp. 5–10.

44. In Philo, Abraham is passingly depicted as the model of the true proselyte, whereas in the rabbis he is the great missionary. See my *Philo's Place in Judaism,* p. 85, and Wilfred L. Knox, "Abraham and the Quest for God," *Harvard Theological Review,* XXVIII (1935), 55–60, and my expanding note, "Abraham's Knowledge of the Existence of God," ibid., XLIV (1951), 137–9.

45. See "Adiebene," in *Jewish Encyclopedia,* I, pp. 191–2, and its literature and references. We know the fact of the conversion, but absolutely nothing of the process.

46. See Foakes Jackson and Kirsopp Lake, *The Beginnings of Christianity,* V, pp. 80–88. The terms for this category vary, and it is not possible to specify what and who they were. Charles Guignebert, *The Jewish World in the Time of Jesus,* pp. 232–7, supposes that Jewish legalism impeded their becoming full proselytes; my hunch is that it was, rather, male circumcision, as indicated by the large number of women converts. Moore, *Judaism,* I, "Conversion of Gentiles," pp. 323ff., repays close study.

47. See Moore, *Judaism,* I, p. 346, and the references there given. See also *Jewish Encyclopedia,* "Antoninus," I, 656–7.

48. Moore, *Judaism,* I, p. 384 states that "Jews did not send out missionaries." It would have been more prudent to say that we have no evidence of Jews sending out missionaries. In Moore's view, conversion was a consequence of the widespread dispersion of the Jews, and the attendant proximity to Gentiles.

The statement of Judah Goldin (*The Jews,* p. 139) that Paul "was a man of means and could undertake frequent journeys" is not buttressed by any citation.

49. See note 44 above. I find it hard to comprehend the figure of Abraham as a missionary unless the age that so conceived him possessed missionaries.

50. The little data in Josephus (*e.g. Antiquities of the Jews,*

XII, 125–6) deal with the negative and the overt, and reflect nothing of the possibly positive.

51. T. H. Gaster, "Samaritans," *Interpreter's Dictionary of the Bible*, IV, pp. 190–97, correctly stresses that "our knowledge of the Samaritans is imperfect." The article can be supplemented for the Rabbinic period by "Samaritans," *Jewish Encyclopedia*, X, pp. 669–81, esp. p. 671. The rabbinic materials (in which the Samaritans are ordinarily denominated Cuthites, from Cutha, II Kings 17:24) provide evidence for what Moore, *Judaism*, I, aptly calls "the durable animosity" between Jews and Samaritans, but little penetrable light on day-to-day relations; I know of no study of the matter. Incidents such as that noted in *Antiquities of the Jews*, XX, 118ff., of battles between Galileans traversing Samaria on their way to Jerusalem may well have been characteristic.

52. See the fine study by Ben Zion Wacholder, *Nicolaus of Damascus*, Berkeley, University of California Press, 1962 (University of California Publications in History, Vol. 75).

53. See *The Jewish War*, I, 515–32, and *Antiquities of the Jews*, XVI, 306–10.

54. Guignebert's discussion (*The Jewish World*, pp. 197–202) predates the discovery of the Dead Sea Scrolls, and his discussion of the "Damascus covenanters" is now antiquated.

The plurality of sects, or of quasi-sects, all too often goes unnoticed, despite allusions in Justin, *Dialogue with Trypho the Jew*, and Hegesippus, quoted in Eusebius, *Ecclesiastical History*, IV, 22, 5ff., and Epiphanius, *Refutation of Heresies*, chap. 1, 18–19, 30, and 53. Little can be made of the Rabbinic allusion to "twenty-four *kittot*," Gittin 55b–56a, beyond the awareness therein of divisiveness. The *Minim* (see the summary in *Jewish Encyclopedia*, VIII, esp. p. 595) have yielded almost as many theories as there have been scholars, and while the substance is rather clear, we are totally in the dark as to the provenance and the ultimate fate. The first-century sage Elisha ben Abuyah (known also as Aher) became a "heretic"—on this the sources agree—but we are so bereft of knowledge about his *particular* heresy that we cannot identify it, and hence the diversity of conclusions of scholars. Despite all that has been written on Gnosticism, and the speculations on a pre-Christian Jewish gnosticism, it does not seem to me that the general haze has at all been penetrated. See Lecture IV, note 22. In my own mind there is a clear (!) picture of the remarkable unclarity; I envisage trends and tendencies, often analogous, often different; sometimes they are extreme, sometimes perhaps restrained; sometimes they are possibly dialectical, sometimes merely intuitive.

Indeed, another issue is equally unclear to me respecting Jewish heresy; when did there emerge that orthodoxy which is a prerequisite to denominating somebody else a heretic? I mean more than merely the chronological problem, but that too enters in. I wish I could remember the source for the statement: "Yesterday's heresy often becomes today's orthodoxy."

55. According to Rabbinic tradition the schools founded by these earlier contemporaries of Jesus differed on 365 points of law (see Louis Ginzberg, *Meqoma shel ha-Halacha*, 13ff.). A heavenly voice ruled in favor of the school of Hillel; one regrets that such a convenient way of settling disputes seems no longer available.

The acuteness of the controversies led to the ancient judgment that the one Law had thereby become two. The schools became hostile to the point where members of each school distained to worship with members of the other; see "Bet Hillel," *Jewish Encyclopedia*, III, 115–6; Judah Goldin, *The Jews*, p. 138, cites Yebamot 1:6 (in other editions it is 1:4; in the Talmud it is 13b), which declares that adherents of the schools intermarried, this in support of a contention that "academic divergence was never permitted to disrupt the peace and unity that both schools pursued." I believe this latter contention is at variance with the full data.

56. The role of the client-king is itself ambiguous. Let it simply be noted that the Romans deposed Archelaus, that they designated Agrippa I as king, and that Agrippa II managed, with Roman consent, to become the king.

The dual role of king-high priest of the Maccabean age does not apply to Herodians, who lacked the genealogical prerequisite for the high priesthood; Agrippa II, indeed, seems to have had the right, or else usurped the privilege, of deposing or appointing the high priest (*Antiquities*, XX,

179, 197, 203, 213). He could not stem the rebellion against Rome; he became a nonparticipant, but pro-Roman; after the war he removed to Rome.

Josephus spends a great deal of space in recounting Agrippa's admiration for *The Jewish Wars.*

57. I Mac. 15:15ff. reflects the mandate that imperial officials, on application of the high priest, should extradite mischievous refugees. The account in Acts supposes that government officials do not enter into the picture, but that the high priest simply writes letters to the synagogues.

58. The Hebrew term is *nasi.* The office appears to be post A.D. 70. One requirement, as also in the case of the *resh galuta,* "head of the Exile," was putative descent from King David. It appears that at Jamnia the leading role played of Johanan ben Zakkai was temporary, an interim tenure since Gamaliel II, the lineal descendant of Hillel and of David, was deterred by the Romans from assuming the post. But the entire matter is most obscure, with the obscurity increased by the complementary office of the *ab bet-din,* a sort of vice-*nasi.* Rabbinic tradition ascribed the two offices, the presidium over the Sanhedrin, to a time as early as the Maccabean period, and modern scholars have expressed a variety of doubts, which aggregate to the conclusion that the post A.D. 70 practice was anachronistically put back into the earliest period, at which time in reality the king-high priest presided. Suffice it that the offices, even if ancient, which I doubt, cannot be traced consecutively, and are notably absent from Josephus. K. Kohler, "Nasi," in the *Jewish Encyclopedia,* IX, pp. 171–2, sees in the word "prophet," in *Antiquities of the Jews,* IV, 218, an allusion to the "*ab bet-din,*" and in this way seeks to justify the antiquity of the office. In the passage, Josephus is paraphrasing Deuteronomy 17:8–13, which mentions no prophet; Josephus erred, either through carelessness or through relying on memory.

Yet even if the office and the title existed prior to 70, manifestly with a king and a high priest both extant, the role was different from what it was after 70, when these two offices became defunct.

59. The Rabbinic proof rests on Exodus 15:1 (*Mekilta Shirah,* beginning). The Gospel proof (Mark 12:18–27 and parallels)

rests on Exodus 3:6. See other items adduced by Moore, *Judaism*, II, 382ff.

60. The Gospel passages, in my judgment, reflect not misunderstanding, but a polemical negation.

61. These "rules" are summarized in Herman L. Strack, *Introduction to the Talmud and Midrash*, pp. 93–8. See also Moore, *Judaism*, I, 248–9, and, for the Rabbinic sources and relevant literature, III, p. 72, n. 14.

62. Literature is cited in my *Philo's Place in Judaism*, p. 16.

63. See Carl Siegfried, *Philo von Alexandria als Ausleger des alten Testaments*, pp. 168ff.

64. There was a sizable early-nineteenth-century literature which predicated Alexandria as the source for Rabbinic exegesis, and, as in the case of Bruno Bauer, for Christian origins. See my "Isaac Mayer Wise's 'Jesus Himself,'" *Essays in American Jewish History*, pp. 325–58, esp. pp. 327–30. Occasional twentieth-century scholars revert to a theory of Alexandrian origin: N. J. Weinstein, *Zur Genesis der Agada*, II: *Die alexandrinische Agada*, and David Daube, "Rabbinic Methods of Interpretation and Hellenistic Rhetoric," *Hebrew Union College Annual*, XXII, 239–64.

65. This is very common in the literature. The assumption is that the Rabbinic exegesis was a standard, and that other types conformed or else deviated. My own view is that exegesis was broad, and encompassed all types of Judaism, and that, out of the broad and variegated, the Rabbinic later emerged as a rather disciplined and more or less controlled system. In the case of Paul, the issue is complicated by the disputed matter of whether or not he was indeed a student of Gamaliel, as reported in Acts of the Apostles 22:3; see Morton S. Enslin, "Paul and Gamaliel," *Journal of Religion*, VII (1927), pp. 360–75. I am among those who doubt that Paul was a student of Gamaliel. As to Paul's being a Pharisee (Philippians 3:5), rather than challenge the authenticity either of the verse or of the purport, as some have done, I would contend that one needs to understand the label Pharisee from Paul's content, and not his content from the label. We are completely in the dark respecting Pharisaism in the Greek Dispersion. See Lecture III, pages 127–28.

66. It is somewhat unclear to me whether it is the priesthood, which improperly controlled the Temple, that is repudiated, or the Temple itself. The former is intelligible to me, the latter not at all, except in the sense that the repudiation of improper priests amounted in effect to a repudiation of the Temple.

The sparse information about the Temple of Onias IV at Leontopolis (see "Leontopolis," *Jewish Encyclopedia,* VIII, pp. 7–9) yields no data relevant to this immediate issue, for that dissident movement was substantially different and unique. See Lecture II, note 3.

67. I do not mean the term in the technical sense of an *ethnos,* which term has its appropriate context, but in a more general sense, this in default of a term that would be readily suitable. Juster, *Les juifs,* I, 414ff., lists the many Greek and Latin terms for the corporate entity.

68. Wilhelm Bacher ("Academies in Palestine," *Jewish Encyclopedia,* I, pp. 147–8) notes correctly, respecting a putative "university or academy—an institution composed of the scribes . . . there is . . . no certain information." One wonders if the academies of later times, at Jamnia and Usha, and at the Babylonian centers which arose in the third Christian century, are responsible for an anachronistic implication that a university or academy existed in the early part of the first century. That there was an early scholastic tradition seems unmistakable; it is the formal impression that the word "academy" implies that seems to me to be open to challenge.

Moreover, the unhistorical aspect seems to me underlined in the Rabbinic tradition (*Erubin* 13B) that supposedly the schools of Hillel and Shammai debated for two and a half years over the question whether it would have been better for man not to have been created.

69. Partisanship beclouds the meaning of this term, as the multiple theories disclose. The literal rendering is collective, that is, "people," not "person." Since the Gospels portray Jesus as associating with outcasts, the term is interpreted by some Christians as an outcast, and these consider the Rabbinic sentiment (Abot 5:2), a contemptible arrogance. Jewish scholars defend the sentiment on the basis that Judaism in

its very essence required at least a minimum of education and hence he who lacked the minimum was thereby impeded from piety. In current Yiddish and modern Hebrew, the phrase *am ha-aretz* means simply an ignoramus. Did the ancient term mean something more, as for example, a rustic bumpkin? I confess that I do not know, and am unenlightened by the many explanations I have read. Baron, *Social and Religious History of the Jews*, I², p. 414, n. 36, and II², p. 413, n. 24, provides the literature and the sources.

Were the rabbis condescending? Why not? Were not the anti-Nicene fathers equally condescending—or worse—to their opponents? Condescension is all too human, and regrettably universal.

70. See Lecture IV, note 34, in connection with Krister Stendahl, *The School of St. Matthew*. To anticipate, I am prone to accept the frequent hypothesis that there existed something kindred to "testimonies"; a "school" of Christian exegetes, however, seems to me an overstatement.

71. See "Angelology," *Jewish Encyclopedia*, I, pp. 583–97. I do not know what to make of the assertion in Acts 23:8 that the Sadducees deny the existence of angels and spirits. No confirmation of this is found in Josephus or the Rabbinic Literature; Moore (*Judaism*, I, 68) supposes that it was the "exuberant angelology and demonology which flourished in the age and was cultivated in apocalyptic circles" that the Sadducees repudiated. Angels, after all, appear in Scripture; how could the Sadducees, who were literalists, repudiate what is in Scripture? Acts 23:8 seems to me mistaken.

72. Theodore Gaster, "Demons," *Interpreter's Dictionary of the Bible*, I, pp. 128–34, devotes a brief section (B5, pp. 132–3) to "hostile angels." I have found it difficult to assess the viewpoint in Martin Werner, *The Formation of Christian Dogma*, which seems to me to present a thoroughgoing identification of sin and evil with demonic possession; it seems to me that Werner makes the identification too encompassing, as if there were no differentiation possible between evil and such possession, and, also, that the views of the post-Pauline Gnostics are too readily attributed to Paul himself.

Respecting I Corinthians 11:10, the discussion in Lietzmann, *Handbuch zum Neuen Testament*, IX, pp. 54–5, and the literature there cited, indicates the ambivalences among the commentators, and their reluctance to consider these angels as demons. The association of "the angels" with the "sons of God" of Genesis 6:1ff. is possible only by excessive straining; the common aspect would appear to be the erotic bent of some angels, similar to that of the "sons."

73. It has been a surprise to me to discover that there are modern scholars who are totally unaware that the office of the exorcizant of demons was provided for by Pope Cornelius in the third century, and that the office, first under the minor orders and then the province of the priest, persists in principle; reinterpreted prayers for the exorcism of demons still precede the baptism of children in the Roman Catholic ritual into our own times.

Lecture II

Palestinian Judaisms

There were several competing versions of Judaism in the first century. Of these only one, Rabbinic Judaism, has survived to our day. During most of the first century, Rabbinic Judaism was an inchoate movement, acquiring its clearest sense of direction only after A.D. 70, after the Temple was destroyed and the priestly cultus came to an end. Before 70, the various groups and sectaries—the appropriate nomenclature is elusive—existed either in conscious rivalry with each other, or simply supplemented each other. After 70 the Sadducees had no reason to persist, and they disappeared,[1] and the Essenes, identified by many modern scholars with the Qumran community, were wiped out. Hence the only surviving form in Judaism was Pharisaism, surviving, we may say, as Rabbinism. About the year 90, at Jamnia, there took place an assembly of Rabbinic sages, who there and then reorganized a harassed and chaotic Judaism. They successfully charted a future for Rabbinic Judaism, this centered in the synagogue and in its liturgy of prayers, and in an ever deepening and broadening immersion in Scripture.

JUDEA VERSUS JUDAISM

If we were to make the somewhat arbitrary distinction between the history of Judea and the history of Judaism in the first century, our first step would necessarily be to distinguish between the works of Josephus on the one hand and the Rabbinic writings and other literatures on the other hand. It is from the writings of Josephus that we construct our view of the history of Judea, of the reigns of the children and grandchildren of Herod, of the Roman procurators, of the Zealots, and the chain of affronts by Romans to Jews and Judaism with the subsequent resentments, and the ultimate open rebellion which resulted in the destruction of the Temple in 70 and terminated in the capture of the final surviving fortress, Masada, in 73. We would scarcely be able, however, to discern from the pages of Josephus any prospect of that abiding reconstruction of Judaism which the name Jamnia[2] represents. *The Jewish War* was written about 75, and *Antiquities* about 95; *Antiquities* repeats much that is in *The Jewish War*, but Josephus terminates his *Antiquities* without giving a second version of the end of the rebellion covered in *The Jewish War*. *Antiquities* ends at 66, though Josephus appends a note congratulating himself on finishing his chore. In *The Jewish War*, after narrating the fall of Masada, Josephus provides a brief narration of the disorders in the Jewish community in Alexandria; its leaders were murdered by some Zealots (*sicarii*) who fled there, but these Zealots were overcome, and apparently executed, though by whom we do not know. Next Josephus tells of the decision by the Romans to destroy the Temple of Onias.[3] He proceeds to give a brief account of the action of the *sicarii* in Cyrene, who were put down by the Roman governor Catullus (prominent Jews in Alexandria and Rome, including Josephus himself, were arrested at the instigation of Catullus, but divine retribution overtook the Roman in the form of a complicated and incurable disease). Josephus terminates *The Jewish War* without a word respecting the ongoing Judaism of the post-70 period; he only assumes it. Similarly, he closes his auto-biography, *The Life*, with a mention of his own marital and social status, but he does not say a word about ongoing Judaism. Most surprising of all, toward the end of *Against Apion* (II, 193–8), Josephus writes about the Temple as if it were still operating, though he wrote this work no earlier than 95.

To Josephus, then, we can look primarily for events, but not for clear information on the doctrines, institutions, and underlying currents that fashioned Rabbinic Judaism. Despite what he tells us about Pharisees, Sadducees, and Essenes—indeed, his account is apologetic and partially untrustworthy[4]—my statement as made requires very little modification.

When one speaks of Rabbinic Judaism one necessarily speaks in the next breath of Rabbinic Literature.[5] We need to remind ourselves, first and foremost, that Jews have called this literature *Torah she-be'al pe*, The Oral Torah, and that in principle it should have remained oral, but it began to be committed to writing toward the end of the second Christian century. The literature, however, hearkens back to sages who flourished even prior to the first Christian century, and their teachings, as well as those of the first-century sages, are incorporated within the pages of compilations made in the second century and also even later. Whereas Josephus concentrates on events and ignores religious institutions, the Rabbinic Literature ignores events and concentrates on religious institutions. The Rabbinic Literature, as I have said, lacks a clear and defined historical bent or any pretension to historical narration, with the result that an array of lacunae and problems confront us respecting chronology and relationships in the chain of Rabbinic Judaism. This can be seen in the unclarity and confusions which the tradition provides about itself. Thus, we encounter the reports on the sequence of sages in disordered and confusing ways. On the one hand, Johanan ben Zakkai, whose great activity is from 70–90 at Jamnia, is found listed as a direct disciple of Hillel, an older contemporary of Jesus. On the other hand, Hillel had a son, Simeon, about whom we know little more than his name and that he headed the Sanhedrin (*Shabbat* 15a). Simeon's son, Gamalicl (usually called Gamaliel I), who figures in Acts of the Apostles, also fails to be listed in the recorded chain of sages found in Ethics of the Fathers I:2. But Gamaliel I is known from other passages to have been most prominent in Jerusalem in the second third of the first century. Indeed, he is asserted to have been the head of the Sanhedrin—a datum which some have challenged. Of Gamaliel's son, Simeon, a little is known, for Josephus mentions him, as does Ethics of the Fathers 1:17. But why are the generations, Simeon ben Hillel, Gamaliel ben Simeon, and Simeon ben Gamaliel, omitted in favor of telescoping matters into a supposed direct relationship between Hillel and Johanan? We do not know.

The fact seems to be that we are able to see developments that ultimately came about in Rabbinic Judaism, but we are without the means of seeing clearly, precisely, and historically what the process of development was. The Rabbinic Literature represents a mature Rabbinism, into which are interspersed allusions to proto-Rabbinism[6] and to early Rabbinic personalities, but we are denied the ability to trace the growth of religious offices, of religious institutions, and of religious doctrines. This is true not only respecting the *halaka*, the strictly legal matters; it is especially true respecting the *haggada,* the anecdotal, interpretative materials.

The general procedure of modern scholars has been to try to peer back from the late date 175, when the Mishna was recorded, to the possibly early preparatory stages, even while they are aware that dates such as 90 and, further back, 70, constitute curtains which cut off vision and prevent a clear sight. Indeed, those who have gone carefully into the question of dating make the reasonable contention that even if we were able to allocate a particular Rabbinic sage to a particular generation, the circumstance that some particular halaka is attributed to him, or some haggadic fancy traced to him, this in no way gets us beyond an inherent *probability* as to the time and place of the origin of these halakic or haggadic matters. Perhaps this seems a startling statement. It arises, however, from researches which have demonstrated that in the multitudinous pages of the Rabbinic Literature, the same halakic innovation or haggadic novelty is attributed variously to sages of different generations and ages. Moreover, both Jubilees and Josephus are repositories of earlier embellishments of Scripture, some of which reappear in the later Rabbinic Literature; there these embellishments are attributed to the Rabbinic sages, who flourished long after Jubilees and Josephus were written. Indeed, it is on the principle of the difficulty or even the impossibility of dating much or most of the Rabbinic materials that scholars have not hesitated to look for parallels between Rabbinic Literature and the New Testament even in the utterances of Rabbinic sages who lived three or four hundred years after the time of the composition of the Gospels, for such Rabbinic utterances could possibly have originated earlier than or contemporaneous with Jesus.[7]

Since it is possible only to a limited extent to associate the teaching attributed to some sage with a given age, and since

90 and 70 stand as curtains obscuring our vision, then it follows that we will always be in some area of great uncertainty as to the stage at which the Rabbinic tradition stood prior to 70.

"NORMATIVE" JUDAISM

To add to the complexity of these matters, we need to reckon with a facet of modern scholarship which, curiously, all too often seems to me to have gone on unobserved. George Foot Moore coined the phrase "normative" Judaism to describe that Judaism reflected in the Rabbinic Literature. He justified the term "normative" on the premise that this was the literature which Jews preserved throughout the ages, and down to our time. In this sense the "normative" literature is distinct from Apocrypha, Pseudepigrapha, and the Hellenistic literature which Jews did not preserve. In Moore's own context, he was arguing against the presentation of Judaism in Bousset's book, *Religion des Judentum in neutestamentlichen Zeitalter.*[8] The case which Moore made against Bousset (in "Christian Writers on Judaism," *Harvard Theological Review*, XIV (1921), pp. 197–254, esp. pp. 241–8), was partly on the basis of Bousset's method and partly a case of *ad hominem.* Respecting the *ad hominem*, Moore questioned whether a man as young as Bousset, then twenty-eight, had had sufficient maturity of study, and was possessed of sufficient leisure in the midst of preparing his new courses, to produce a book that could be a responsible work. Moreover, Moore contended that Bousset's lack of first-hand acquaintance with the Rabbinic Literature, and his necessary reliance on the pre-Strack and Billerbeck anthologies,[9] deprived Bousset of a sufficient personal authority by which to approach Judaism; to Moore's mind Bousset's description of Judaism was the equivalent to denigration. Bousset's sources were primarily Apocrypha, Pseudepigrapha, and Hellenistic literature. Respecting methodology, Moore raised the question whether the appraisal of Judaism should be made from the literature Jews did not preserve, or from the literature which they did. While Moore's book, *Judaism in the First Centuries of the Christian Era: The Age of the Tannaim*, does not hesitate to call on the testimony of Apocrypha, Pseudepigrapha, and Philo, it is constructed and shaped primarily by the Tannaitic literature.

Moore was not the first to level sharp criticism against Bousset. The initial major criticism came in 1903 from a Jewish scholar, Felix Perles, in a book, *Boussets Religion des judentums in neutestamentlichen zeitalter kritisch untersucht*. Perles had two principal criticisms to make. The first anticipated Moore's, contending that since Bousset had no firsthand knowledge of Rabbinic Literature and was innocent of having read large portions of it in sequence, he was disqualified from writing about it at all. The second was that Bousset's attributing to the Rabbinic Literature the character of a dry legalism, which was a burden to the people, was in Perles's mind a distortion of Judaism. Bousset, in his book, *Volksfrömmigkeit und Schriftgelehrsamkeit*, also published in 1903, defended his procedure, by asserting that one must differentiate between the popular piety reflected in Apocrypha and Pseudepigrapha, his supposedly legitimate topic, and the academic, scholastic tradition which the later Rabbinic Literature represented. Of course, the issue of the chronological problems within the Rabbinic Judaism also entered into Bousset's defense.

Among the minor issues raised in this debate, two are worthy of our attention: First, much of the Pseudepigraphic literature is eschatological, while the overriding tone of Rabbinic Literature is non-eschatological and even contains portions which specifically repudiate eschatology. Second,

Jews did not preserve this eschatological literature. Is it legitimate to attribute to Judaism of the age of Jesus the broad eschatology of the Pseudepigrapha, in light of the non-eschatology of the normative literature? Again, as to the denigration of Judaism, the Rabbinic Literature is avowedly legal literature. The nineteenth-century German scholarship, as represented by Bousset and Schuerer[10] and others, seemed to Moore in sharp variance to motifs found in the earliest Christian literature, both the New Testament and early patristic literature. In this early Christian literature, one finds a usual contention that Christianity represented an unbroken continuity with the Judaism of the previous ages, and Jesus, even in controversy with fellow Jews, is never depicted as over and against the Judaism of his age. In the nineteenth-century literature, on the other hand, one finds a contrast drawn between the supposed massive, monolithic legalism of Judaism and the complete freedom of Jesus from any legalism, with the result that Jesus is conclusively depicted as over and against his inherited Judaism. Moore commented quite acidly on the shift from the oldest view of "continuity" to the nineteenth-century theory of rupture. He also raised the question of the propriety of describing an entire religion by a single phase of its character, its legalism. Essentially, Moore was raising the question of whether the German scholars of the nineteenth century were describing the Judaism of the age of Jesus accurately and responsibly and with the detachment that ought to abide in scholarship, or whether they were looking at Judaism with the eyes of a Martin Luther and in the light of the argument of Paul in Galatians and Romans. One might even go beyond Moore in this regard and make the comment that, for all his difficulties with the Law and his ultimately turning away from it, Paul seems to have not one word to say along the lines of the criticisms of Jewish legalism which these nineteenth-century scholars made. They seem to have assumed that there was some kind of inconvenience or burden in the Law, so that, by implication, it was not principle but merely convenience which animated Paul.

The fact must be faced that value judgments on Judaism, as distinct from a detached description of it, constitute an ongoing reality in much of modern New Testament scholarship, despite Moore's valiant effort to correct an infelicitous trend.[11] To the extent that Christian scholarship tends to denigrate Judaism, and Jewish scholarship to glorify it, there is always the possibility that, in the one or in the other, there will be some measure of distortion. Scholarly subjectivity is the major obstacle to comprehending the Rabbinic Literature.[12]

Let me indicate as clearly as I can where my personal sympathies lie. If I were asked to comment on the chief difference between the attitude toward Judaism in the Christian scholarship prior to Moore's time and that after it, I would say that, prior to Moore's time, there was almost no effort to be fair to Judaism, and since Moore's time, there has been a considerable effort, and considerable attainment, especially in America and Britain. There is still a great distance to go, but I have every confidence, possibly naïvely so, that that ability of scholarship to correct itself will some day bring about the assertion of detachment and objectivity even in this field.

THE LEGAL CHAIN OF TRADITION

What is more to the point than the value, high or low, of the legalism of Judaism is the question of how the legalism of Judaism can be understood respecting the possible phases that it may have gone through in the first Christian century.[13] My meaning may be perhaps a little clearer if I again raise the question of the Book religion, the question of the proof-text, and the question of a growing tradition. It is related of Hillel the elder, who flourished in the late first pre-Christian century and into the first Christian century, that he was a Babylonian by birth, and that he came to Judea, where at one of the academies he engaged in a discussion of a particular legal point not covered in the Bible. The people with whom he was engaged refused to accept a series of three biblical prooftexts which Hillel fluently offered them. Unable to persuade them through prooftexts, Hillel then said, in support of his position, that he had "received" it from his predecessors, the sages Shemaiah and Abtalion.[14] Once Hillel cited this bit of received "tradition," he achieved the persuasion that his prooftextings failed to achieve.

There is always difficulty in knowing if an anecdote of this kind is meant by the talmudic sages to be taken as purely historical or not. But even if the anecdote is legendary, there is surely historicity in the contrast that the anecdote sets up between an inherited tradition, transmitted from a past generation, and the mere prooftext as offered by a contemporaneous generation. What is significant is that in the beginning of the first Christian century there already existed a sense of "authoritative tradition." How old it was by then is beyond ascertaining.

What would appear to be the outstanding contribution of the first Christian century to the process of growth and development in Judaism is the stabilization both of the inherited tradition and of principles of scriptural interpretation, so that the two, as it were, could go hand in hand, instead of seeming to clash. The effect of such stabilization is this: the student of Rabbinic Literature discovers in Rabbinic Judaism, as early as the end of the first Christian century, an architectonic structure of surprising force. Rabbinic Judaism seems to blossom in breadth and in depth and in system and in grand synthesis, as a consequence of a peaceful evolution, accomplished from within, and marked by no inner violent upheavals.

The clue to this quiet evolution seems to me to lie in the essential nature of this Rabbinic Judaism, in some circumstances and in some characteristics of the Literature that seem deliberately designed. For example, the Maccabean revolt is never narrated in the Rabbinic Literature, nor is the revolt against Rome handled by any more than allusion, nor the destruction of the Temple dealt with except by reference, and the Bar Kochba uprising concentrates on the spiritual leadership provided by Rabbi Akiba and not on the Bar Kochba himself. Rabbinic Judaism neglects history, for its concentration is on religion. One needs only to list certain key phrases to summarize the drastic nature of this religious reformation: the Temple destroyed, priesthood unnecessary, the synagogue vital, the rabbi essential, animal sacrifice gone, and prayer a surrogate for it.

Now this drastic alteration, whatever debt it may owe to events or to personalities, owes its ultimate debt to the circumstance of the Book. Without the emergence of the Bible and its centrality in the late post-Exilic period, such a drastic alteration of Judaism in the first century would never have taken place.

THE IMPORT OF A SACRED SCRIPTURE

It seems to me that far too little attention is paid to the underlying issue relevant to any tradition that has a sacred Scripture which is deemed to be ancient. The issue is this, that the later generations are faced inevitably with a need to find some viable harmony between the demands, or the opportunities, of the new age, and the presumed eternal verity of the ancient. The pious communicant of the later time is necessarily obliged to acquire his own sense of the existential relevancy of the ancient text to his own life, for without this relevancy the ancient text serves only as an object of an antiquarian adoration. The communicant, unlike the modern scholar, can never stop at the question, what does the ancient text mean; he must go on to ask, what does it mean to *me?*

It is normal for three positions to emerge. One position is retentive of the words of the Scripture in their literal sense, and the answer to the question, what does it mean to me, takes the form of adjusting the present life to the ancient formulation. At the other extreme, there is the position which holds that it is the intent of Scripture, as discerned by interpretation, which is relevant to the present life; in effect, the literal meaning of Scripture recedes in importance, though not necessarily so in theory. The middle position involves that of a certain self-limitation, of a certain self-imposed restraint, binding Scripture to the present at the same time that one binds the present to the ancient past. The process in all three positions involves fixing on some particular view or principle respecting the meaning of the ancient Scripture, and some quantity, large or small, of imputed elasticity supposedly inherent in the Scripture. None of the three positions, of course, repudiates Scripture, or ever asserts anything other than the fullest fidelity to it.

SADDUCEES AND PHARISEES

We can perhaps see this basic issue most clearly by turning now to the Sadducees and the Pharisees, and later to the Qumran community. Respecting the Sadducees, we first need to remind ourselves that we know a little about their negations, and almost nothing about their affirmations. Erwin Goodenough proposed that the Sadducees (to whom he felt Philo had a relationship) believed in immortality, even while they denied resurrection; this is possible, but quite undocumented. The Sadducees, whom we might denominate as the first historic exemplars of Bible literalism, represent a viewpoint recurrent in the Judeo-Christian history for which the Protestant term Sola Scriptura is an apt phrase. Far more important than certain calendar differences which arose between the Sadducees and the Pharisees is the crucial point as to whether or not the Book, admitted by both to be sacred and conceived of by both as authoritative, is or is not susceptible of any elasticity, and whether the prescribed norm was to be an undeviating loyalty to the literal text, or whether the norm was to lie among the illuminating deductions which inventive minds would infer from Scripture. The Sadducean literalism offered the theoretical danger of rigidity, of an inability to cope with new events and new needs; the Pharisaic method offered the theoretical danger of excessive elasticity, of caprice, and possibly even of license. Pharisaic non-literalism itself necessarily needed to develop some viable controls as the respective adherents of some basic positions debated the question of just how much elasticity could be allowed. The great teacher Shammai can be said to have been a "strict constructionist," and the greater teacher Hillel the exponent of a more elastic position.

PHARISAISM AND RABBINISM

But were Hillel and Shammai Pharisees, or were they rabbis? Neither is ever spoken of by the title "rabbi," for they flourished before the word became a title. I raise the question to emphasize that we do not know exactly how much Rabbinism owes to Pharisaism as a matter of organic, genetic connection; it is unclear. Obviously, Rabbinism flourished by extending into its broad and remarkably well-defined system that impulse in Pharisaism which asserted the legitimacy of interpreting Scripture. Perhaps what in Pharisaism may have been no more than a sense of direction, and a precedent, served as a prologue to Rabbinism. Yet where Pharisaism ends and Rabbinism begins[15] involves a borderline which may be of interest to modern scholars but was probably quite unnoticed in the surging Judaism of the first century. Indeed, the chief overt aspects of Rabbinism—the rabbi, the synagogue, the liturgy in the synagogue, the evolution of the political power of the Rabbinic patriarchate—may well have represented uneven growths, a forest of trees of different kinds and of different sizes, so that we are today unable to say what in the first century was a full-grown oak and what was simply a stripling poplar. Respecting Pharisaism itself, we need to acknowledge that we deal with a number of uncertainties.[16] Was it a thoroughly organized movement with its brotherhoods, or instead, or else in addition, an impulse, rather than essentially an organized movement? Was Pharisaism in 150 B.C. the same as Pharisaism in A.D. 50? Might Pharisaism have spread from Judea into the Dispersion, either as a movement or as an impulse, and did Pharisaism in the Dispersion, as possibly exemplified by Paul (Philippians 3:9), undergo enough modification to differentiate it from Judean Pharisaism? We do not know.

THE SYNAGOGUE

These unclarities might well be epitomized in some of the current debate about the origin of the synagogue. While the archeologists have discovered no synagogue edifice earlier than the second Christian century, and even though Yadin has identified a chamber at Masada as possibly a synagogue, the allusions to the synagogue in the first-century Christian literature make it plain that the synagogue already existed prior to the second Christian century. So, too, clear allusions occur in Josephus, in *The Jewish War*, II, 285–6, and in *The Life*, 276. Moreover, the scholarly views on the synagogue attribute its origin to a range beginning with the Deutero-nomic reformation in 621 B.C., through the Babylonial Exile, and to a new theory that insists that the synagogue did not exist as late as the time of Ben Sira.[17] This latter view does not commend itself to me in the slightest, except possibly in one respect, that the synagogue *as an edifice* may not have existed in Ben Sira's time, but the synagogue as a place of study of Scripture, and thereby removed only by a step from prayer, surely must have existed. It was quite impossible for the Book to be adulated without there developing a place, an institution, where the Book was taught by a specialist, first called the scribe and later the rabbi. If by synagogue we mean the *act* of assembling to hear Scripture expounded, then necessarily its origin must be looked for no later than in the early post-Exilic period. The related question of when the synagogue came to be a separate edifice, and then came to be a highly ornate edifice, is quite different from the problem of the origin of the synagogue. Whether or not the narrative in Luke 4:16–30 of Jesus reading from the scroll of Isaiah in the synagogue in Galilee is historical,[18] there is every pre-sumption that the practice of reading Scripture at a gathering place, which Luke clearly has in mind, in no way violates probability or possibility. The fact that Scripture *was* read and expounded at that time is as unmistakable as is the obscurity of the evolution of the systematic readings[19] of the Pentateuch on the one-year or three-year cycle, known from later times, and reading of the stipulated prophetic section, the *Haph-tara*,[20] also known from later times. These systems may pos-sibly be later than the first century, but the practice of read-ing Scripture cannot be. It is quite reasonable that system arises as a sequel to antecedent practice.

THE SERMON

Similarly, there may well have been a development, even prior to the first Christian century, from the random halakic or haggadic inquiry connected with scriptural reading into the structured homily, the archetype of that unique development in the history of religions, the sermon. The Rabbinists of modern times seem to be agreed that the initial scriptural elucidation was halakic rather than haggadic, yet I have the suspicion that their statement is not without some difficulty, for the antiquity of the haggadic elaborations in Jubilees and in Josephus persuades me that the haggadic was quite as ancient. Possibly what the Rabbinists mean is that the sequential compilations of the individual halakic pericopes represent something of greater antiquity than the compilations of haggadic fancies. On this there is universal agreement: the halakic *midrashim* were compiled earlier than were the haggadic *midrashim*. But the scholars are quite unable to trace the steps which led from a bare explanation of the biblical phrase or verse into an expanded, thoroughly worked-out discourse on the phrase or verse.

However inspirational or hortatory the sermon came to be, in its basic intent it seems to me to have been necessarily pedagogical. The expository discourse based on something found in a sacred Book seems to partake of the school lesson as much as it does of religious exhortation. Since the Bible was the inspiration, then necessarily the preacher was like the teacher. He inquired with ever-increasing profundity into the meaning of the Scripture, and the inquiry led to the disclosure of a range of facets of meaning only hinted at in the scriptural verse.

THE SPIRIT OF RABBINISM

If in its legal aspects this process of inquiry led to casuistry (which, mistakenly, has come to have a pejorative overtone) and to a preoccupation with what a modernist may consider unnecessary fine points, nevertheless, to comprehend Rabbinic Literature and the spirit of Rabbinism one must notice the extraordinary illumination which such inquiry attains, both in frequency and in abundance. The Rabbinic Literature, in its form, namely Talmud or Midrash, lacks the grandeur of the Prophets or Job or Psalms; the Rabbinic religion, on the other hand, represents an advance beyond biblical religion. A lack of sympathy for the method of Rabbinism has betrayed more than one Christian scholar into a failure to recognize the content that the constrained method produced. Moreover, it is as partisan and one-sided to assess Rabbinic religion from the standpoint of Paul as it is to assess Paul from the standpoint of Rabbinic convictions. Again, the supposition that the concrete forms of teaching that are characteristic of Rabbinic Literature, namely aphorism and parable, are in themselves less worthy than abstract philosophizing has led to the curious paradox of the willingness of nineteenth-century Christians to scorn the Rabbinic parables and at the same time to adulate their counterparts in the Gospels. Obviously, not every Rabbinic parable is worldshaking, nor is every aphorism free from the possibility of being merely witty rather than trenchant, and I am by no means contending that every item in Rabbinic Literature is necessarily of intrinsic, ongoing merit. I am only saying that the manner of Rabbinic Literature does not necessarily render it any less profound than the content of Philo, and I am contending that the total effect of Rabbinic Literature and the total thrust of Rabbinic teaching comprise a religiosity of stupendous value.

MYSTICISM

The pristine bondage of the Rabbinic Literature, especially the *Gemara*, to an exclusively oral form, entailed the procedure in the academies of interrupting acute halakic discussions with anecdotes about the authorities engaged in these discussions, this probably as a mnemonic device. These anecdotal digressions and divagations ought in themselves to have prevented the nineteenth-century scholarship from its misinterpretation of Judaism as only a legalism, and the further misinterpretation of Rabbinic Judaism as devoid of mysticism. (I must confess here to a personal ambivalence, in that my own bent is rationalist and non-mystical, and at the same time, I find a fascination in the study of mysticism; indeed, I think that it is the mysticism of Philo which attracts me even more than the other aspects of Philo.) What ought to be striking, at least to my mind, is this, that the Rabbinic Literature, though legal, contains so many direct allusions to both theoretical and practical mysticism as to make it astounding that the nineteenth-century scholarship failed to notice them. The quantity of mystic or quasi-mystic material in the Rabbinic Literature directly and explicitly reproduced is relatively small,[21] but the quantity is quite large enough to indicate a considerable breadth and depth of mystic background. This is the case respecting the mysteries of creation, the character of the First Adam, that curious angel Metatron (about whom conflicting theories in abundance exist), and the lore of the "chariot."

Now these matters have all been investigated by scholars in a variety of ways, and naturally an extensive bibliography

could be compiled of the secondary literature relating to
Jewish mysticism. There is not the slightest disagreement that
the roots of such mystic tendencies lie in the period antecedent to the first Christian century. What defies assessment
is the extent and depth of this mysticism in the first Christian
century. It would seem reasonably clear that fully developed
mystic systems as such did not exist in Palestinian Judaism
and it is quite likely that the occasional Rabbinic mystic utterances reflect either individuals or else limited circles, and
perhaps the words sporadic and scattered might well characterize such tendencies in the first Christian century. We
often encounter the modern book review which chastises the
author of a study in economics for not dealing with philosophy, even though the author has stated specifically that
philosophy is outside the immediate orbit of his limited study.
Similarly, it may well be that the legal thrust of Rabbinic
Literature precludes any preoccupation with the mystic
traditions in Judaism as outside its legitimate orbit, and it is
therefore somewhat frivolous to lament that the legal literature abstains from satisfying our curiosity about mysticism. It
is bad scholarship to fail to grasp the idiosyncrasies of the
Jewish legal literature. It must therefore suffice to say that we
face the paradox of abundant clues to the existence of first-
century mystic tendencies, but their contours defy our assessment for the given age.

THE SANHEDRIN

Even a word as well known to us as *Sanhedrin* confronts
us with a methodological problem. There is a Talmud tractate
that bears the name *Sanhedrin*. Josephus alludes to the
Sanhedrin from time to time, as for example, the trial of
Herod after his execution of Hezekiah, in approximately 43
or 42 B.C. The first use of the term *Sanhedrin* in Josephus re-

lates to the decree of the Roman governor of Syria, Gabinius, and his division of Judea into districts numbering five, each of which had a Sanhedrin. Josephus comments in one sentence that the "people, removed from monarchic rule, lived under an aristocracy." Elsewhere, as in *Antiquities*, XI, 111, Josephus seems to mean by this Sanhedrin "aristocracy" simple priestly rule. The parallel passage in *The Jewish War* uses the term *Synod* rather than *Sanhedrin* for these five councils.

Since 1902, scholarship has been strongly influenced by the view of Adolph Büchler, who so interpreted some of the discordancy in the Rabbinic materials as to assume that there were two *Synedria*, which were different in character and function and which officiated side by side, the one political, and the other religious. Much of the scholarly discussion of Sanhedrin has rotated around the supposition of these two diverse Synedria, and one might say that it has been the political Sanhedrin which appears in the accounts in Josephus and the New Testament, and the religious Sanhedrin in the Rabbinic sources. Again, the Bet Din (court of law) established at Jamnia in 90 is often viewed as in some sense a continuation of the Sanhedrin, but of which of these two, one might hesitate to say. It is held that it was the political, not the religious Sanhedrin which condemned Jesus. (Is it relevant to cite the frivolity that among Jews of Houston it has been frequent to say that it was the Galveston Jews who did the crucifying!?)

On the other hand, the view of Burkill in the *Interpreter's Dictionary of the Bible* must be reckoned with—that the Rabbinic Literature reads back into the period before 70 suppositions about the Sanhedrin which characterized the Bet Din *after* 70; if this view is extended in its implication, then the supposed distinction between the two Synedria would tend to become dissolved. If I understand the situation respecting the hypothetical two Sanhedrins, I would comment that Josephus gives us far too little data for us to fashion any secure view of the Sanhedrin from him, and that the Gospel materials are simultaneously vague and also fraught with the possibility of unreliability, since the Gospels were written rather far removed in time and place from the trial of Jesus, and are marked by palpable tendentiousness. The endless debates that have gone on as to whether the Sanhedrin of the trial of Jesus had or did not have the right to pass a sentence of death are capable of explanation only on the basis that we do not have enough information about the Sanhedrin to know what the facts were. There is, moreover, the possibility, so often pointed out, that the Gospel contention that the Sanhedrin did not have the power to pass the death sentence (John 18:31) is an untenable, apologetic explanation of why it was that the Romans, rather than the Jews, executed Jesus. I would suppose that the present heightened interest in the Sanhedrin among Jews and Christians rotates around modern apologetic necessities stemming from the deicide charge, with the resultant wish of involved persons either to challenge the authenticity of the Gospel accounts or to defend it, and not from any intrinsic interest in the history and development of the Sanhedrin itself. At any rate, there are strong reasons for regarding as no longer tenable the frequent supposition that there were two Sanhedrins that has been prevalent since 1902. The reasonable conclusion to my mind seems to be that we do not have sufficient information through which to be precise about the Sanhedrin in the first Christian century.[22]

THE SYNAGOGUE LITURGY

When we study the development of liturgy, we again confront great areas of darkness. That liturgical prayers accompanied the Temple service is indirectly well attested, this by the mere existence of the Book of Psalms. There is no information at all available on the transfer of liturgical elements of Temple worship to the synagogue.[23]

There is even a jumble of contradictory data about when the Shemoneh 'Esrēh,[24] the "eighteen benedictions," came into fixed use. Indeed, there are first-century sages who are on record as having protested against prayer in a fixed formulary way. It is well known that the Mishna itself abstains from reproducing the eighteen benedictions. The Patriarch Gemaliel II, who flourished at the end of the first century, appears to have instructed a certain Simeon Ha-Pakoli to assemble or edit the eighteen benedictions, and to make the recitation of the eighteen incumbent on everyone in the three daily services. Granted that the "eighteen benedictions" were the core of the synagogue liturgy and that that liturgy came to be enriched and extended and broadened, and granted that at least portions of the eighteen benedictions have a high antiquity, I for one am quite unable to see precisely what the synagogue liturgy was in the period before 70.

Another pillar of the liturgy is the Shema ("Hear O Israel"), and its array of benedictions. The assertion has been made[25] that in Josephus the recitation of the Shema is already known, and there ascribed as an injunction from Moses, Antiquities, IV, 8:13. This assertion goes quite beyond what Josephus there states, for Josephus in that section does not mention the Shema at all. Josephus in that passage has Moses merely enjoin two daily periods of prayer; the Rabbinic tradition, however, attributes to Moses an injunction for three daily prayer periods.[26] Furthermore, Josephus speaks of the reading of the Law in a septennial cycle, whereas the settled practice in Rabbinic times became for Babylonian Jews to read the Pentateuch in an annual cycle, while in Palestine it was to be read in a triennial cycle. There is, in

addition, evidence of second-century proposals that would
have made the cycle vary between two and a half years and
five and a half years.[27]

No one should be surprised that there is such unclarity and
vagueness. It is inherent in the situation that so long as the
Temple was standing, the synagogue was only a supplement
to it and, prior to 70, still at a stage that in some sense must
be considered incomplete; it was only after the Temple was
destroyed that the synagogue became the major institution
and that disparate practices were worked through to fixity—
overcoming discordant usages, and conflicting opinions of
the Rabbinic sages.

ETHNOCENTRICITY: UNIVERSALISM AND PARTICULARISM

A factor which I find very difficult to weigh is the possible
distinction between an ethnic group, with religion as its basis,
and a community that is primarily a religious community, in
which the ethnic factor is of less significant consequence. I
find I am always cautioning myself against reading the
modern age into the ancient one. I suppose that one of my
difficulties ensues from encountering, in some of the Christian scholarship, contrasts between a "universalistic" Christianity and a "particularistic" Judaism, which I have felt to
be unviable. These contrasts rotate around interpretations of
Paul, and his words about "neither Greek nor Jew." Two
things seem to me crystal clear. The first is that Jews never
lost their ethnic sense, and Paul also did not. The second is
that the Jewish religious sense was always potentially universalistic, and this for the simple reason that the scattering
of Jews throughout the world made it inevitable that some
cognizance had to be taken of humanity, and hence in some
way to temper the ethnic sense. To me, the specific point at
which the Christian claim of universalism fails most sharply

is this, that granted that Paul tends to liquidate the tradition of the Jewish ethnic sense, I do not see that Christianity completely escaped possessing a somewhat similar, somewhat analogous sense of a particular community. Indeed, for the Church to be the mystic body of Christ meant that it was an entity distinct from the rest of the world, and much as outsiders were welcome to come in, it was into an inside that they were welcome to enter. I have said elsewhere that I do not believe it proper to set Jewish particularism and Christian universalism over and against each other, for, on the one hand, there were universal tendencies in Judaism, and on the other, there were quite particularistic tendencies in Christianity. In my view Christianity emerged not as a pure universalism but as a new particularism.

I read with approval the assertions of both Juster and Moore that the Jewish patriarchate which developed at the end of the first Christian century was ethnic rather than limitedly religious, and I see no reason to combat this view. Yet I wonder from time to time if there is not a viable distinction between the overt organization of groups, such as the Jewish *ethnos* in the Graeco-Roman Dispersion, and the religious thinking within that ethnos which might well have transcended the ethnos itself. For example, there could be no doubt that a Philo, who went on a mission to Rome on behalf of the Jewish community of Alexandria, was a loyal member of the ethnos; at the same time, the definition which Philo gives of a Hebrew, namely one who sees a vision of God, seems to me completely without ethnic limitation. I often wonder if we do not interpret the ethnic sense of the Jewish people in the first Christian century almost exclusively as a counterfoil to the anti-ethnic Christian universalism, not of Paul, but of nineteenth-century analysts. Certainly in my reading of Rabbinic Literature I am quite aware of a strong ethnic sense; yet when I read Josephus, and his obsequious

aspersion of the Jewish loyalty which culminated in the rebellion against the Romans in 66, I find in him an accentuated
ethnocentrism which is in contrast with the universalism
which I recurrently find in the Rabbinic Literature. It leads
me to wonder whether the narrow perspective of Josephus
does not lead to an inadvertent distortion, that the ethnocentricity inherent in his writing does not adequately reflect
the universalism which I find not only in IV Ezra, but also
in so much of Philo. The Jewish tradition itself speaks frequently of the seven laws of the "sons of Noah," [28] which
are regarded as those laws obligatory on all mankind in con-
tradistinction to the total array of laws binding on the Jews
alone.

When I ask myself what is at stake in this inquiry into
universalism and particularism, then surely a modern partisanship of modern apologists, on whatever side, scarcely merits
attention. The only legitimate interest is the question of how
accurately and responsibly we can understand the nature of
this entity, Rabbinic Judaism, and within that context, how
responsibly we can understand that portion of its development which took place in the first Christian century. Do we
fully and adequately understand first-century ethnocentricity?
I doubt it.

QUMRAN

Respecting the Dead Sea Scrolls and the Qumran community, I would take it that by now the so-called battle of
the Scrolls is ended, and we live in a state of armistice, though
perhaps the peace treaties have as yet not been signed. It still
appears that from time to time there are border raids by
isolated partisans, but it seems to me that, at the moment, only
minor skirmishes are being fought. To my mind, the appropriate way to approach the Scrolls is to say that prior to

their discovery, we already had the bodies of literature, Apocrypha and Pseudepigrapha, Hellenistic Jewish literature, and Rabbinic Literature, which threw light on the Judaisms of the first Christian century, and now we have, in addition, the attestation of the Scrolls. An understanding of the first Christian century is incomplete without the Scrolls; it is also true that a study on the basis of the Scrolls in isolation, as if what we antecedently possessed is to be aside, or ignored, is clearly a misdirection.

For all that the Scrolls do illuminate one aspect of Jewish life in the first century, even in that aspect which they illuminate, we deceive ourselves if we think they provide full illumination. It seems to me quite probable that if we were miraculously to recover *everything* that was written and preserved and maintained and copied in the Qumran community, then the sectarian documents which have survived would turn out to be only a small portion of a very much larger entity. Yet even if we possessed that entirety, and even if we sifted through the various allusions to the Essenes in Josephus and in Pliny and in Philo and the Church Fathers, and persuaded ourselves about what is historically reliable,[29] we would still fall short of being able to estimate to what extent the sectarian documents in the Qumran community represent a tiny or medium-sized or large portion of the Jewish population, and, comparably, to estimate to what extent the religion in the Scrolls represents a minority group or something more than a minority group. On the one hand, I have not found myself persuaded that in any one single item of overwhelming significance the religion reflected in the Scrolls is absolutely unique. On the other, the Qumran documents do constitute a kind of inwardly consistent single variety of the plural varieties of Judaisms that existed in the first Christian century. I would set Qumran in the position of holding to the intent of Scripture as seen through interpretation, while the literal meaning of Scripture recedes in importance.

I have written on other occasions to express my dissent from the methodology whereby alleged parallels between the Scrolls and the New Testament are interpreted as signifying a particular and direct influence of the Qumran community on earliest Christianity. I have raised the question of the legitimacy of assuming an antecedent source for everything in the New Testament in general, and of regarding the Scrolls as this rich source in particular, for I have contended that this procedure seems to ignore the large element of creativity within the New Testament writers. I have also commented that, since the Qumran community represented *a* Judaism, we should scarcely be surprised to find in it broad reflections of what would be found in *any* Judaism, namely the influence of Scripture and the influence of the Jewish tradition.

As I have reviewed the literature on the Scrolls, it has seemed to me that much of the warfare has rotated on the wish of a particular scholar to isolate some single item as unique to the Scrolls, and then he is countered by another scholar who denies the accuracy of this attribution of uniqueness, and then goes on to supply his own nomination for what is unique. I have often thought that if the Scrolls could have been accompanied from the start by a Strack and Billerbeck, then much of the warfare would not have arisen. In our context, it might be useful to raise the issue of quantity, and to tabulate, in terms of pages, just how extensive the sectarian documents are. To that end let me list the sectarian documents as the Manual of Discipline, the War of the Sons of Righteous against the Sons of Darkness, the Thanksgiving Psalms, the new Psalms, and the contents of the Commentaries to Habakkuk and to Nahum. On the basis of the ordinary printing of modern Hebrew books, I would tabulate this sectarian data as encompassing between 35 and 45 pages, depending, of course, on the size of the type. In extent—that is, in quantity—the Scrolls do not vie with the hundreds of pages of the Pseudepigrapha, Rabbinic Literature, and the like, but are relatively brief.

The matter of quantity is an objective measurement; that of the quality of the testimony of the Scrolls is a more subjective one. This is the case even when one disregards the lacunae in the text, the illegible sections, and the unintelligible ones. I wonder if it is possible to say that, while the Scrolls give us almost no clear light on any historical events and persons, they still do give us reflections of theological viewpoints. In this absence of the historical, I have found it quite impossible to form in my own mind any pattern of a way in which the theological ideas of the Scrolls were a cause which produced effects; to my mind they seem to me rather to be the effects of antecedent causes, and the Scrolls themselves seem to me to have been without palpable sequel. It is by no means the case that the Scrolls are without interest or without value; it is that they are without tremendous consequence, whereas the incident of Hillel and his appeal to the tradition he had learned from Shammai and Abtalion was fraught with consequence. We can see in early first-century Judaism the impulses which developed into Rabbinism and Christianity. Qumran, though, represents a dead end. One must beware of arguing from the circumstance that the Scroll community came to nothing that the Scroll doctrines were either totally marginal or totally idiosyncratic; I do not believe that such an argument could be made. But the Scrolls do seem to be some digression which turned into a cul-de-sac, and, indeed, seemed fated to. I do not know any way of estimating the extent in breadth or the influence in depth of the theological premises of the Scrolls in the context of first-century Judaism. I am quite willing to believe that Qumran might be described as having been of some considerable import prior to 70, though we cannot be sure. What

I think we can be sure of is that after 70, the theological ideas, like the organized group itself, receded in importance and ultimately came to be dissolved.

SUB ROSA ART?

The discovery at Dura-Europos of the synagogue which dates from the third century is significant mostly because of the mural paintings. These have seemed to be in all defiance of what was known from Rabbinic Literature, from Philo, and from Josephus, respecting the virtually universal Jewish prohibition of pictorial art. Erwin Goodenough has set forth a theory that while the main lines of Jewish expression and attitude were hostile to pictorial art, the murals at Dura-Europos are indicative of a widespread, sub rosa, popular Jewish religiosity which did not eschew the pictorial. This theory would suppose that on the one hand there existed the developing normative tendency, ultimately guided, directed, and even governed by the rabbis, which looked askance at art, and on the other hand there was the popular tendency which not only had practiced it, but broadly encouraged it. If I understand correctly, Goodenough's argument in part deals with the circumstance that second-century synagogues, such as those at Bet Alpha and Bet Shearim, present mosaics which depict Helios and the signs of the zodiac, this within Palestine. While such synagogue decoration is different in its form from the direct pictorial representation of Old Testament scenes that we find at Dura, Goodenough appears to hold that the impulse which led both to the decorations, on the one hand, and to the pictures, on the other, was the same, and that only the forms were different. This theory necessarily rests on the supposition that there existed a sub rosa popular culture that was at variance with the authority of the developing Rabbinate. Professor

Ephraim A. Urbach[30] of the Hebrew University, in dissenting from Goodenough's view, makes the point that as early as the first century pagan idolatry was no longer the problem to Jews as, for example, it had been in the second pre-Christian century. It was firmly established not only in the Judaism of the second century, but also in Christianity, that emperor worship, the acme of idolatry, was totally inadmissable, and was so axiomatic as to need no additional restatement. In this context, the decoration of the Galilean synagogues so completely failed to smack of idolatry that the rabbis had no occasion to oppose it vigorously. Urbach, then, denies totally the premise of Goodenough. Urbach offers a chronological explanation for his viewpoint, whereas Goodenough's explanation rests on supposed diametrically opposed impulses within the same time period. Moreover, Urbach is able to cite passages from the Rabbinic Literature in support of his position, but Goodenough's contention rests on inferences and not on any such citations.

Moreover, Goodenough's full theory is very much broader, for he sees in the decorative motifs, which on all hands are acknowledged to be present, the reflection of a sub rosa, *mystical* Judaism. Accordingly, he gives a consistently mystical interpretation to the decorative motifs, though almost never possessing literary sources to cite in justifying this mystic interpretation. The labor that went into the twelve volumes, *Jewish Symbols in the Graeco-Roman Period*, represents a tremendous attainment by one scholar. What Goodenough has essayed to do has been to give a literary explanation of non-literary materials, but without possessing the ancient sources to justify his modern literary interpretation. His attainment is scarcely diminished when one must say plainly that he has placed more reliance on Jungean psychology than he has on clear and unmistakable sources.

To my mind there is also a constant confusion in Goodenough's procedure between symbol and mysticism, for even in his own distinction of the difference between objective and subjective religions, I do not see that so-called objective religions were necessarily without symbols, or that such symbols, even if they possessed some over-meanings, necessitate a theory of a thoroughgoing mysticism. In Lecture III I will discuss points at which it has seemed to me that Goodenough has gone astray in his view of Philo; here I must express the judgment that he has overinterpreted and thereby misinterpreted, and that he has proceeded beyond legitimate restraints into untenable inferences.

NEW TESTAMENT AND RABBINIC JUDAISM

In Lecture IV I shall speak in greater detail about early Christianity in its own terms. Here I speak about it in relation to Judaism. I have long had the opinion that it is virtually impossible to recover the Judaism of the age of Jesus, the Judaism of the age before 70. Nevertheless, a few themes seem to be clear. It seems clear to me, for example, that earliest Christianity grew out of the Judaism of the synagogue and not out of the Judaism of the Temple. Indeed, if we were to speculate on how we would describe Christianity if it had chanced to come to the same cul-de-sac that the Qumran community did, and had become dissolved at 70, then I am persuaded that we would view it as a facet of late Pharisaism or early Rabbinism.

Let me raise a question that seems to me to be seldom asked: What illumination do the documents of early Christianity provide for our understanding the ultimate flowering of Rabbinic Judaism? Do the Epistles of Paul and the Gospels throw any light on Rabbinic Judaism?

Let me first pursue those elements which seem to me to be affirmative. The strongest statement that I would make is that despite whatever connection earliest Christianity had with the Zealots,[31] Christianity as a distinct movement was basically a Book religion. The circumstance that the purpose for which Scripture is cited in the Christian documents is quite diverse from the purpose of the rabbis in no way affects the validity of this conclusion. On the simplest level, one need only look at those printed versions of the New Testament wherein the quotations from the Old appear in boldface type while the rest of the material is in normal type to see the abundance of the influence of Scripture on the literature of the new movement. Moreover, such scriptural paraphrase and citation is almost invariably non-literal.

In the second place, the conflict stories in the Gospels, even when these have been metamorphosed in the growing Christian tradition from an intra-Jewish debate into a supposition of Christian-versus-Jewish conflicts, carry with them the overtones and the substance of the types of inner Rabbinic disputes known elaborately from the Rabbinic Literature. Indeed, Mathhew 23, with its denunciation of the Pharisees and its prohibition of the title rabbi, should be a clue to us of an awareness in the growing Christian literature of the emergence of Rabbinism to Jewish hegemony.

Next, let me venture a judgment I would find very difficult to buttress by citation: the Gospels give us greater insight into the inner Jewish religious life than do the pages of Josephus. Again, however much the Christian tradition may have metamorphosed the motifs regarding the Jesus of history, the depiction of him in the Gospels as a teacher with disciples makes it easier for us to understand the development of the Rabbinic tradition with its chain of teachers and their disciples.

Even the Epistles of Paul make their contribution in this respect. However we may choose to interpret that difficult phrase, Philippians 3:5, *kata nomon pharisaios* (whether Paul was saying that he was a Pharisee or that his attitude toward Scripture was kindred to that of the Pharisees), there is confirmation in his Epistles of the growth of that kind of Book religion which Rabbinic Judaism represents. Indeed, as I have written elsewhere, the early New Testament literature, but in particular the Gospels, strikes the usual Rabbinist as territory so familiar that often he is unaware of pitfalls, for he too often assumes that in the Gospels he is fully within the ambit of Rabbinic Judaism.[32] The Epistles of Paul and the Gospels teem with so multitudinous an array of peculiar —that is, particular—problems, that a reckless Rabbinist often stumbles, this through a mere unawareness of the particular.

I have also noted elsewhere that very few Rabbinists have ever shared the total skepticism toward the Gospels that marked some of the more extreme nineteenth-century Protestant scholars, for the supposition that an author such as Mark could have created the Jewish setting of his Gospel out of thin air or simply out of imagination remains unpersuasive to those of us who have worked in Rabbinic Literature.[33] The paradox may be put in this way: familiarity with Rabbinic Literature is the greatest persuader of the relative reliability of the Gospel accounts, but, on the other hand, an intimate acquaintance with the Gospels inevitably recalls that host of significant problems which constitute the nub of nineteenth- and twentieth-century Gospel study.

Similarly, I have already mentioned the circumstance that the Rabbinic tradition, the so-called Oral Law, was conceived of as divine, whereas the Corban narrative, especially Mark 7:8, delineates it as human. It is hard for me to believe that this latter delineation is accidental, or that it rests on genuine misunderstanding; it seems to me rather that it is deliberatively tendentious and combative. It does not rest, then, on an ignorance of the Jewish contention of the divine origin of the Oral Law; it is rather so deliberate a denial of the divine nature of the Oral Law that it necessarily reflects a knowledge of the Jewish affirmation.

One must reckon, moreover, with the circumstance that certain motifs, few in number but highly developed, present their own attestation of Christian literature to Rabbinic developments. Consistent with the Christian experience of coming to believe that Jesus had first made a preparatory appearance and would then return in the near future, Christianity altered the older Jewish messianic expectation from the single appearance into the two phases. Yet even this alteration, or embellishment, reflects its actual base, the common messianic motif. When we become aware that the adaptation of the messianic motif among Christians goes to the point of contravening and contradicting the usual array of Jewish messianic expectations, we cease to expect to find views in the Rabbinic Literature identical with those offered in developing Christianity.

Moreover, the lack of historical awareness in the Christian literature is comparable to the lack of historical awareness in Rabbinic Literature, and this also contributed to alteration. Thus, as Professor Fritz Baer[34] of the Hebrew University has pointed out about the Gospel incident of the cleansing of the Temple, one could not infer from the narrative that Herod's Temple was the complex of structures that in fact it was—the equivalent of what we would today call a civic center. Rather, the Gospel narratives conceive of the Temple as though it were a tiny pagan edifice, greatly restricted in size, and quite isolated from the adjoining towers and fortresses and other imposing buildings. Looking at the modern archeologists' re-creations of Herod's Temple, whether in line-drawings or in replicas, it is difficult to believe the evangelists had ever seen the Temple or had any clear understanding of what it was.

But still pursuing the question of the use of Christian

literature for understanding Rabbinic Judaism, in considering the Epistles of Paul, one must begin by noting that late Pharisaism/proto-Rabbinism represented an impulse which was the exact antithesis of that of Paul. Thus, whereas to Paul's mind the laws of Moses were passé and null and void, and hence the Law needed no further development and no refinement of its legalistic requirements, the Rabbinic tradition worked on exactly the opposite premise, that the Law was eternal and hence cried for a clarification of the legalistic requirements. With this theme of the invalidity of the Law so central in Paul, one could scarcely expect the content of Paul's Epistles to overlap with that of the rabbis. To the extent that Paulinism or quasi-Paulinism informs the Gospels of Mark, Luke, and John, this Pauline emphasis creates numerous situations of apparent unrelatedness between early Christianity and Judaism. Perhaps simply to understand that Paul and Rabbinism are antithetical provides a key for us, for we can reasonably conjecture that the views are antithetical because of some measure of direct confrontation, and the earnestness with which Paul pursues his anti-legalism is explicable because the same age witnessed an earnestness in legalism.

But we need to be very wary in the matter of the possible relationships. The double problem exists in looking at the Christian legalism reflected in the Gospels, particularly in Matthew. First we must understand it in relation to Paul, and only then may we understand it in relation to developing Rabbinism. The Sermon on the Mount, and especially Matthew 5:17, "Think not that I came to destroy the Law or the prophets; I am not come to destroy but to fulfill it, and not one jot or tittle will pass from the Law," presents its own problem within the development of Christianity. Protestant scholars ascribe this material to Matthew, not to Jesus, and the legalism in Matthew can perhaps be interpreted as in the flow of post-Pauline developments; it is an innovation, a created Christian legalism[35] not directly related to the preceding Jewish legalism. If this is so, and if the two versions of legalism provide some elements that are somewhat similar, it is easy to miss what is divergent and distinctive and different in the two. We must understand that the presence of somewhat analogous motifs in the two legalisms does not necessarily represent the influence of one on the other; moreover, what at first glance seems to be analogous can turn out to be quite diverse. For example, in the Rabbinic tradition it is held that the Sabbath rules can be suspended for what is described as *pikuaḥ nefesh*, danger to one's life. That can mean, for example, that the limitation on bodily movement on the Sabbath to 2000 ells could be set aside if one needed to go to a doctor who was 2500 ells away. On the other hand, to declare that the Sabbath is made for man and not man for the Sabbath, and that the son of man is lord of the Sabbath, both denotes and also connotes something quite different from the mere suspension of the Sabbath regulations by the rabbis in instances of emergency. Accordingly, it does not seem to me to be sound to regard somewhat analogous motifs either as identical or as common in origin.

The compendia of Rabbinic materials first arose in the thirteenth century for polemical purposes (as was the case with Ramon Martini's *Pugio Fidei*). This gave way to the only indirectly hostile, then to more deliberately illuminating compendia of the seventeenth century, and culminated in Strack-Billerbeck in the twentieth century. These compendia have a utility only when they are used with extreme delicacy. Very often that utility has seemed to me to be necessarily limited to what is implicit in the circumstance that earliest Christianity was a Judaism and therefore shared in large measure that which was the property of all Judaism. Even so, the specific differences that distinguish Christianity are factors never to be forgotten. The broad elements held in common are more implicit than explicit and often without direct demonstrable significance. The legalism in Matthew does not seem to me in substance to illuminate the Rabbinic legalism; the Jewish legalism is a direct outgrowth of Pentateuchal law, the Christian a newly created entity ensuing after Paul's abrogation of the Law. The author of Matthew reveals his awareness of the divergency of the legalisms, and he is eager to maintain the divergency; on the other hand, in a context in which legalism has been challenged on principle, he invokes the scribes and the Pharisees as sitting in the seat of Moses, and in the same paragraph endorses legalism but also warns against the Pharisaic forms, to the point of prohibiting the use of the title rabbi (Matthew 23:2-8).

As to the converse, the question of the significance of the Rabbinic Literature for illuminating the New Testament, I should think the situation is exactly similar, except in one regard. Inasmuch as the Gospels, arising after the Epistles of Paul and not before them, represent a second stage in the development of Christian literature, but presuppose a Judean setting, they are characterized by the premise that the reader possesses certain information and that he understands such matters as the Messiah, baptism, eschatology, the kingdom of God, and what a synagogue is. Perhaps the readers of the Gospels, when they were written, possessed such knowledge. For the modern reader of the Gospels, such relevant information is not to be assumed. Data about customs, practices, procedures, and theological views culled from the Rabbinic Literature can help us understand many of the implicit suppositions of the Gospels. But the methodological error that seems to me to be constantly repeated in the scholarship is the movement from the legitimate generalities into illegitimate specifics, through the failure to recognize that in the specifics, the context, the tone, and the impulses have drastically changed.

Notes

1. The disappearance, like much else respecting the Sadducees, is not documented. The rise of Karaism in the eighth century, with some similarities to Sadduceeism, prompts the occasional suggestion, which I heard repeatedly from my teacher, Erwin R. Goodenough, that there was some "subterranean" direct connection between the Sadducees and the Karaites. The unpublished mimeographed notes of a course in history of another of my teachers, Jacob Mann, p. 5, contains this sentence: "Though the Sadducees disappear as an organized party, their ideas did not entirely die out; some people used to read their works in private, which finally culminated in the 8th century Karaism." This is, of course, completely speculative; no evidence is available to sustain the suggestion.

2. Jamnia (*Yavne* in Hebrew) has ceased to be merely a place name and has come to be the symbol for the reorganization of Judaism implied in the end of the temple cultus and the priesthood and in the rise of the synagogue and the Rabbinate. As a symbol it has become invested with a range of

activities touching such things as the synagogue liturgy, the calendar, and the possible final canonization of Scripture. It is, however, impossible to be precise about what took place at Jamnia, and the word as a symbol seems to me to represent oversimplification and exaggeration. The final canonization there of Scripture rests on the Mishnaic tradition (Yadaim 3. 5) that the sanctity of Song of Songs and Ecclesiastes was accepted at Jamnia on a celebrated day (the deposing of the patriarch Gamaliel II), but there is abundant evidence (see Moore, *Judaism*, I, 242–3) that there was not true finality at Jamnia. That Jamnia 90 is of utmost significance is beyond dispute; yet we should be wary about knowing too much about it, and avoid attributing to one occasion developments which took place over a much more extended period of time.

3. This temple, at Leontopolis in Egypt, was built by the fugitive priest Onias IV, about 154, on being deprived of the high priesthood which should have been his. It represents the only known instance of a deliberate founding of a temple by Jews in addition to the Temple in Jerusalem. Little is known about it, and it appears to have been of little importance even to Egyptian Jews. The Mishna (Menahot 13:10) seems to regard it as only quasi-legitimate; see Baron, *Social and Religious History of the Jews*, I, pp. 218–19; the relevant literature is cited on p. 394, n. 11.

4. Untrustworthy, because in an apologetic interest, he equates these groups with classes of Greek philosophy. Moreover, the quantity he gives is very small. The conflict in the data on the Essenes between Josephus and Philo leads me to prefer the partially untrustworthy Josephus to the totally untrustworthy Philo in this one regard. See below, note 29.

5. On the premise that Christian readers may not be intimately acquainted with this literature, a brief list and characterization may be in order. It is designed to spur recollection, rather than to introduce and expound in detail.

    i. The Mishna is a compilation of legal requirements, set down in writing about A.D. 175–200. It is arranged on *topics*, in six major divisions, with appropriate subdivisions. In manner, a mishnaic statement is laconic to the point of terseness; it cites the legal opinions of sages, often in unresolved dispute with each other; ordinarily it abstains from quoting a scriptural basis for the legal opinion. The term *tanna* ("teacher") is used to allude to a rabbi who flourished early enough to be mentioned in the Mishna.

2. The Gemara discusses the Mishna respecting such matters as the hypothetical scriptural basis that a *tanna* could have rested his opinion on; in the case of divergent opinions, it settles on its preference for the *halaka* ("the way"), that is, the one opinion accepted out of the diversity; it proceeds to make new legal inferences from the Mishnaic formulation. Mishna plus Gemara equal Talmud. Two versions, or recensions, of the Talmud have been bequeathed to the modern age; the dominant recension is the Babylonian, completed about 500; it is normally cited without specifying "Babylonian." The Palestinian, normally cited either as Palestinian or Jerusalem Talmud, was completed about 450. A sage of the age of the Gemara is an *Amora*.

3. Midrash ("inquiry") is a generic term for scriptural exegesis, resulting from "inquiring" into the meaning of the sacred text. *The* Midrash is the assembly of such exegesis, arranged not topically but in the chapter and verse order of Scripture. The oldest such works are legal, i.e. halakic: The Mekilta ("container") to Exodus, the Sifra ("book") to Leviticus, and Sifre ("books") to Numbers and Deuteronomy; as older collections, the halakic midrash is *tannaitic*, that is, it cites the earliest sages. Much later there were recorded the haggadic ("narrative," as distinct from halakic) *midrashim* (plural of midrash), with their embroidery, embellishments, and hortatory homilies, in the *Midrash Rabba* ("great" Midrash, though the term *rabba* is disputed), to Genesis, Exodus, and so forth.

4. Another tannaitic collection, *Tosefta* (or Tosifta, "addition"), assembles the quasi-Mishnaic utterances which failed of inclusion in the Mishna; an individual verse of the Tosefta is known as a *baraita*.

In a good many passages in Rabbinic Literature, out of cognizance that Scripture was possessed by Christians, the Oral Torah was regarded as uniquely a Jewish possession and in theory it was never to have been committed to writing, for to do so could conceivably have made it, like

Scripture, available to Christians. Implicit in this viewpoint is that Christians used and interpreted Scripture wrongly. I mention this only to underscore the term "oral" in the phrase Oral Torah.

6. I have no recollection of where I first encountered this term. It enters into frequent conversations I have had, and have, with my colleague, Ben Zion Wacholder, an expert rabbinist, in allusion to the Rabbinism prior to Hillel. It is a vague term, of course, for it deals with a most vague and indistinct period. It is used in contrast with the maturing Rabbinism which is relatively (but only relatively) more distinct.

7. See Bernard Bamberger, "The Dating of Aggadic Materials," *Journal of Biblical Literature*, LXVIII (1949), 115–23.

8. Editions in 1903 and 1906; revised in 1926 by Hugo Gressmann with a new title, *Die Religion des Judentums im späthellenistischen Zeitalter*.

9. See below, page 100, note 12.

10. See Schuerer's chapter, "Life under the Law," in *A History of the Jewish People in the Time of Jesus Christ*, II, 2, pp. 90–125. To this Israel Abrahams wrote a reply that would be judged convincing if only it had convinced. It can be set down as something destined to endure eternally that the usual Christian commentators will disparage Judaism and its supposed legalism, and Jewish scholars will reply, usually fruitlessly. I have addressed myself to this topic in three or four essays, and do not intend to pursue this any more beyond this one time, preferring to conclude that with those Christians who persist in deluding themselves about Jewish legalism, no academic communication is possible. The issue is not to bring these interpreters to love Judaism, but only to bring them to a responsible, elementary comprehension of it.

I recognize that the matter is of crucial importance to very many Christian theologians, for if Jewish legalism was other than reprehensible, then the conflict stories in the Gospels call for a reappraisal which can involve some reluctance. Furthermore, the tenability of Paul's strictures about the deficits in the Law would seem to cry for some reassessment.

Modern ecumenism, in addition, necessarily discountenances a spirit of condescension on the part of adherents of one religion to another and to the latter's adherents. Some Christians "solve" the problem by conceding virtues to Judaism in the age long after Christian origins, but suppose that in the age of Jesus and Paul there was a convenient low point. This is the procedure of Francis Burkitt, *The Gospel History and Its Transmission*, pp. 169–74: "I do not think we need deny the real spirituality of the Rabbinical religion because we believe what the Gospels say about the Scribes, or that we need disbelieve what the Gospels say about the Scribes in the first century because we recognize the real spirituality of the Rabbinical religion. We have a right to believe that the spiritual descendants of the Scribes whom Jesus denounced perished in the two Revolts [66–72 and 132–135] during the century after the Crucifixion. . . . The spiritual ancestor both of the Jews who became Christians and the Jews who developed the Rabbinical religion is represented by the Scribe who was 'not far from the Kingdom of God.' "

But why not take Gamaliel I as typical? Or must he, and the Scribe not far from the Kingdom of God, be regarded as exceptions? And was the admitted spirituality of Hillel transmitted in such a way as to by-pass the age of Jesus? And did the Prophets and the Psalms go unread in the age of Jesus?

When I was first struggling to understand Paul, and was mystified at how a Jew could asperse the Law, and how Christians, in the light of his influence, could persist (contradictorily?) in speaking of "God's law" and the like, I told my teacher at Yale that I fell short of understanding it all. He replied—I remember a certain smugness—that Jews were *under* the Law, but Christians were *above* it.

In the Judeo-Christian tradition the recurrence of smug condescension ("triumphalism"?) is only too well attested. Is it any wonder that, apart from their skepticism, so many modern men, regarding the Judeo-Christian tradition, paraphrase the words of Shakespeare, "a plague on all your houses"?

11. In my "The Jewish Scholar and Early Christianity," *Jewish Quarterly Review*, Seventy-fifth Anniversary Volume, 1967,

p. 476, I wrote: "It is not my obligation to the Pharisees to guard their reputation from the assessment of them in some lamentable Christian scholarship; my obligation is to the truth and to sound scholarship, not to the Pharisees. I must not distort Pharisaism affirmatively simply because some Christian scholars distort it negatively."

12. Is it not tragic that much of Claude G. Montefiore, *Rabbinic Literature and Gospel Teachings*, is devoted to questions of the subjectivity (that is, the bias) of interpreters? Repeatedly he feels the need to point out a Lutheran pre-occupation in Strack-Billerbeck, resulting in a judgment passed on "works" in the rabbis, from the vantage point of "faith."

13. If we are to assume, as I think we must, that Jewish post-biblical legalism was born, developed, and matured, then we would be enlightened by being able to see and trace this growth. Various histories of the halaka have been written, these by modern, scientific scholars, as distinct from older traditional scholars; see the Bibliography in Baron, *Social and Religious History of the Jews*, II, p. 432, n. 16.

As Baron correctly notes (ibid., p. 427–8, n. 6), "even the best versed Talmudic scholar still suffers from a lack of critical editions. . . ."

Even if it were possible to be certain about the date and historical reliability of supposedly early materials, these seem to show us broad trends respecting the methods of halakic inference, rather than providing us with a clear, genetic view of the progressive unfolding of it. Indeed, one can doubt whether prior to 70 the halaka unfolded at all systematically, and that there is any true relevance in the implication of the word genetic. The situation seems to be this: We can notice certain trends, though often without being able to date them, and occasionally we can date certain passages by reason of the *Sitz im Leben;* all this is by no means negligible, but at best a few drops in the bucket.

My colleague Ben Zion Wacholder has written a study (to be published in *HUCA*), the first of several he projects, this one denying that the Mekilta is authentically a Tannaitic composition. Dr. Wacholder's view is this, to put it simply, that the entire Rabbinic Literature stands in need of a new approach, and the secondary literature is often a recapitulation of previous untested opinions, all of which probably stand in need of revision. If he is right, much that hitherto has been assumed to be stable is in reality either merely supposition or even wrong. And if this is the case respecting the period after 70, how much more does it apply to the period before 70?

14. Pesahim 66a; P. Pesahim 33a. The precise issue was this, when Passover fell on a Sabbath, was the slaughter of the paschal lamb a higher obligation than the prohibition of labor on the Sabbath? The account tells that Hillel undertook to prove by three scriptural citations that Passover rules took precedence over the Sabbath, but his auditors, "the sons of Bathyra" were unconvinced.

15. I hold the question to be a modern one, not an ancient one. Attendant on the issue, at least as I see things, is that the hostility in the Gospels is directed to Pharisaism, not Rabbinism, and this may well provide us with a clue to the circumstance that in the age of Jesus, Rabbinism had as yet not come to its triumph. The uses of the word rabbi applied to Jesus, as in John 1:49 and 6:25, and as applied to John the Baptist in John 3:26, fall short of being a title; awareness of the term as a title in Matthew 23:7-8 seems to me unmistakable, for the passage in my view does not authentically reflect Jesus or his age, but the sub-apostolic age. Others (e.g. Pierson Parker, "Rabbi," *Interpreter's Dictionary of the Bible*) classify Matthew 23:7-8 with the non-titular tone of Gospel passages.

At least some of the adulation for the Pharisees by modern Jewish scholars represents a defensive reaction, not only to shield the Pharisees from Gospel slurs, but to go on to exalt them. Matthew Black, "Pharisees," *Interpreter's Dictionary of the Bible*, III, pp. 774-81, is replete with unreliable generalizations, and the reactive tendency of Jewish scholars can be gauged by quoting his estimate: "Pharisaism is the immediate ancestor of Rabbinical (or normative) Judaism, the arid and sterile religion of the Jews after the fall of Jerusalem." I am personally a descendant of this Rabbinical religion, the sterility of which was not so complete as to prevent my being born. Black's article is not only unreliable, it is disgraceful that it should have appeared in the same dictionary to which I and some dozen other Jews contributed. Had I known of Black's article in advance, I might have declined to contribute. But see my "Understanding & Misunderstanding: Prepossession versus Malice," in *Dialog, A Journal of Theology*, Vol. 6, Autumn 1967, pp. 284–9.

Perhaps I should add this word, that Christians should be aware that the role of the modern American congregational rabbi is a product of the modern age, and that role is no clue at all to the ancient title or role. The latter carried no congregational responsibility, and no clerical functions (marriage and burial), but implied expertness in Scripture and in law and lore. The rabbi of ancient times was a sage rather than a functionary.

16. Black glosses over the uncertainties. Moreover, his hostility to the Pharisees leads him to untenable conclusions in what he includes, and his omissions are striking.

17. See Ellis Rivkin, "Ben Sira and the Nonexistence of the Synagogue: A Study in Historical Method," in Daniel Jeremy Silver, ed., *In the Time of Harvest: Essays in Honor of Abba Hillel Silver on the Occasion of his 70th Birthday*, pp. 320–55. To my mind, Professor Rivkin seems to beg important questions, to deal somewhat superficially with others (e.g. the relation of the Scribe to the Law is scarcely handled adequately, as in Rivkin's differentiation between authority in the Law and authority over it), and to stack the deck in trying to find a distinction between synagogue and *proseuche*. For a more tenable view of the many real problems related to the synagogue, see Isaiah Sonne's remarkably fine "Synagogue," *Interpreter's Dictionary of the Bible*, IV, 476–91, and the excellent bibliography.

18. The view that Luke 4:16–30 is not historical is a problem in Gospel relationships and rests on the assumption that Luke has freely expanded Mark 6:1–6 and has placed it at the beginning of Jesus' public ministry, rather than midway as in Mark 6:1–6 and Matthew 13:53–58.

19. See Moore, *Judaism*, I, 299–300, and III, p. 99, n. 76.

20. Ibid., pp. 300–301.

21. See, for example, Gershom G. Scholem, *Major Trends in Jewish Mysticism*, chap. II, "Merkabah Mysticism and Jewish Gnosticism," and, for our context, especially pp. 41–3.

22. Hugo Mantel, *Studies in the History of the Sanhedrin*, especially in Chapter II, "The Sanhedrin in Rabbinic and Greek Sources," and Chapter VI, "Jesus, Paul, and the Sanhedrin," ably assembles the data in the primary sources and the discordant views in the scholarly literature, and makes an admirably patient effort to penetrate the confusions. The difficulty for me is not so much Mantel's solutions as the implication which seems to guide his work—that solutions are possible. Mantel (p. 92) supports Büchler's view of two Sanhedrins. But see T. A. Burkill, "Sanhedrin," *Interpreter's Dictionary of the Bible*, IV, pp. 214-8, with bibliography, and his judgments on the uncertainties and the moot matters. The latter arise from the former, plus the perplexities contributed by the trial of Jesus. My point is that the issues respecting the Sanhedrin are everywhere obscure, its role prior to 70 remains most clouded, and the available data are an invitation to divergent scholarly interpretation.

23. Abraham Cronbach, "Worship in NT Times, Jewish," *Interpreter's Dictionary of the Bible*, IV, 894–903, with a short bibliography, abstains from directly inquiring into the historical question, probably because the early history of the tendency to a fixed liturgy is so obscure.

24. See "Shemoneh 'Esrēh" in *The Jewish Encyclopedia*, XI, pp. 270–82. Later literature is cited in Baron, *Social and Religious History of the Jews*, II, p. 376, n. 34.

25. In J. D. Eisenstein, "Shema," *The Jewish Encyclopedia*, XI, pp. 266–7.

26. The Rabbinic Literature romantically ascribes the institution of the three daily prayer periods to Abraham (morning), Isaac (afternoon) and Jacob (evening); see "Prayer," *The Jewish Encyclopedia*, X, pp. 164–71. The allusions to the Essenes in the article should be taken with a grain of salt.

27. See Moore, *Judaism*, I, 299.

28. See "Laws, Noachian," *The Jewish Encyclopedia*, VII, pp. 648–50. W. D. Davies, "Law in the N T," *Interpreter's Dictionary of the Bible*, III, p. 98, is among those who see the threefold decree of the Apostolic Council (Acts 15:20) as related to "the Noachian commandments which Judaism laid upon all men." This relationship, if admissible, seems to

me tenuous, and at most one of intent rather than a matter of direct, substantive connection.

29. I cannot take seriously what Philo tells about the Essenes in *Quod Omnis Liber Probus Sit*. On the one hand it is apologetic. On the other, it conforms with his pattern that the three types of perfection, by teaching, intuition, and practice, are exemplified in Scripture by Abraham, Isaac, and Jacob. Of these the Therapeutae (in *Concerning the Contemplative Life*) exemplify the Abraham type of perfection, and the Essenes the Jacob type. See my "Parallelomania," *Journal of Biblical Literature*, LXXXI, 1 (March 1962), 1–13.

30. See his "The Laws of Idolatry in the Light of Historical Facts in the Third Century," in *Eretz Israel*, V (1958) 189–205. In an English synopsis of the Hebrew essay there is found (ibid. 94*–95*) this statement: "Goodenough's ideas on a popular mystical religion collapse completely." (Goodenough's views are found in *Jewish Symbols in the Greco-Roman Period*, Vol. IV, pp. 2–44.) Urbach cites the principal relevant literature on Dura and on synagogue archeology. See also Joseph Gutmann, "The 'Second Commandment' and the Image in Judaism," *Hebrew Union College Annual*, XXXII (1961), pp. 161–74, and Jean Ouellette, "Le deuxième commandement et le rôle de l'image dans la symbolique religieuse de l'ancient testament essai d'interprétation," *Revue Biblique*, LXXIV (1967), 504–16.

31. S. G. F. Brandon, *Jesus and the Zealots*, argues for an intimate connection, and views the "pacific Christ" as a device designed to deny the true historic circumstances. See below, Lecture IV, pages 190–91.

32. See my "The Jewish Scholar and Early Christianity," *The Jewish Quarterly Review*, 1967, pp. 473–81, esp. p. 477. I would here add that between the age of Jesus and the last of the four canonical Gospels there are traversed the period from Jesus to Paul, the age of Paul, the rise of parties, including Gnostics; overtones, or more than overtones, of all these are present in the Gospels. Jewish scholars have tended to overlook such factors. Furthermore, through unacquaintance with the Gospel process—the priority of Mark and the use of Mark by Matthew and Luke—they tend to ignore the distance in time and space between such later

Gospels and the Palestinian scene, and to treat all four Gospels as if they are simultaneous in time and the creation of a single author; see, for example, David Daube, *The New Testament and Rabbinic Judaism*.

The "original Aramaic" has beguiled a good many Jewish scholars. For example, "Let the dead bury their dead" (Matthew 8:22) is alleged to rest on a mistranslation of the Aramaic, and should really be read as "let the *people of the place* (*m'tha* in place of *mēthaya*) bury the dead," thus depriving the Gospel passage of its bite. This proposal, from Felix Perles, is dutifully recorded by Klostermann *ad loc.*, and is rejected, but it has entered into the *res gestae* of scholarship. On the other hand, H. P. Chayes, *Markus Studien*, with its far-fetched effort to demonstrate that a basic Hebrew gospel underlay Mark, is deservedly completely ignored in the scholarship. Except for Montefiore, Klausner, and Schoeps, Jewish researchers have almost entirely neglected the Christian scholarship on the Gospels; see, as an example of such neglect, Asher Finkel, *The Pharisees and the Teacher of Nazareth*.

33. *We Jews and Jesus*, pp. 61–77, 80–81.

34. Baer's article appeared in the Hebrew periodical *Ziyyun;* see my synopsis of it in *New Testament Abstracts*, 12, 1 (Fall 1967), 31–2.

35. I am quite aware that many Protestants deny that any legalism at all inheres in the Sermon on the Mount. See, as typical, G. Bornkamm, *Jesus of Nazareth*, pp. 102–5. If Bornkamm were exceptional, one could be astounded by the sequence of his arguments. He is, however, typical of a particular kind of Protestant mind which demands that Jesus and Christianity be insulated from legalism. Bornkamm seems to concede this (pp. 223–5) in his scanty Appendix II, "The History of the Exposition of the Sermon on the Mount."

There is an abundance of essays which seek to demonstrate that there is no essential difference between the Sermon on the Mount and Paul's attitude to the Law. On the dilemma Christians seem to face, between a Gospel mandate for law and a mandate from Paul against it, see as an example, p. 286, column 2, in Grayston, "Sermon on the Mount," *Interpreter's Dictionary of the Bible*, IV, pp. 279–89.

On my personal insistence, with Bacon and others, that Matthew's legalism is a genuine one, see below, Lecture IV, page 209, note 27.

Hellenistic Judaism

In the preceding lectures, and in the succeeding one, I have assumed that we possess some common store of knowledge, and that I could proceed directly to my problems of certainty and uncertainty. I do not think that this assumption is valid for Hellenistic Judaism; in this lecture, then, in part I will be deliberately expository[1] and in part I will argue for a certain complex of views.

Any discussion of the Hellenistic experience of Jews entails the consideration of a distinction between events, social factors such as anti-Semitism, and Jewish self-government on the one hand, and the religious response to the Hellenistic encounter on the other. Scholarship has diverged, and has created unsettled issues in the realm of the religious factor.

The most fundamental issue, often marked by rabid partisanship on the one side or the other, I touched on in Lecture I: Whether or not there was any significant difference between the native Palestinian Judaism and the Judaism of the Dispersion. Were the differences only superficial, and did they involve only Hellenization in language but no more than that? Or did portions of Hellenized Judaism, as for example, Philo, represent so extensive and deep a penetration of Judaism by Hellenistic philosopy and religion as to have resulted in a transformation of Judaism into a religion significantly different from Palestinian Judaism?[2] Still another question exists: even if it were granted—as it is not—that Philo does represent a Hellenization that is extreme, then to what extent is Philo to be regarded as typical of Hellenized Judaism, or as exceptional?

PHILO

For all that I have my own special opinion in those matters, I confess that I do not always know how to steer my way through the complexities. If much of my discussion rotates around Philo, it is, I hope, with adequate recognition that he was an individual and not necessarily representative of all Dispersion Jewry.[3] Yet as the person who bequeathed to us the largest quantity of materials, running thirteen books (curiously, twelve volumes) in the Loeb Classic edition, Philo seems to me to represent for modern scholars a kind of organizing factor around which the many attendant issues might be focused.

We do not know Philo's dates, even though they are customarily given as 20 B.C.–A.D. 40. Writing in approximately 39, after the riots broke out in Alexandria when the ship bearing Agrippa I to Judea touched the Egyptian port, Philo describes himself as an old man. On the supposition that he may have died shortly thereafter, possibly in 40, and that an old man in those days was possibly 60 years old, then Philo's birth would be approximately 20 B.C.[4] In his adult career, he was a first-century Jew.

PHILO'S WRITINGS

It is customary to divide the writings of Philo into several categories. The first of these is often called the historical works, his account of the persecutions in 38–39 in *Against Flaccus*, his *Legation*, the description of the Therapeutae in *Concerning the Contemplative Life*, and the treatise *That Every Good Man Is Free*, which closes with a mention and description of the Essenes. A second category of writings consists of his *Questions and Answers* to Genesis and Exodus, which take the form of citing verses in the biblical sequence and an immediate explanation, moving most quickly from a laconic, literal explanation into a complex, allegorical one.

It is in the third and fourth categories that a great deal of confusion is apt to arise, as I have learned in my teaching. Philo wrote a number of treatises that are classified under the rubrics, "The Exposition of the Law," this the third category, and also a fourth category, a number of treatises classified as "The Allegory of the Law." The first distinction between the "Exposition" and the "Allegory" to be noted is that in the "Exposition" Philo writes on topics, such as *Concerning Creation, Concerning Abraham, Concerning Moses, Concerning the Decalogue, Concerning the Special Laws*. These essays are all biblically based, but the shape of the particular essay is determined by the topic. In the "Allegory," each essay bears its own title, such as *Concerning Dreams, Concerning the Migration of Abraham*, and the like, but here Philo's procedure is to begin an essay with a series of consecutive biblical verses and to have his essay shaped by the accident of the sequence of the words, phrases, and sentences. The confusion that I have found to be widespread is this, the diversity in the nomenclature has misled students, especially beginning students, into dividing Philo's biblical writings incorrectly, into the allegorical and the non-allegorical; rather, all his biblical writings are allegorical. The "Exposition" is quite as allegorical as the "Allegory."

PHILO'S BIBLE

Philo, in his treatise *On Moses*, hearkens back to the origin of the Septuagint as contained in the Letter of Aristeas, an origin which in the view of most scholars, but not all, is legendary.[5] The Letter of Aristeas states that in the reign of Ptolemy Philadelphus, around 250 B.C., Demetrius of Phaleron, the celebrated librarian at Alexandria, persuaded Ptolemy that the library was incomplete without the Jewish Bible. Demetrius thereupon secured royal consent to bring to Alexandria seventy-two priests as fluent in Greek as they were in Hebrew. On arriving, these men first engaged in a kind of Platonic symposium with Ptolemy, and then set about their task of translation, yielding a version so accurate that, in effect, the Greek is every bit as reliable as the Hebrew. Indeed, the Letter of Aristeas (302ff.) implies that the new translation might well be considered, to use our modern phraseology, an authorized translation, and that its wording must not be changed, on penalty of becoming accursed. Philo, in repeating, though with some divergencies,[6] the substance of this legend, appears to do so with high approval. If we were to extract from the story of the origin of the Septuagint one single datum, that in 250 or by 250 B.C., the Pentateuch was rendered into Greek, then, between the time of translation and Philo's birth, an interval of 230 years, we must reasonably reckon with the permeating influence of the Greek translation among Greek Jews, and with the rise of an

exegesis of the Greek Scripture. It seems to me reasonable to
suppose that Philo inherited both the so-called Septuagint
and also some history of its interpretation. I believe this to
be the case for two reasons. First, Philo, in a number of
scattered passages, alludes to having heard particular bits of
exegesis from his predecessors, so that he himself is not the
creator of the totality of the allegory which he presents.
Second, I would assert that so architectonic is the total structure of Philo's allegory that it impresses me as beyond any
likelihood that one single mind constructed it, and I would
incline rather to the view that however much Philo adds,
he begins with the legacy from his past.[7]

PHILO'S ALLEGORY

I have been personally both repelled and fascinated by
Philo's allegorical method. But I think it is necessary to state
at this stage that the allegorical method and the content
provided by that method need to be looked at in quite diverse
ways. The word "allegory" means to say another thing. It
is well known that allegory as a method was developed by
the Stoics from earlier impulses, usually in respect to Homer,
and it is the common view that Philo borrowed the method
and the general disposition. The person who has read only
Paul's allegory in Galatians 4:21-26 can have only the barest
inkling of the tremendous range and complexities of allegory
elsewhere.

Such allegory, whether in the Stoics or in Philo, results in
this: the very points at which the ancient and respected texts
create problems for the intelligent promptly cease to be problems through the application of this method. Once such
encountered difficulties become eased, the allegorist can move
on to a voluntary and unrestrained application of the method.
Accordingly, much of Philo's allegory is, first, devoted to

the purpose of dissolving troubling passages, but, second, it has proceeded into opening new and startling vistas. Allegory enabled a Philo to introduce into the supposed meaning of Scripture the broadest array of religious and philosophical ideas. As an example of the first, the liquidation of difficulty, the bare text of Genesis 12:10–20, describing the need of the patriarch Abraham to sojourn in Egypt because of the famine, involves the patriarch in the assertion that Sarah, his beautiful wife, is in reality his sister. On the literal level, Philo, without a word of blame for Abraham, castigates Pharaoh for his violation of the universal laws of hospitality; in his allegory, Pharaoh represents the hypocritical mind which aspires to virtue, Sarah, even to the extent of making an effort to deprive the progressing mind, Abraham, of that precious possession. As an example of the second, the opening of new horizons, the incident of the covenant "between the pieces" of Genesis 15 becomes in Philo's hands an exposition of the Pythagorean problem in geometry of how to divide with equality.

Philo derives the mechanics of his allegory in a very great many instances from the supposed etymology of the Hebrew names of biblical characters or places. Thus, while Abraham is still Abram and a resident of Ur, which is the great center of astrology, Abraham is initially an astrologer; allegorically he is the "high-soaring father," a good, precise translation of Hebrew *Abram*, since *ab* means father and *ram* means high. The justification of the allegorical quantity which Philo assigns to biblical characters usually rests on the supposed Hebrew etymology of their names; while the Hebrew *ab-ram*, is quickly recognizable, in countless other instances it is very difficult to discover just how Philo managed to derive his meaning, for his etymologies are often as bad Hebrew as the one on Abram is good. The moot question as to whether or not Philo knew Hebrew is often affirmatively predicated on that portion of the etymologies which seem to make sense, while the negative case is predicated on that portion of the etymologies which do not. The issue becomes complicated because Philo gives us Greek etymologies too—for example, for the words *theos* and *nomos.* Philo's Greek etymologies are as capricious as some of the Hebrew ones, but no one doubts that Philo knew Greek. (I have previously made two suggestions. First, the Hebrew knowledge displayed in Philo is not necessarily his own, but may well rest on a kind of *notarikon,* or list of biblical names, and the attendant Hebrew "etymologies," such as was discovered by Deissmann[8] for a slightly later period. Second, the issue is quite unimportant, for if Philo knew even a usable amount of Hebrew, which I doubt, at no time does he exhibit anything of significance related to such putative knowledge, for his expositions of Scripture are invariably of the so-called Septuagint and never of the Hebrew text.)

ASSESSMENTS OF PHILO

Yet much more to the point in all this is that his writings, except for the historical ones, are all deeply rooted in Scripture, and again it is the Book religion which animates and shapes, and even dictates, the tremendous religious expansion that Philo represents. This is so easy to see that it is a truism, and yet it seems to me that the commentators on Philo have all too often ignored this elementary fact. It is by ignoring this that Wolfson constructs a Philo who is wholly a philosopher, as if a character of the medieval Renaissance; and Reitzenstein scorns him as if the epithet eclectic is unduly to honor Philo, and Schuerer denominates him a psychologist, and Goodenough finds him the repository of a mystic Judaism which is thoroughly Hellenized, and Belkin asserts that there is no essential difference between a Dispersion Jew like Philo and the Judean rabbis.

I have come to suspect that, in large measure, these and also other differences in the interpretation of Philo do not represent the wide and sharp disagreement that might at first be inferred. On the one level there is among the scholars the tendency to accentuate some particular motif, in the context of recognizing the other motifs, and hence, in part we get among the scholars different ways of formulating a somewhat similar assessment. On another level, the differing assessments emerge from the particular interests of the researcher, so that a man with a philosophic bent like Wolfson would yield an apparently different Philo from that of a *Religionsgeschichtlicher* like Reitzenstein.

TORAH AND NOMOS

What seems to me anomalous can be illustrated in the procedure of Erwin Goodenough, to whom we are indebted for many books, among them *By Light, Light, The Jurisprudence of the Jewish Courts in Egypt,* and *The Politics of Philo*. Yet Goodenough seems to me not to raise and confront the very fundamental problem involved in a Book religion. That problem can be stated as follows: for some reason obscure to us, the Jews of Alexandria gave to their translation of the Pentateuch the name *Nomos,* Law. To Alexandrian Jews, as to us today, the word "Law" has a ring that is quite different from the Hebrew word *Torah,* Revelation. Had the Alexandrian community been completely segregated from the rest of that teeming Greek and Egyptian city, possibly no issue would have arisen. But Alexandrian Jews were involved in the local law of Alexandria, and in the overarching Roman law, and members of the Jewish community were exposed to the Platonic and Stoic inquiries into the nature of law, and as a consequence, the issue arose inevitably—in what way was the *Nomos* of the Jews to be compared with the practical laws of Alexandria and of the Roman hegemony, and in what way could it stand the philosophical scrutiny which Plato and the Stoics had made of law in general? The issue was even more complex because of the peculiar circumstance that the first book of the *Nomos*, Genesis, is almost totally without legislation, and indeed, if legislation is present, it is limited to what the rabbis call the seven laws of Noah or the injunction to circumcision in Genesis 17. Genesis is almost entirely narrative, except for the few poems; in what sense could this book of narration justly be included in a five-part book called the Law?

Simple as this question is, the answer to it involves a good many complexities. One of the complexities, for example, is the question of the audience for whom Philo was writing. The assumption has existed, since Massebieau[9] expressed the opinion in 1889, that the Exposition of the Law was written for Gentile readers, and if that view is accepted, then this body of writings is a sort of apologetic corpus which may be devoid of that authenticity that is all too often absent from the work of apologists. On the other hand, the view of A. Tcherikover,[10] that there is no evidence that Gentiles ever read Jewish works, and hence a Jewish audience must be envisaged even for the Exposition of the Law, would imply that the Exposition was not written for outsiders but was a work of edification for those inside. In my own opinion, the Exposition was written for that portion of the Jewish community which was rapidly being assimilated, and either in the midst, or on the verge, of apostasy, and it represents an effort by Philo to retain those whom the Jewish community seemed destined to lose. If my view should be right, then there is still an implicit apologetic motif to Philo, but then the thrust of this motif is quite different from what it would be if we take the view of Massebieau. Indeed, the issue of the audience comes to be the question of the authenticity of the content, whether one deals with an artificial arraying of materials so that they will sound impressive to outsiders, or whether the writings represent a profound effort at self-understanding.

Moreover, another aspect of the problem needs to be faced: that by the very nature of the Pentateuch the inquiry was obligated to turn up an answer to the question of the relationship of the patriarchs of Genesis, who lived before the age of Moses, to the laws beginning in Exodus 20, which came in with Moses. This is not a theoretical question, but a real one. The reality is proved by the circumstance that Philo faces up to it, Paul makes specific inferences from it, and the rabbis make their quite different inferences from it.

Viewing the problem from still another direction, if Philo's writings reflect currents within the Jewish community, then there is the inescapable question of the relative quality of the Mosaic laws and the other laws, the Alexandrian and the Roman, in an at least partially open society. This would be all the more acute if the Stoic philosophic inquiry into the very nature of all law was part of the knowledge of Alexandrian Jews. Indeed, we can start with the observation that, as was known to Philo, virtually all societies have laws that are analogous to each other relating to murder, robbery and burglary; therefore respecting these, one might promptly imply the possible absence of uniqueness in the Mosaic laws; or, again, if we reckon severity either as an asset or a deficit, then a comparison of Mosaic laws with other laws respecting severity requires some setting of Mosaic laws over and against other laws. The Mosaic laws did not enjoy in Alexandria the safety or luxury of isolation.

However much Philo reflects philosophy, or psychology, or legal theory, I am persuaded of this: if Philo had not had the Book to defend and the Book to explain, he would have had much less reason to write than he had, and he would have written much less than has survived from him. Since allegory was his method, it enabled him to read into Moses the ideas of Pythagoras, of Plato, and the Stoics, and even to conclude that these latter were plagiarists of Moses. While there can be no question but that there is ample material in Philo for philosophical analysis or for psychological inquiry and for a host of other problems that have attracted generations of researchers, all this should not becloud the one central fact that Philo is the devotee of a Book religion and that the Book for him goes under the name of *Nomos*, and virtually everything that he writes is in some way related to or even dependent on the centrality of *Nomos*.

SCRIPTURE: ANTIQUARIAN OR EXISTENTIAL?

In Philo's approach to the Book, we encounter, so it seems to me, an extreme case of the necessarily dual approach by any devotee of a religion to the Book sacred in that religion: that the devotee must balance the heritage and authority of the past with the need or the opportunity of the moment. This past authority in a Book that is ancient largely takes the form of that which is historical; that is to say, it deals with events that occurred long ago, including the event of revelation. The contemporary authority, on the other hand, is the response of the late reader of the ancient Book, a response that is in some ways existential. A person immersed in a Book held to be divine must necessarily find in it much more than merely the action of God in the past; he must find some way of discovering his own intuitive, and thereafter reasoned, responses to the meaning of the divine Book for him; he must feel that he finds the meaning within the Book itself. A merely antiquarian study is not a characteristic of the devotee of a living religion; it is characteristic only of the modern research scholar. Philo represents an extreme regarding this normal dual approach, in that for him the role played by history is relatively insignificant. It is not simply for the sake of rhetoric that he asks, "What significance is there in the migration of an Abraham?"—that is, in the fact that one man long ago moved from one place to another. To Philo that ancient journey of Abraham could be significant only if it was a spiritual journey which he, Philo, could also make. Note that here Philo does not liquidate the history of Abraham's migration; he only de-emphasizes that which is historical in favor of that which is existential. Yet along with this particular de-emphasis on history, elsewhere Philo stands on the threshold of actually liquidating history, and occasionally even crosses it. He does this, for one single example among others, when he speaks of the conflicts between Sarah and Hagar; he informs us that Scripture is not interested in relating the backyard quarrels of two women, and he proceeds to tell us explicitly that Sarah and Hagar are not historical characters.

The *Nomos* which Philo is endeavoring to explain is really not the *Nomos* of Moses but the *Nomos* of Philo. Once, in a lecture, in response to a question, I ventured the judgment that Philo would have carried water on three shoulders had that been possible. The *Nomos* to him was both historical, and at the same time also non-historical, yet curiously the *Nomos* was in addition his own ultimate historicizing of even what he has previously interpreted as non-historical. This last verges on being so self-contradictory as to challenge any endeavor to explain it, yet let me try. Respecting the matter of Sarah and Hagar, it is in the course of a particular essay, *Concerning Mating for the Sake of Erudition*, that Philo presumes to deny that the incident is historical. On the other hand, his view of Abraham as the progressing mind, which necessarily needs a general liberal education, forces him to view the Abraham of Genesis as having historically acquired that education. Accordingly, Hagar is not a historical woman, but only the "encyclical studies" that you and I can also master. Yet the Abraham of ancient history attained his perfection by going through the historical step of mastering those encyclical studies. This is a clue to what I mean.

During the period that Abraham was mated with Hagar, he was able to beget only Ishmael, who shot his arrows but seldom hit the bull's eye, and hence Ishmael is the Sophist; when we, you and I, are in college, the most we can beget is sophistry. It is only when we go on beyond college that we are able to duplicate Abraham's historic achievement, namely to mate with Sarah, virtue. We too can imitate Abraham's spiritual journey, of departing from Ur, astrology, and proceed on to true belief, and mate with Hagar, and possibly also with Sarah, for we too possess within ourselves some facets of Abraham's innate gifts. Perhaps I have now adequately indicated the meaning of the phrase, the historicization of the non-historical. It is non-historical in the sense that Philo knows as well as you and I know that, historically, Sarah and Hagar never actually were true philosophy and encyclical studies; it is historical, however, because we can repeat the spiritual experience of our historical forebears in the allegory of the account about them in Scripture.

It would be methodologically easier for us if we could neatly distinguish in Philo, in all that he wrote, among the historical, the non-historical, and the historicization of the non-historical, but the fact is that he does not always so distinguish, and often he blurs matters. The inevitable conclusion I keep coming to is that he blurs them because they are blurred in his own mind. I do not say this in derogation. It seems to me, rather, the necessary end result of the process whereby the historical has indeed come to be the existential, and then the existential historical, since for a fervent Jew the historical cannot totally disappear.

Perhaps the most striking of all the passages in Philo is his thrice-repeated statement that God has mated with Sarah,[11] and with other matriarchs. In one of the three passages, that in *Cherubim*, Philo advises us, as a prelude, that he is about to induct us into a mystery which is quite beyond the average man and, as a mystery, it is incumbent upon those that hear it not to babble about it. Despite some of the involved figures and the contorted devices which Philo here uses, this is all crystal clear, especially when we recall that Sarah is virtue, for Philo means that it is with virtue, not the woman Sarah, whom God mates. Indeed, as generic virtue, Philo uses a prooftext, Genesis 18:11, "there had ceased with Sarah the manner of women," to declare that Sarah had been restored to virginity. This "virgin-birth" narrative can easily delude one into literalism, and thereby into distorting Philo's intention, which is purely theosophical.

Shall we call this thrice-repeated motif merely existential, or does it involve also the historicization of the non-historical? To the latter I would reply strongly in the affirmative.

But for all the many forays into the language of the mysteries—we must recall the statement of Reizenstein[12] that Philo knew all the principal doctrines of the mystery religions and spoke their idioms—we must not be diverted from the question of Philo and his understanding of the Pentateuch. To the implicit question, in what way is Genesis a book of laws, Philo supplies his answer. He tells us that Genesis is the book of the law of nature; the patriarchs served in the role of *nomoi empsychoi*, laws embodied in men; the succession of the three of them, moreover, illustrates the three graces with which men are potentially endowed, namely an ability to learn, intuition, and practice. Aristotle had antecedently suggested that the three capacities could explain the native equipment by which individual men arrive at perfection. I would imagine that a Rabbinic Jew would readily applaud this view of Genesis, providing he could grasp it, for it is an exalted view; a Judean rabbi could say, so far so good.

THE PARTICULAR LAWS

But in discussing the Laws of Moses, which begin in Exodus 20, Philo makes some statements which are astounding, and which I imagine a Rabbinic Jew would find uncongenial. He classifies the laws of Moses as "particular laws" and these by definition are imitations of, or substitutions for, the law of nature of Genesis, and hence inferior to it. Philo does not hesitate to argue that the laws of Moses are superior to the Gentile laws in two regards, first, that they are everywhere the same, and second, that they are eternal and unchangeable, and for these two reasons they represent the best possible imitation of the law of nature. They are, however, in a grade below that of the law of nature.

The laws of Moses, however, represent a vehicle, a device that can be understood if we will conceive of three classes of men. First, if you chance to be a rare person of supreme gifts, then, at least in principle, you are able to live by the law of nature, this through following a proper dialectic (*orthos logos*), correct and free from error. From Philo's standpoint, a Hebrew is a person who through proper dialectic alone rises to the vision of God, whether he is a Jew or not.

But it is a reality that few of us possess the capacity for proper dialectic, totally free from all error. Indeed, there are those who fall short of even elementary capacities. Such bereft people can fit into the second class, for whom the laws of Moses are a prescribed way, a substitute for the in-

dividual and free way of *orthos logos*. Accordingly, even
though we may be unlettered, if only we faithfully observe
the laws of Moses, then *coincidentally* we are living like
Abraham, for Moses in his laws simply recorded what
Abraham did. That is to say, even an unlettered Jew, who
has never heard of allegory and who belongs to the group
that Philo scorns, namely the literalists, can unconsciously
live like Abraham.

In between the handful of the supremely gifted and the
abundance of the unlettered, there is the third class, those of
us of superior mentality, who in following Moses so as to
live like Abraham, are not compelled through personal limitations to do so by mere coincidence and in complete unawareness. Rather, the laws, like the narratives, are subject
to allegory, and the allegorical meaning of the laws rises
into the law of nature. This third class, the superior people,
consciously live like Abraham, and in obeying Scripture,
do so while understanding the laws of Moses in their allegorical sense.

It was absolutely impossible for Philo to have come to this
conclusion, to have set it forth with remarkable clarity in
his treatise *Concerning Abraham,* and to have reflected it
in almost everything he wrote, without his calling upon his
rich erudition in the Greek civilization to guide his exposition
and buttress his contentions.

THE GREEK AND THE JEWISH IN PHILO

In his array of philosophical explanations, Philo might be
described as thoroughly Grecian, but the explanations he
offers clarify religious intuitions that are undeviatingly Jewish. He is a good Platonist when it comes to explaining how
prophecy works; he is thoroughly a Jew in his assertion that
prophecy exists, and that a historical record of it is available.

Respecting authentic Judaism and Greek philosophical explanations, Louis Ginzberg made the suggestion that what Philo was doing was turning normal Pharisaic doctrine into Greek philosophical concepts. Moreover, if I understand Professor Wolfson correctly, especially in his view on Philo's Judaism as representing "a collateral version of Pharisaic Judaism," Wolfson seems to imply the same sort of thing."[13] If by these suggestions there is meant that Philo's Hellenism is only that of form, and never that of any substance, then I believe there is reason to object.

In the first place, in the mere transition from the one mode of expression, namely the so-called native Palestinian into the Hellenistic, there takes place at least a subtle transference in what we might call stance or attitude. Thus, to move from the vocabulary of one civilization into the vocabulary of another is quite impossible without absorbing the overtones of the civilization into which one moves. If I understand Philo right, he is saying something like this, "We Jews of Alexandria, loyal to our inherited Judaism, have come to understand it in the light of those themes, motifs, and comprehensions that are intimately part of us, for they are part of our new environment, and part of the intellectual horizons that have become natural to us. It is not that we are changing our religion, but rather that we are understanding it from a new perspective."

There are a number of comparable examples in the case of Judaism in the United States. When, under the influence of the Social Gospel of the Protestants, Reform Jews began to speak of Judaism as "prophetic religion," they were in no sense becoming Protestants, but they were beginning to understand their inherited Judaism in the light of that motif in Protestant theology which at that juncture had come to some notable prominence. Somewhat similarly, American Jewish theologians in our time are using some of the thought patterns of Protestants as various as Kierkegaard, Niebuhr, and Tillich in their expositions of their present theological stance respecting Judaism.

On a different level, if it is legitimate to distinguish between thought patterns and the content of these patterns, as I believe it is, the medieval philosophers, Jewish or Christian, who fashioned their reconciliations of revealed religion with Aristotelianism, stopped short at that point in Aristotle in which "creation out of nothingness" was involved. Though some modern biblical scholars have challenged the idea that the first chapter of Genesis truly represents *creatio ex nihilo*, to the medieval mind that notion was the accepted implication of Genesis I, with the result that the philosopher reconciling his traditional religion with Aristotelianism found at this point an insurmountable obstacle. Faced with the necessity of choosing, he chose Genesis over Aristotle, even while utilizing unlimited measures of Aristotelianism elsewhere.

The thought patterns are only one aspect of the wide array of factors making up a religious communion, and other factors, such as the religious rites, the religious calendar, and the religious organism, that is, its organization and institutions, all can have a relevancy quite the equal in impact, if not in importance, to the intellectual patterns. When religious borrowing takes place in a tradition that has an exclusivist tendency, as I have said, it can be set down as a general rule that what is palpably alien and inconsistent is never borrowed. Yet the question of what *is* palpably alien needs to be envisaged from the standpoint of the person within the situation, and not from the standpoint of an analyst considerably removed from it in time and also removed from it geographically. If to us in our day the aggregate of Platonism and Stoicism that a Philo borrowed seems alien to Judaism, then it is methodologically wrong for us to deny the borrowing; we must rather conclude that that which strikes us as

alien did not strike him as alien. Such borrowing, startling to
a later age, took place only in the context in which the borrower was totally unaware that he was borrowing.

THE MYSTERIES

If we ask, did Philo borrow from the Greek mysteries
or not, it seems to me that the question is incorrectly
stated. The issue is quite different. The proper question,
I think, should be, did he borrow from the Greek mysteries so significantly and substantially as to feel that he
ruptured the essential Judaism which he had inherited and
for which he was so eloquent a spokesman? Had the answer
that Erwin Goodenough given been this, and this alone,
namely that Philo borrowed from the mysteries primarily, or
only, the stance and attitude of Greek intellectuals to the
Greek mysteries, and that Philo applied to his Judaism facets
of such an intellectual approach, then I believe that Goodenough's position might not have come to be challenged.
Where I would myself challenge Goodenough is his repeated
assertion that Philo goes beyond this, and that Philo is a
repository of reflections of sacred meals, and of the organization of Judaism into mystic-like *thiasoi*.[14] While it would not
have surprised me had Philo gone to this length, it seems to
me that there is no evidence that he did so, and that Goodenough's suggestion that he did not borne out by the texts.

Yet if we state what it is that Philo did, using the evidence
we *do* have, then we can assent to Goodenough's conclusions
to that extent, and, after modifying Goodenough, proceed
to agree with him. If Philo approached Judaism in a way
comparable to that in which a Greek intellectual approached
the Greek mysteries, as seems the case, it is in the context
of Philo's explicit and repeated statements that the Greek
mysteries are totally wrong, and that they are totally to be

rejected. Yet Philo asserts that the only true mystery is Judaism. I have seen no evidence that Philo made any alterations in the calendar, ceremonies, in the legalism, or in the ethnic feeling. What was altered was not his Judaism, but his understanding of it.

PHILO'S ANTECEDENTS AND SEQUELS

What seems to me to be elusive in the case of Philo is the double question of what it was along this line of alteration that Philo inherited from his Hellenistic past and what it was that he bequeathed to later Jewish generations. If it is right that the architectural structure of Philo's allegory implies that he inherited portions of it, then we must presuppose some antecedents of Philo. We could therefore envisage Philo as standing within a tradition of a Hellenized Judaism that was earlier than his time, and in relation to which he emerges as a clarifier and, in some sense, as a systematizer. I do not know of any broad and direct evidence that would support this assertion. There are some patterns of thought similar to Philo in the Wisdom of Solomon, IV Maccabees, and also the Epistles of Paul. This inclines me to envisage a blend of Judaism and Hellenism antecedent to Philo, a blend much broader than Philo himself. In such a chain[15] of Hellenized Judaism, Philo represents a significant milestone in two respects. The first is that it is in him that the Hellenistic impulse reaches its highest pinnacle. The second is that, so far as we know, he represents the last significant literary expression of this Hellenized Judaism and that, at least within Judaism, that impulse, having once reached its climax in Philo, peters out and then disappears. That Philonism exerted an influence on subsequent Christians is unmistakable, as Bousset[16] especially has successfully demonstrated. The abundance of studies that attempt to show a direct Philonic influence on the

Gospel According to John or the Epistles to the Hebrews have often seemed to me to attribute a specific influence by Philo on such writers, but more properly, as I see it, one should ascribe the influence to the blend of Hellenism and Judaism in which chain of tradition Philo himself stands.

The patristic tradition which asserts, incredibly, that Philo became a Christian, has this truth in it—that this tradition would not have arisen had it not seemed to Christian intellectuals who read Philo that they were reading the work of a man whose spirit was so kindred to theirs that he must have been one of them.[17]

PAUL: RABBINIC OR HELLENISTIC JEW?

The scholarly disputes over Paul and his relationship to Hellenized Judaism or to normative Judaism are destined perpetually to continue.[18] The advocates of the view that Paul was a good Rabbinic Jew, as if he were completely immune to any Hellenistic influence, rest their case primarily on Acts of the Apostles. In the Acts, Paul is a student of Gamaliel, he circumcizes Timothy, he makes a journey to the Temple in fulfillment of a vow, and he speaks fluent Hebrew. In the light of the testimony of Acts, it is not surprising that a substantial line of scholars have interpreted Paul from within the context of Rabbinic Judaism; it is surprising, indeed, that so many have been willing to see Hellenistic influences on Paul. At least three presuppositions seem to me to govern the interpretation of Paul as a Rabbinic Jew: first, the testimony of Acts, second, the assumption that there was no distinctive Hellenistic Judaism that was different in any marked way from Palestinian Judaism, and third, the assumption that to attribute to Paul a reflection of Hellenistic influence is in some way to reduce his authenticity.

There will never be an end to articles that assert, for example, that Galatians II and Acts 15 can be reconciled, or that they cannot be, on the question, was Paul a man of ruthless independence, or an obedient, acquiescent subordinate to the pillars of the Jerusalem church? There will never be an end to articles that will demonstrate that there is no essential tension between Paul's assertion that he was an apostle from God and not from man, and his willingness to be the agent who participates in the broadcasting of the apostolic decree of Acts 15, at which apostolic council it is Peter, not Paul, who speaks in behalf of Gentile Christianity. An opinion in this area reflects prepossession and disposition, and the issue will never be settled. Accordingly, while it is my own opinion that it is Paul's Epistles and not Acts that are the true clue to Paul, I find this old controversy increasingly of less and less significance. It seems to me a matter of antiquarianism, for while I do hold that Paul was a Hellenistic Jew and not a Rabbinic Jew and while I am among those who would not credit the portrait of Paul in Acts, the reason I find this only an antiquarian issue is that I find Paul so completely individualistic and so inventive and creative that the question of his background, whether the one or the other, is a very subordinate matter. For, even in asserting that I would not yield on the question of Paul's being a Hellenistic rather than a Rabbinic Jew, it seems to me that the important thing is that Paul was Paul. In this light, neither the Rabbinic nor the Hellenistic influence is to my mind as significant as the spontaneous creativity which I believe I see in Paul himself. When I try to explain the character of this creativity and individuality to myself, it becomes much more intelligible to me if Paul were a Hellenistic Jew rather than a Rabbinic Jew, and I am able to grasp some major elements in Paul from the one standpoint that I find elusive to grasp from the other standpoint. But again this is a question of only limited significance.

PHILO AND PAUL

There are scholarly works that point to some notable parallels in the thought of Paul and the thought of Philo; for example, in the scholarship of Wilfred L. Knox.[19] There is, indeed, a somewhat extreme opinion, that of Gerald Friedlander,[20] which attributes to Paul a direct literary dependency on Philo. I am not able to take this last viewpoint with any seriousness whatsoever. I think, however, it can be granted that there are ample echoes of Paul in Philo or Philo in Paul that bind the two of them to a somewhat common background. We know nothing about the date of Paul's birth and we have only guesses as to when he died; in fact, the matter of his having met martyrdom at Rome is an inference from the ending of Acts of the Apostles and far less than an established fact. But that Paul and Philo are roughly contemporaneous seems to me to meet no difference of opinion.

Yet along with the statement that the two were both Hellenistic Jews, living in approximately the same time span, and that there are parallels in their writings, there are also some specific differences that should be noted. I would take it that Philo was a much better educated man than Paul, though not possessed of a better mind. I would take it that Philo was a relatively calm, relatively detached person, whereas Paul was a highly active, a highly intense person. I would take it that Philo was a prudent, restrained thinker and that Paul was an intuitive, volatile thinker. I would point out that eschatology permeates the Epistles of Paul and that eschatology is virtually absent from Philo, and where it is present, it is neither vivid nor immediate. Perhaps the contrast between the two can be put in this way: if we speculate about what would have happened had Philo come to the Christian convictions that Paul came to, one thing that we can be relatively sure of is that Philo would not have traveled around; rather, he would have sat down to write a treatise. If it is replied that Paul's Epistle to Romans is in its own way a treatise, then I would retort that it was occasioned by circumstances, by Paul's urgent need of self-exposition, and that it was not the product of an antecedent lifetime of writing treatises. The two men are so different that, having just contrasted them, I must go on to say that making a contrast between them is basically preposterous.

Yet even as one dismisses the question of whether Paul was a Rabbinic or Hellenistic Jew as mere antiquarianism, there still remains some relevancy to the historian in his understanding of the first Christian century. If it was an act of intuition whereby Paul identified the Christ with the *logos*, either directly, if Colossians is by him, or indirectly, if it is not, then our horizons are considerably broadened when we contemplate that great development in the Jewish idea of *hochma*, which became identified with *torah* and in turn with *sophia* and with *logos*. Whether the *logos* in Philo was simply a putative metaphysical entity, rather than a reality, may continue to be hidden from our eyes; to Paul, the Christ *logos* was the reality which he experienced. Again, even as we abstain from investing Paul with the content of Philo or Philo with the content of Paul, we are still enriched by seeing the range of possibilities that a fertile mind could encounter and contend with relating to the Christ *logos*. That which is unique in Paul, and I am one of those who believes there is much, is unique within the broader context of what Paul shares with his Hellenistic environment and shares with fellow Hellenistic Jews.

THE RELIGIOUS QUEST

It has seemed to me to be valid to ask what the religious problem is that each, Paul and Philo, is trying to solve. When we ask that, we are thrown into the question of environment as environment impinges on the individual. It seems to me that before Paul found Christ, he was looking for something, and the Christ was the answer to what he was looking for, and we can understand what he found only if we ask ourselves what he and others were looking for. Similarly, if we raise the question of Philo's religious quest, then we must see it in a somewhat comparable way. The answers which each found are shaped in part by the environment and in part by the personality of each man. Perhaps one may put it that Philo and Paul have it in common that they are both looking for the God of today, and not the God of the ancient revelation to Moses. Again, the Book is the inspiration, for the Book, dealing with God, was perforce existential as well as historical. Persuaded, then, that the God of Scripture was a living God, both Philo and Paul, as devotees of the Scripture, needed a sense of having communed with Him. For each, for both, the quest was for the God who in some way could raise man above corporeality, above bondage to death, and, freeing man from attachment to the given moment, would bring him into relationship with eternity, and into eternity itself. The obstacle to man's rise was not only man himself, but also man's environment, and since man understood himself in terms of his environment, man and environment were intertwined. The view of man common to Philo and Paul is more dualistic than monistic, and the salvation which both sought is analogous to the quest in the pagan mysteries which, since the two were Jews, they could not credit with any possibility of helping them. Philo's

answer to his quest emerges in terms of his being something
of an academician, and hence he utilizes Platonism and Stoicism to explain how the individual can, through observing
the Laws of Moses, rise above corporeality and into communion with the *logos*, the immanent aspect of the tran-
scendent God. The explanation, though, is the afterthought
to the sense of personal experience, for mere explanation and
nothing else is fruitless; that is, Philo goes through the tedium
of explanation because he has himself personally experienced
the *logos*. Philo is, as it were, content with a more or less
static, unhistorical answer, in that for him the *logos* is time-
less and immune from time, even though at given moments
Philo has had the experience. The answer for Paul seems to
have been rooted in event, that is, the event of Jesus. Accordingly, for Paul the encounter with the Christian tradition as
it was unfolding in his time, coupled with the view that
Jesus was in some sense divine, led him to identify the *logos*
he so desperately desired with this Jesus. Since the career of
Jesus was to Paul an event that has occurred, it is in history
that it has occurred, in a history so recent that it has occurred
within Paul's own experience and lifetime, and it fits into the
history of Jewish revelation as the most recent and climactic
occasion. While both Paul and Philo each feel certain that
he has encountered the *logos*, the encounter for Philo, since
it is philosophical rather than event-centered, is calm, detached, and speculative; for Paul it is a vivid, highly charged,
intuitive, personal experience of the divine, which has in-
truded into the flow of time. If I were to put this in another
way, I would say that Philo was contending that the ancient
equivalent of a Ph.D. course in philosophy would bring the
gifted student into occasional mystic communion with the
logos; Paul was saying that an event, and the experience of
the event, have enabled him to shortcut the mechanical im-
pediments of academic study, and they have given him the

direct encounter, and the encounter now permeates his being and compels his actions and dictates his intentions, thoughts, movements, and activities. Philo seems to me to have the full assurance that he has at times encountered the *logos*, whereas Paul, by contrast, is completely possessed by the *logos*.

If all this is right, as I am persuaded it is, then the scholarly issues ought not to lie in the domain of passages here and there in Paul and Philo which echo each other; we should take it for granted that two Hellenistic Jews living about the same time and in a somewhat similar environment would reflect aspects of that same environment. Instead the issue is the distinction between the sense of historical experience that characterizes Paul and the non-historical contemplation that characterizes Philo.

This crux of historical experience or its absence, if it is a valid distinction of the two, can begin to explain some other differences. For example, since it is Philo's contention that the Laws of Moses are the best possible imitation of, or substitution for, the law of nature, Philo sees no reason to abrogate these "particular laws." In the well-known passage, *The Migration of Abraham* 89–93, in which Philo takes to task certain Alexandrian Jews who feel that since they have penetrated to the law of nature and need no longer observe the particular laws, Philo applauds them for their knowledge of the law of nature, yet he also chides them for failing to observe the particulars. Little as we know about these Alexandrian philosophical defectors from the laws of Moses, it seems reasonable that their conclusion stems from philosophy and not from event. Paul, on the other hand, impelled by event, proceeds to an even more drastic position respecting the law of nature and the laws of Moses. I see no direct connection, of course, between Paul and these "allegorizers."

I have read in many places efforts to explain the background of Paul's surprising contention that the laws of Moses are not only not the proper vehicle for attaining salvation, but indeed are an impediment and, in that sense, evil; I have myself seen nothing to persuade me that Paul is here working out of any antecedent influence, and I incline rather to think that this is a product of Paul's own creativity. To Protestant interpreters Paul seems the opposite of what he has seemed to the line of Jewish interpreters, for Protestants view him as the acme of penetrating acumen while Jewish interpreters view him as kindred to a blasphemer; yet I would still think that the impartial observer would need to credit Paul, not only with tremendous inventiveness and a scintillating mind, but also with tremendous courage. In speaking of his courage, I do not have in mind what seems to me to be the pedestrian challenges which Paul is depicted in Acts as having thrown down to Jews of his time, or his twice receiving thirty-nine stripes; the courage, rather, seems to me to lie in his readiness to challenge his inherited Judaism at its most central point, the laws. Surely this is an act of bravery much beyond daring to enter Hellenistic synagogues, as Acts depicts him doing.

Denying as I would the direct influence of Philo on Paul, I would nevertheless state this: Philo reflects a facet of Hellenistic Judaism in which the laws of Moses were inevitably set over and against the law of nature, but Philo was able to work out for himself a satisfying harmony. Paul on the other hand, working in terms of the same contrast, saw no conceivable harmony, and indeed saw the two aspects, especially in the light of his personal experience, as antitheses. Where Philo was impelled to harmonize, Paul was moved to envisage the inescapable necessity of a choice of one over the other.

Whether or not the account in Acts is historical of Paul on Mars Hill, and whether or not the analysts are right in asserting that Luke either does not understand or else distorts Paul's theology, this much I think is inescapable: The motif in Paul's speech on Mars Hill, namely, that that god, deemed by the philosophers to be unknown, is both known and knowable, adequately represents a primary element in Paul. I would even suppose that Paul could have made the same kind of speech to no other than the circle of Philo's disciples, for Philo, in putting limits on man's philosophical knowledge of the divine, allocates God Himself to the realm beyond man's possible rational knowledge.[21]

CONTENTMENT IN TRADITIONAL RELIGION

Erwin Goodenough's contrast between objective and subjective religion is worth some consideration. In objective religion, the communicant is satisfied through his faithful performance of rites and ceremonies, and has no need to gain a sense of personal communion with God; in subjective religion, the sense of personal communion is the nub of the personal religion. This contrast does seem to me suggestive, but I also find more wrong with it than right with it, for I do not think it is tenable, except with considerable modification. I do not believe that the so-called objective type of religion lacks its own form of quasi-communion with God, and I do not believe that subjective religion is devoid of rituals and ceremonies. Any effort to compare Palestinian Judaism with Hellenistic Judaism on the basis of the rubrics of objective and subjective religion seems to me wrongheaded. Nevertheless, there seems to me still a sense in which the comparison is appropriate and viable: the one type, the objective, can foster a satisfaction with and contentment in the traditional religion, while the other, even when the person begins as a loyal communicant, reflects an unsatisfaction in, or dissatisfaction or discontent with, the placidity of his inherited religion. Does this give us some clue to Paul, and, indeed, to other intuitive mystics?

I do not see the contrast between the Rabbinic Judaism, on the one hand, and the Hellenistic Judaism, on the other hand, as a horizontal one, however much they had in common and however little they differed in externals. I see the contrast, rather, in vertical terms: a religious tradition with any antiquity is going to have periods in which contentment with the traditional will be followed by periods of discontent. Next, the expression or substance of the period of discontent afterwards comes to be a matter of contentment and even institutionalization. Paul represents discontentment; the Christianity which ensued after Paul came to be (in part) an institutionalization of Paulinism. It is noteworthy that the Pastoral Epistles deal with church organization, and not with one individual's wrestling with the implications of his personal experience of the *logos*.

THE END OF HELLENISTIC JUDAISM

Scholarship too often fails to confront the problem of what happened to Hellenistic Judaism. The assumption need not be challenged that Philo is the last eminent literary representative of it and that in a sense the chain of Hellenistic Jewish writings terminates with him. What happened that wiped out Hellenistic Judaism? Did the emerging Rabbinic tradition manage to exert such *de facto* leadership as to assert a Hebraic hegemony, bringing to Hellenistic Jews a renewed knowledge of the Bible in Hebrew, and resulting in the elimination of the Septuagint or the other Greek versions, even Aquila, from their usage? Did they lose great numbers in the uprisings of 112, which we know about dimly, and in the backwash of the Bar Kochba rebellion? Did they become assimilated into the Gentile population? Did they in large numbers become converts to Christianity, because they saw in Christianity an adequate form of Judaism, satisfying to themselves and not at variance with their ancestral inheritance? We do not know. I have encountered very little interest in this, to me, significant question.

Had it not been that Christianity preserved the Hellenistic Jewish writers and fashioned what we usually call the Alexandrian canon, and maintained copies of Philo and of Josephus and of other writings, we would not know from the normative Jewish tradition and its literature that a Philo existed or a Josephus existed or that a Wisdom of Solomon was written or that IV Maccabees was composed. It was Christianity that preserved these writings. Perhaps one might conclude that Christianity in the Hellenistic world was the spiritual legatee of the Hellenized Judaism which did not have within itself the capacity to muster survival factors.

We may gain some perspective from the observation that Jewish Christianity in Palestine withered, for it lacked survival power; Hellenistic Judaism withered, too, since it lacked survival value.

It is my feeling that when any two civilizations encounter each other, as in the encounter by the Jewish civilization of the Greek civilization, they fail to understand each other completely. They thereby fashion an intermediary civilization which is perhaps crystal clear to its adherents, but always fraught with some sense of being alien to those in the respective civilizations who have not been part of the encounter. It is in such terms that a Paul and a Philo seem so un-Jewish to so many Jewish commentators, and so un-Greek to so many classical commentators.

The result of the demise of Palestinian Jewish Christianity and of Hellenistic Judaism has been that the surviving Rabbinic Judaism and the surviving Hellenistic Christianity came to maturity in distinctively different environments. Fed by opposing views of the laws of Moses, and each undergoing its tremendous and significant inner development, they came to be quite incapable of communicating with each other, especially when, centuries later, mature Rabbinic Judaism and mature Christianity re-encountered each other in Europe. It is only in the past century and a half, and, indeed, only in the past few decades, that the two have been able to find a beginning way of conversing with each other. If I comment that hitherto much of this beginning dialogue has reflected the will to converse rather than the ability to do so, I say this not in despair, but only to indicate authentic difficulties.

Notes

1. Let me briefly indicate the scope of Hellenistic Jewish literature: first and foremost, the Septuagint, and then the later renderings. Next, certain historians, e.g., Demetrius, Eupohemus, Artapanus, Jason of Cyrene (from whom the author of II Maccabees made an excerpt); II Maccabees, III Maccabees; poets such as Philo "the elder," (not the same man as Philo of Alexandria); a playwright, Ezekiel; philosophers such as Aristobulus and Wisdom of Solomon; a homilist such as IV Maccabees; random works such as the Letter of Aristeas; and such works as Josephus, *Against Apion*. One should add the interpolations into the Sybilline Oracles. Much of the above, and also some Greco-Samaritan literature, is preserved only in fragments in citations in Josephus, Clement of Alexandria, and Eusebius. The standard study of these is still J. Freudenthal, *Hellenistische Studien*, I, 1875. I commend most warmly Baron, *Social and Religious History of the Jews*, II, pp. 183–210, and the relevant notes, especially for bibliography. The bibliography by Goodenough and Goodhart in Goodenough, *The Politics of*

Philo Judaeus, pp. 127–321 is broader than Philo. Addenda are found in Ralph Marcus, "Recent Literature on Philo (1924–1934)," *Kohut Memorial Volume*, pp. 463–491. Louis Feldman, *Recent Research on Josephus and Philo* is a most worthy supplement; Feldman provides annotations and makes judgments, and I admire his balance and prudence.

2. For a discussion of these matters, see my *Philo's Place in Judaism*, pp. 4–5.

3. In at least two ways Philo cannot be representative. First, he is, by and large, the last literary representative of the Graeco-Jewish literary tradition, and he represents a highly sophisticated manner compared with his predecessors, as any reading of the fragments preserved in Josephus and Eusebius quickly reveals. Second, he alone of all these writers, even including the author of Wisdom of Solomon, exhibits a full, rounded and authentic knowledge of Greek writers, so that where they provide echoes and overtones, he provides responsible citations and paraphrases.

4. See Erwin R. Goodenough, "Philo Judaeus," *Interpreter's Dictionary of the Bible*, III, pp. 796–9. I regard this as a most unsatisfactory article. Possibly space limitations hampered Goodenough. But here, as in his *Introduction to Philo Judaeus*, he seemed incapable of deferring his special opinions until he had provided an appropriate introductory context for them, but blended them into the elementary exposition where, in my judgment, they intrude.

5. For more recent literature, see Baron, *Social and Religious History of the Jews*, I, p. 384–5, n. 38, and Moses Hadas, *Aristeas to Philocrates*, pp. 86–90.

6. Chiefly, Philo attributes an arrival at identical phraseology by the 72 translators to divine guidance, whereas Aristeas has the translators compare their versions and harmonize them. The legend about the translation grew in scope and in the miraculous (see Hadas, *Aristeas to Philocrates*, pp. 70–84), and also elicited the scorn of Jerome for the latter.

7. I base these conclusions on their reasonableness, for I know of no compelling evidence. In my *Philo's Place in Judaism*, pp. 16–17, I discuss the theory by Hölscher that there existed Hellenistic compilations of scriptural interpretations, and I

followed Rappaport in rejecting the suggestion, since there is no evidence for such compilations.

8. See my *Philo's Place in Judaism*, p. 12. The Adolf Deissmann reference is to *Veröffentlichen aus der Heidelberger Papyrus-Sammlung*, I, *Die Septuaginta-Papyri*, . . . , 1905, pp. 86–93.

9. In "Le classement des oeuvres de Philon," *Bibliothèque de l'École Etudes* . . . *Sciences religieuses*, Paris, I (1889), pp. 1–91.

10. In his "General Observations" in the Hebrew *Sefer Zikkaron le-Johanan Lewy*, pp. 139–60, he seems to me to make a convincing case that there is almost no evidence that Gentiles read Graeco-Jewish writers.

11. *Mutation*, 137–8, *Cherubim*, 48, and *Allegory of the Laws*, III, 219. See my *Philo's Place in Judaism*, p. 174, n. 340.

12. In *Die hellenistischen Mysterienreligionen, 2nd Ed.*, p. 41.

13. See my *Philo's Place in Judaism*, pp. 1, 4.

14. When studying under Goodenough, and working through his *By Light, Light*, where these contentions first appeared, I challenged them as not borne out in the Philonic texts cited. Moreover, Goodenough worked primarily in the Exposition and abstained from the gathering of full Philonic data from the Allegory, and thereby was led into a good many inconsequential errors. It seemed to me that, on confrontation, Goodenough was persuaded by the passages I brought to him, but only for the period of the confrontation. Similarly, in *An Introduction to Philo Judaeus*, he seems (pp. 203–4) only momentarily to reckon with objections raised to his interpretations and proceeds (pp. 205–10) to re-state his position as if it were unchallenged.

15. I see no direct chain from any of the Graeco-Jewish writers, especially respecting the elaborate allegorizing. While Aristobulus is similar in intent, he is far removed in method and scope. An as yet unpublished paper by Professor Irwin Batdorf of United Seminary, Dayton, deals very competently with this question of Aristobulus and Philo.

16. In *Jüdisch-christlichen Schulbetrieb in Alexandria und Rom.*

17. A former student, a Christian from a staunch Fundamentalist background, once assured me that Philo reads like an au-

thentic Christian except for the absence of a specific mention of the Christ!

18. See Lecture I, note 65. My views on these matters are to be found in *The Genius of Paul*. In brief, I there considered Paul's position to have been most extreme, as one would expect from an intuitive religious genius, and that a later age handled this extremism by neutralizing it. Three writings accomplish this in different ways: James, by espousing works along with faith; Acts, by describing Paul as a normative Jew who always conformed to his inherited Judaism; and Matthew, by introducing a legalism, no longer that of Moses, but now emanating from Jesus.

19. In *St. Paul and the Church at Jerusalem* and *St. Paul and the Church of the Gentiles*.

20. In Gerald Friedlander, *Hellenism and Christianity*, pp. 84ff.

21. This is frequent in Philo. For example, "Everything which is subsequent to God man can apprehend; God alone is unapprehensible" (*The Posterity of Cain*, 168).

Lecture IV

Christianity

PRECISE HISTORY AND THE RESEARCHER

When I began the serious study of the New Testament, my objective was clear. It was to discover, on a basis of tenable scholarship, how and when and why it was that Judaism and its daughter, Christianity, came to a parting of the ways. I must emphasize that it was not to discover approximately what had happened, nor what in general had happened, but, rather, precisely what had happened. The two words, approximately and precisely, in their opposite implications, permeate much of this lecture.

If, at the time I began, my background in the Judaism of the age of Jesus was tolerably good, by contrast my store of information about Christianity was exceedingly tiny. I knew almost nothing about Paul, except that in some vague way he had been responsible for much or most of what Jews have regarded as the negative outcomes; I had at that time never read any of his Epistles or Acts of the Apostles. About Jesus I had a slightly greater store of knowledge, for I had already read Mark—read but not studied—and had skimmed through Klausner,[1] and I had the general feeling, shared by a good many American Jews, that our Jewish Jesus had somehow, probably illegitimately, been appropriated from us by the Christians.[2]

I embarked, then, on a quest for precise history. Surely, I thought, someone like myself who had already been inducted into the Higher Criticism of the Old Testament, and, under Julian Morgenstern, into a radical aspect of that criticism, was susceptible of openmindedness regarding the New Testament. The union seemed ready at hand, namely, that of an open-minded, scientific student and the material itself, and consequently precise history would surely have to emerge. I do not think that it was ever my assumption that my Jewish eyes would see better than Christian eyes, but only that they would see from a different angle.

My quest for some mastery was double, that of learning the documents, which as yet I did not know, and a scholarship about them which, I assumed out of my knowledge of Protestant Old Testament scholarship, would be broad, encompassing, and honest.

I then had a clear program of study ahead of me, and that program proceeded to move along very much as I imagined it would—almost. When I began work in New Testament there was certainty in my mind that the Graf-Wellhausen hypothesis about the Old Testament, especially respecting the four major documents, J E D P, was right. Yet as I began to work more deeply in the "intertestamental" literature, in Josephus, and in Philo, and in Rabbinics, the conviction began to grow in me that the documentary hypothesis as usually stated was a modern construct, anachronistically superimposed upon the Pentateuch, and not in accord with what seemed to me to be the realities of the Near Eastern scene and the realities of the Hebrew mind. Not that I was by any means retreating to traditionalism; to the contrary. Rather, I was coming to the opinion that the phenomena which created the Graf-Wellhausen hypothesis were truly present in Scripture, but that the hypothesis was not providing an answer convincing to me. What this meant, in context, was that I could not continue to accept the Higher Criticism of the Old Testament without personally challenging it at many significant points. Accordingly, I also became unconsciously disposed to challenge the Higher Criticism of the New Testament—provided, of course, that I was to learn it responsibly and fairly.

DETACHMENT OR INVOLVEMENT

Another change, not in my program but in my basic purposes, was brought on by outside events. There is an involvement which I believe is more American than European—the occasional withdrawal from the ivory tower. I began my studies in New Testament just before the start of World War II, and I received my Ph.D. shortly after it ended. The Hitler experience of us Jews, and the baffling problem of Jewish-Christian relationships, whether directly or only obliquely related to Hitler, brought me into certain situations wherein either my opinion was solicited, or at times I felt impelled to volunteer that opinion. Was there, and is there, such a thing as a detached, objective opinion in this area? Perhaps I should put the issue in two related questions: Have Christian judgments on Judaism and Jews been fair and tenable? Have Jewish judgments on Christianity and Christians been fair and tenable? It is a reality, of course, that New Testament materials are critical of and even hostile to Jews and Judaism, and as a consequence there are substantial portions of the New Testament scholarship that amount to vindications and extensions of New Testament attitudes. There are, on the other hand, some Jewish attitudes or pre-possessions that are scarcely charitable to Christianity and Christians. The paradox of detachment within involvement has constantly harassed me.

The matter of detachment in the midst of involvement has been a most intrusive factor along two lines. One of these has been the need to try to learn and absorb the character of Paul. It is difficult enough for a modern person, a product of the French Revolution, the Enlightenment, and modern secular education, to try to recapture the ancient times and distant places. How much more difficult it is for a Jew, bred affirmatively in Judaism, to set himself resolutely to try to grasp a mind and a career which argues that the laws of Moses are an impediment to righteousness and are no longer valid. That, as a Reform Jew, I have much in common with modernist Christians does not alter my affirmative relation to the Laws, for though I do not abide by them, I do not consider them an impediment to righteousness. The intrusive factor operates, also, through the Passion narrative and the subsequent developments, due to which I too am among living Jews who was called a Christ-killer by neighboring children.

How can such intrusive factors be reconciled with detached scholarship? To what extent do they jeopardize, and have they jeopardized, that antecedent intention, to learn exactly what happened, in a purely objective and historical way—that is, in a precise way? Again, to what extent is reliable scholarship, whether mine or someone else's, affected by the alternatives of a Christian adulation of the Gospels and a Jewish lack of adulation of them, by the alternative of some commitment to the figure of Jesus and a lack of any commitment? If there is any answer, it would seem to me to go along these lines, that the New Testament documents are realities and they are susceptible of study, and the most one can do is to study them honestly, testing one's own tentative or definite conclusions against the totality of a thorough, and magnificent, scholarship.

For what it may mean, I should say for the record that I was never, never at all, taught New Testament by Jews, but only by Protestants. I have read books by Jewish authors, and also by Catholics,[3] but my teachers in New Testament have all been Protestants. It was under Protestant guidance that I absorbed the works on the theology of the New Testament and on "Introduction," and my frames of reference still remain with this orbit, however much I have departed in details.

THE ELUSIVENESS OF HISTORY

Even though one remains within the general framework of Protestant Higher Criticism respecting the literature and theology of early Christianity, if his bent is history, *precise* history, he encounters some immediate, inescapable problems, due to the sparseness of reference in the New Testament to clearly known incidents in the history that we know, however imperfectly. Forgetting momentarily the acute critical problems which we must notice later, we begin by observing that, of the twenty-seven books of the New Testament, only the four Gospels and Acts purport to narrate events. The Epistles of Paul narrate only indirectly, as in Galatians. Acts terminates with Paul's arrival at Rome, and hence the New Testament lacks historical narration after that event completely. Cannot we say that all this is a bare minimum of narration?

If it were viable to distinguish between Christian history and Christian literature, then a focused discussion on first-

century Christianity could regard the literature as a body of
diverse source materials from which a careful student could
excerpt some history, much the same way as we might possibly excerpt history from the books of Samuel and Kings.
Yet before we can use the literature for any organic understanding of the history of first-century Christianity, we need,
of course, to have some sense of what is first-century literature
and what is not. On this level, there is a series of vexing
questions which are both important but also pedestrian, such
as the old issue of whether or not Colossians and Ephesians
are by Paul himself and therefore safely within the first century, or else works of a later time and possibly from beyond
the first century. These problems I would call chronic, rather
than acute.

What has constantly preoccupied and even troubled me
is not the intertwining of questions of history and literature,
for this intertwining is simply a fact. Rather my difficulty is
the equivalent of a paradox, that on the one hand we possess
only a bare minimum of data, and on the other hand the
question of isolating precise history seems to me to continue
to hold the center of the stage of the accumulated scholarship.

The motive behind the desire for precision on the part of
Christians has been and is somewhat different, perhaps, from
my own. My own is to try to understand accurately an admirable religion which is theologically alien to me. For the
Christian student, if Christianity is anything, it is a religion
based on the premise that in the long history of the revelation
of God the culminating revelation of Him in Christ was
conceived of by early, orthodox Christians as an event that
actually took place, and that the event took place within the
lifetime of persons flourishing in the first Christian century,
who were still living at the time the earliest literature was
being written. While even in the first century there were

those Christians whom we call Gnostics[4] who were already prepared to liquidate Christian history or to dissolve it into symbol, as Philo was prepared to do with Hebrew history, if I understand the main thrusts of Christian thought, especially in the first century, it has been to assert that the climactic event of revelation occurred in history. Once this is understood, it becomes readily comprehensible that so much of modern Christian scholarship on early Christianity has focused on the question of the tenable or untenable historicity of the contents of the quasi-historical books, that is, the Gospels and Acts, and the possibility of amplifying the history from the non-narrative materials.

Yet, different as the motives may be, the materials are the same and most of the facets, or the process of study, are similar, or even identical.

It seems to me that at least three separate questions have arisen in efforts to fix precise history. The first two deal with what I will label external events, and the third with what I will call internal. The first questions is this: is it possible so to handle the total materials as to answer the questions of historical tenability and reliability? The second is, is it possible to array the reliable data to indicate or even describe some genetic sequence, so that we understand not only that certain events happened, but what the direction and flow of those events was? The third, the internal question, is that of the supernatural, not only regarding the matters of miracles and wonders, but greatly transcending these, the question of the historicity of the Incarnation.

DIFFERENT TYPES OF PROBLEMS

There arose in my mind at an early stage that there is an important, even essential difference in the character of the problems in the Gospels on the one hand, and the prob-

lems in Paul, on the other. The problems between the
Epistles and Acts I will touch on below; at this point we
can say this about Paul, that for the most part we are
confronted with some clusters of incompleteness and of uncertainty, but all this lies in an area of relatively broad reliability. For example, in studying the travels of Paul, when
we are confronted by a north Galatian hypothesis versus
a south Galatian hypothesis, or the question of how many
trips he made, our uncertainties are primarily caused by inadequate information, not dubious information. Even if Paul's
precise travels occasion problems to scholars, they have
been almost unanimously certain that Paul founded a church
at Galatia. On the other hand, in the case of the Gospels,
we are confronted with large areas of utter uncertainty, and
only a restricted area of certainty. Did Jesus make a single
visit to Jerusalem, which the Synoptic Gospels record, or
the plural visits, which John suggests? Is the route of the
journey to Jerusalem in Luke right, or the route depicted in
Mark and Matthew, or are two different journeys intended?
And there is the problem that the resurrection appearances
in Mark and Matthew seem to be located in Galilee, while
in Luke and in John they are located in the vicinity of
Jerusalem. Such problems are abundant to the point that
they arise in virtually every pericope. Where the Gospel
accounts are plural and out of accord with each other,
whether in matters of petty and negligible detail or matters of
great significance, scholarship has been faced with the necessity either of trying to reconcile divergencies, or else of
selecting out of plural versions one single version which
could be correct and the other presumably incorrect, or
else of concluding that all could be correct or even all incorrect.[5]

The Synoptic Problem

I have clear recollections of reading in the nineteenth-century scholarship[6] reiterated assumptions that if only the Synoptic problem itself could be solved, then the discovery of which documents, such as the hypothetical Q, were prior to others, would in turn bring scholarship nearer to certainty about history, this on the premise that earlier writings would be freer of the legendary and theological strands which are found in the later writings. At the end of the century, the Synoptic problem seemed to have been solved, and there then seemed to be no place to go. There was an air of finality; not only had the scholarship dutifully recorded every single deviation in one Gospel from the other Gospels, but on the assumption that Matthew and Luke, respectively, used Mark and Q as sources, the commentaries provided boundless efforts to explain the origin and significance of each and every deviation. No body of scholarly literature to my knowledge is as vast, as careful, as relentless as is the detailed examination of all the phenomena in the Gospels. But the solution of the Synoptic problem, however affirmative it was respecting the literature, was devastatingly negative respecting history, for it was the view, as can be seen from Schweitzer,[7] that the Gospels reflected the developed Church rather than Jesus himself.

Form Criticism

As I see it, two different responses ensued upon the devastating negativism of nineteenth-century Gospel scholarship, the one "pneumatic"[8] exegesis, and the other Form Criticism. The pneumatic exegesis has by and large handled the historical negativism by what seems to me to amount to a repudiation of it, that is, by wishing away the problems that created the negativism. Form Criticism, on the other hand, attempted to meet the negativism by first defining it, and by seeking thereafter to penetrate beyond it. It was no less than a supposedly objective discipline, which, through a knowledge of the way in which folklores develop, could solve the problems in history by first categorizing the Gospel materials, and then by searching for the manner in which each pericope in the Gospel has its own history of birth, growth, and development. Using the data on this birth, growth, and development, it was believed the successive layers of legend, theology, and interpretive embroidery could be peeled away, and purest history emerge to light. Such was the theory.

I began my work in New Testament at a time when Form Criticism was newly arrived in the United States. I was at that time reading endlessly in Benjamin Bacon, Frank Porter, Bernhard Weiss, and Johannes Weiss, and working through the commentaries by Klostermann; I read about Paul not only in Nock and in Kirsopp Lake, but also in Machen, and I studied Jülicher on the parables. I labored through Burney, *The Poetry of Our Lord,* and I took the theories of Torrey, in *Our Aramaic Gospels* seriously enough to scrutinize every paragraph, and I read the attacks on him, and also the scorn with which some of the University of Chicago scholars, such as Goodspeed, treated his views. I was immersed in the "social setting" in the work of Case and Riddle on the one hand, and in Cumont and Reitzenstein on the mystery religions on the other hand.

When I encountered Bultmann and Dibelious and Form Criticism, I had the feeling that these disciplines were especially designed for me in particular, and I recall vividly the difficulty I had in assessing the review by Henry Cadbury of Bultmann's *Geschichte der Synoptischen Tradition* in the *Harvard Theological Review,* XVI (1923), "Between Jesus and the Gospels," pp. 81–92, for I had worked through *The Making of Luke-Acts*, and Cadbury was (and is) one of the great names to me, especially since I had read his study of the medical language in Luke. Accordingly, though Cadbury attributed to Bultmann "extreme skepticism," I welcomed Form Criticism, and I devoured it—and at the same time was undergoing my personal reassessment of the Higher Critical scholarship. I then began to become aware of a certain prepossession which necessarily affected me.

Let me illustrate by an example from the Tanach, Genesis 19, the account of the patriarch Abraham's bargaining with the Deity. I have never felt, in my adult life, any issue in the historicity, or absence of historicity, in that incident, even while I think it is an important item in Genesis, in that it reflects the theological view that the righteousness of some can save a total community. With such a prepossession about the Tanach, I began to ask myself about my stake in the historicity of items in the Gospels. I had read, of course, in the Commentaries about the temptation of Jesus, that, since there were no disciples present, the information about the temptation, if historical, was necessarily preserved through the medium of Jesus relating it to some disciples; it did not bother me to conclude that the incident is theological or didactic, rather than historical. Form Criticism had its supposedly objective method by which to differentiate between the historical and unhistorical. Yet, in my dilemma of wanting precise history and of finding it constantly elusive, I was discovering Form Criticism to have more of a stake in history than I had, and to be very subjective, rather than completely objective. I found myself concluding that all too often the method argued in a circle, concluding from one layer a datum of where the Church stood, let us say in A.D. 50, and then using that datum to identify other layers as coming from 50. It often seemed to me to neglect the factor

of creativity which could have explained the late origin of
a total item, but simply proceeded under the necessity of
dividing a pericope into hypothetical layers. It tended to
neglect the writing factor in the Gospels[9] and, by concen-
trating on pericopes, it has seemed to obliterate Gospels as
totalities. It presumed to know about Judaism in the age
of Jesus more than I found myself able to know. As to where
the Church stood at 50, any such conclusions rest on the
possibility of winnowing out of Acts such data as can be
certain and unchallengeable, or inferring such data from
Paul's Epistles on the assumption that somehow or other
fixed chronological points can emerge. Yet the chronology
in Paul's writings rests largely on Acts—and almost everywhere I turned I was reading that Acts was fraught with
insuperable difficulties.[10]

A Stake in History?

I found myself tending to the conviction that in reality
there has been, and there can be, no *objective* method
whereby the historical can be separated from the unhistorical,
in either the Pentateuch or in the Gospel materials or in Acts.
My contention was not, and is not, that there are not historically reliable materials in them, but only that there does
not exist in scholarship the tools whereby to make the differentiation. Predisposition, whether of religious conserva-
tism or religious radicalism, necessarily enters in, and so do
the other traits of the individual researcher, so that the assertion of history, or its denial, is a matter more of the personality of the scholar than the clarity of the documents.

Let me revert for a moment to my statement that the
question of historicity of events became one in which I have
come to feel no stake. The point is that I often feel I can
leave questions open and unresolved. For example, I do not
feel the need to make up my mind whether events which

actually took place in the Passion account called to mind such Psalms as 22 and 69 and hence these Psalms are cited, or whether the Psalms were so much part of the ken of the Evangelist so that he created the incidents out of the Psalm passages.

The import of feeling no stake in the historicity of the events in a sense amounted to an invitation to abandon what was originally basic for me, namely, to learn, not approximately, but precisely what had happened.

Overprecision

At the same time that my uncertainties about events were crystallizing, I was reading innumerable theological essays which were designed to explain words, phrases, and ideas. I began to find myself rebelling against an overabundance of subtleties, acute distinctions, and eisegeses[11] which seemed to me to go beyond all reasonable prudence. This was the case especially with Paul; certain essays gave me the impression that Paul had had a thesaurus, or better, a dictionary of synonyms at hand. Interpreters seemed to me to be committing him to a precision which I simply could not take seriously. Again, and here a Jewish bias enters in, I read essays which contrasted him with the rabbis, and while I could smile at the one-sidedness, I had to question the academic worth of comparisons which misstated or distorted the attitude of the rabbis, in contrast with over-subtle explanations of Paul.

Precise history and overprecise theology, quite apart from unimportant issues of bias, began to appear to me as delusions. Precise history seemed to demand being set over and against a merely general history, and precise theology over and against a merely general theology. That is to say, I felt that I could accept, and even begin to formulate, some broad and general history and theology of Christianity, but I was debarred from precision.

There have naturally been some tremendous implications to me in this position. Certain of the refinements of the scholarship have seemed to me so completely speculative as to merit on my part only acquaintance but not familiarity, and flirtation rather than courtship and marriage. I am no longer carried away by the ability of a scholar to tell us exactly where and when some New Testament or Old Testament document was written, and the sources it has been derived and adopted from, and the precise conditions under which the composition issued forth.

I have found myself from time to time oppressed by a theme in the field of New Testament "introduction," one that implies or concludes that one single motive or purpose can identify or characterize a particular piece of writing. I am quite willing to believe that particular motives are recognizable, but I am persuaded that the New Testament literature represents enough complexity so that any given writing must reflect plural motives rather than one single motive. Respecting Luke-Acts, for example, I am quite willing to believe that F. C. Baur was almost on the right track in describing its tendentiousness as an effort from a later time to view the diversity in the early Church as though it was in reality one great harmony, but I am unwilling to believe that that is the one and only purpose of Luke-Acts. I do not believe that the single purpose of the Gospel According to Mark is limited to defining the so-called Messianic secret; I do not believe that the purpose of Ephesians is to provide a covering letter for the publication of the Pauline corpus. The literature in the New Testament seems to me to be too complex for such simplicity. Moreover, we read the New Testament with modern eyes, not ancient ones.

In still another area relating to the Gospels, I find myself skeptical, and even unconcerned. It is the finality with which a great scholar like Streeter was able to allocate the particular Gospels to particular localities, with Mark and Luke emerging from Rome, and John probably from Ephesus, and Matthew from Antioch. I do not feel any stake in these questions: I am only mildly interested in whether John was written in Antioch or in Ephesus or in Alexandria; I am only mildly interested in whether Matthew was written in Antioch or elsewhere. This geographic allocation seems to me to be only of limited relevancy, and surely the circumstance that the Gospels were written at all is much more important than where they were written. I concede that the effort needed to be made to try to discover where they were written, but I have not found myself persuaded by the answers that have been provided, even when these answers have constituted a sort of consensus, and it strikes me that the questions are secondary, rather than primary. So too with the recent suggestion that not only was John the earliest Gospel, but even written in Palestine, and even contains *ipsissima verba*.

It is not that I find myself in perpetual suspended judgment, for this is far from the case, especially about opinions that I am not sympathetic to. For instance, I spent some time on the Mandean bubble because it seemed important to me to know about it and to try to keep it in perspective. I think that the Mandean literature turns out to be unimportant for New Testament study. I suppose it may be that I have rather firm opinions on views I cannot accept or feel I must oppose, but not nearly so firm opinions on what I take to be possible, or reasonable, or probable, or admissible.

A Moratorium on History?

If we did not have a long history of excellent scholarship, then I would approve unreservedly the efforts of scholars to be precise in the solution of New Testament problems. Since, however, there is in the arena of public notice a tremendous scholarly literature which dutifully records the efforts that able men have made, then my reluctance to be too certain is not a prejudgment of the issues, but rather a conclusion to which I found myself driven after weighing the issues.

I cannot say whether it is the sparseness of direct historical pegs or my antecedent disposition which has led me to the conclusion that, respecting Genesis or the Gospels, or Acts, it would be useful to scholarship to declare a moratorium on the search for precise history, and to resume the quest only if and when archaeologists discover literary materials with unmistakable historical pegs which warrant the resumption.

SELF-DETERMINATION

Let me turn now to the question of whether or not a modern student can acquire some sense of the organic growth and development of early Christianity. At some time in the past, I no longer remember just when, the problem shaped itself in my mind as susceptible of approach from two standpoints. The first is to acquire some sense of the affirmative, inner growth of the new movement. The second is to hold this view of the inner growth in balance with an important consideration—namely the progressive growth of the movement away from Judaism and from Jews.[12] Early Christianity could conceivably have felt a positive relationship to the ancient Judaism, and yet have an entirely different feeling toward contemporaneous Judaism and Jews.

By all the testimony, the Pharisees and the Sadducees were quite aware of the difference between them, but they appear uniformly to have assumed that this difference existed within a Judaism common to them. When and how did the Christians' comparable awareness of difference *within* Judaism lead to their awareness of a difference *from* Judaism? What was the situation in the time of Jesus? What was it between the time of Jesus and Paul? What was it in the time of Paul? And after Paul's time, were the awarenesses of difference crystal clear and settled and defined, or were they still fluid? Was there in ensuing decades some dominant judgment that existed side by side with a recessive, opposite viewpoint? Was the ultimate canonization of the New Testament in any way an effect of such awareness, or a cause of it? And how shall we handle the impression John Chrysostom gives us, that Christians in Antioch in the fourth century still were not completely cognizant of the full import of difference?

Much of the controversy about the growth of the Christian movement after the days of Jesus rotates around the antithetical evaluations by Christian scholars of the reliability of the Acts of the Apostles. It has sometimes seemed to me that if we said that first-century Christianity is in some way kindred to a jigsaw puzzle, then Acts has impressed me as providing us with more pieces than would fit in a single puzzle. Indeed, among the unsolvable issues respectable enough to merit confrontation, there is the suggestion of John Knox[13] that Luke-Acts represents a mid-second-century writing, and that the viewpoint and therefore the contents of Luke-Acts are shaped more by the middle of the second century than by the materials which they contain. When we say something of this kind we are immediately back in the area of the futile quest, applicable in so many biblical books, of assessing the relationship between a relatively late document and the earlier period which is described in it, and the even more difficult chore of separating the more ancient material from the younger editorializing or tendentious connective material. I find myself faced by an unsolvable problem of how much in Acts is an accurate history of the early Apostolic Church and how much of its schematic approach is second-century tendentiousness and apologetics.

THE ACTS OF THE APOSTLES: OMISSIONS?

What troubles me most about Acts is not the material that it contains but a host of matters about which it is totally silent. I wish it gave me some idea of who it was that established the churches of Damascus, Alexandria, and Rome. I wish it were more generous in the treatment of all the apostles, instead of confining itself, as it so largely does, especially in the latter half, to the work of Paul. I wish it gave us some clearer insights into Christian worship, some clearer view of how the unfolding community developed liturgically. I wish it told us something about the mysterious disappearance of Palestinian Jewish Christianity from the total Christian economy. I wish it enlightened us directly on the way in which the community made whatever shift it may have made in eschatology. I wish I knew how and when hegemony in the Church departed from Jerusalem. In short, difficult as I find it to deal with what Acts contains, I find the omissions much more perplexing, and even baffling.

Acts and Paul

What remains most elusive for me in connection with Acts is the role of Paul in the early Church. The problem here is not whether Acts makes Paul into a conformist who observes the laws, studies history with Gamaliel, is present at the stoning of Stephen, is a meek and compliant servant of the Apostolic Council, speaks Hebrew, circumcizes Timothy, and journeys to Jerusalem to fulfill a vow at the Temple— all matters which scholars at one time or another have denied. Rather, the problem for me is whether Paul was of the same consequence in his lifetime as his consequence is implied in Acts and in the totality of authentic (or inauthentic) Pauline letters in the canon of the New Testament. Elsewhere I have pointed out that, of the twenty-seven books, thirteen are by Paul, or purport to be by him; I tabulated the number of individuals to whom the risen Christ is presumed to have appeared, and these come to at least 514 (see I Corinthians 15:5–8); after noting that two Epistles are attributed to Peter and one to James and three to John and so forth, we still cannot escape the fact that almost 50 per cent of the New Testament purports to be from Paul. Was he 50 per cent of the Church in his own time? Surely he was not more. If he was less, how much less was he? Here, then, is a point at which the matter of literature and the matter of history so touch each other to create an enormous problem, a problem which to my mind is quite beyond solution, except by either well-based or baseless theories, or by sheer speculation.

PAUL

I suppose there is no character in the history of religion about whom as much has been written in contradictory vein as the great apostle Paul. But in the welter of conflicting opinions, one comes to the point at which he may feel secure in even one more idiosyncratic judgment; and consistent with such license I have myself undertaken elsewhere to set forth the theory that virtually all New Testament literature except Revelation owes to Paul either an affirmative or a negative debt of notable size, whether large or small. It has been and is my opinion that Paul was a religious genius,[14] but one of such an extreme kind that he confronted the Church, both in his person and in the doctrines in his preserved Epistles, with the dilemma of how to retain affirmatively the tremendous contribution that he made and also how to temper that extremity in the interest of the impulse on the part of others to fashion a stable Church. This view rests on the premise that the Paul of Acts is a personality quite different from the Paul of the Epistles, not so much in the missionary journeys he undertook, but in the doctrine, belief, and practice on which he exercised an influence. The old Tübingen pattern, of a Petrine party which represents Jewish-Christianity thesis, a Pauline party which represents Gentile Christianity and "antithesis," and the early Catholic Church as the "synthesis" of these movements, has seemed to me excessively patterned, and excessively conditioned by Hegelianism. I have not been able to find any evidence of stirrings of such magnitude as to justify such a pronounced pattern, even though, of course, we read in I Corinthians of the partisans of Paul, Cephus, and Apollas, and that enigmatic group, the party of Christ. In turning away from such patterned reconstruction, I preferred to speak of Paul and Paulinism as a Diaspora phenomenon of such tremendous consequence that it gave Christianity a second beginning, but this in a context in which the contribution of Paul and Paulinism could be useful to the developing Church in an ongoing way only as this influence was to some extent re- strained and neutralized. I would hazard the guess that if the Church had not neutralized Paul, the Church would not have survived the second century, this for the reason that Paulinism has as much potential for disintegrating a corporate entity as it had for enormously amplifying and shaping and even determining the character of the entity, if it managed to survive.

Yet I must confess that, though this view satisfies me in its essence, it nevertheless leaves me unsatisfied at many points and in many areas, in precisely the same way that the Acts

of the Apostles leaves me unsatisfied. I remain bereft of information that I still desperately desire. Let me cite one
item: How much did Paul know of the unfolding oral material about the career of Jesus, which material ultimately
became the substance of written gospels? (I shall speak of
this material as the Gospel tradition.) There are many who
have preceded me in pointing out that from the Epistles of
Paul alone we should know little more about Jesus than that
he was crucified and that it was believed that he was resurrected and that subsequent to the resurrection he appeared
to his followers, and that he was opposed to divorce. Did
Paul know no more than that?[15] I find this hard to believe.
But if he knew more, why does he not reflect this? Is it
the accident of what he chances to include, or omits as
outside the immediate focus of his Epistles? Or is it the result
of a deliberate slighting of the details of the career of Jesus,
as being of no great consequence to him? I incline to this
latter.

I have made my way laboriously through interminable
studies of particular topics in Paul. The total scholarship is
not only bulky but, qualitatively, it is of the finest scholarship.
What leaves me somewhat unsatisfied with it may be put
this way. Some such studies seem to me to put the cart before
the horse; until we can successfully decide just who and
what Paul was, we are not in position to embark on the chore
of precisely reflecting some aspects or implications of his
thought.[16] Next, if it is legitimate to inch up to the problems
in Paul's thought from various angles so that cumulative data
rather than prepossession alone dominates, then I find myself
faced with a somewhat different kind of dissatisfaction—
which is paradoxical, for often such studies are marred for
me by excessive research and excessive information, and
dubious relevancy. Certainly it is legitimate to try to trace

the Stoic influences on Paul, and the influences of the mystery religions and the Pharisaic influences and all the other possible influences. Yet I wonder if Paul himself would have understood some of the erudition in the clarifying essays. To my own dismay I have had to give up trying to understand the genesis of this or that idea in Paul as previous influence or contemporary environment would explain it, mostly because I have not found these explanations adequately convincing to me, despite the light they throw, for to my mind it is Paul the creative person and not the Paul who was shaped by this or that antecedent who emerged as the second greatest figure in Christianity. I would rather know less about the background and absorb more thoroughly satisfyingly the man himself, rather than let the man become dissipated and dissolved into one more reflection of a complicated and uncertain age.

THE SPREAD OF CHRISTIANITY

It seems to me that factors relating to the content of Christianity, rather than the work only of the men, such as Paul, enabled Christianity to spread. Consider the Jewish and Christian conviction of God's guidance and compassion. Compare this motif with the term "mystery religion." How significant is the age-old and unsettled dispute over whether or not Christianity managed to spread through its resemblance to, or as an actual form of, a mystery religion? To my mind, the quarrels over this are either semantic or subjective. They very often involve either the wish to denigrate Christianity by terming it a "mystery," or else the opposite, to give Christianity a delusively total uniqueness by shielding it from the term. A chain of scholars have given the bases on which they believe Christianity could not possibly have been a mystery religion; these bases are often ingenious and perceptive, but I wonder if they would be completely intelligible[17] to an early Gentile Christian or to the pagan who rejected Christianity.

In the Hellenization of Christianity, as well as the Hellenization of Judaism, it would seem to me that both Hellenized forms were presented to pagans as if they offered a recognizable and persuasive solution of religious problems, and in that sense possessed not so much *novelty* as *certainty*. It would seem to me that Judaism and Christianity were advocated for pagans on this basis: what pagans were looking for, and not finding, was here, and available, and was unassailably truthful. That is, it is not alone that God's eye is on the sparrow, but it is *true* that His eye is on the sparrow: it is true not because I, one person, say so, but because eyewitnesses have attested to it, and, moreover, because that rock of stability, the Old Testament, attests to the truth of it. The similarity of the early Hellenized Christianity, especially Pauline Christianity, to the mysteries is to my mind a problem of no consequence whatsoever, for when one has taken his stand pro or con, he is still within the realm of mere externals; it is hard for me to believe that it was such externals in Christianity that enabled it to triumph. I would contend that it was the Kerygma that enabled Christianity to triumph; it was not the circumstance that the wine and the wafer, and baptism, were rites and ceremonies which could also be found as essentials in the mysteries of Mithra. Persuaded as I am that at least Pauline Christianity and Philonic Judaism appealed to pagans as versions of the mystery religion, I would still say that this is quite unimportant, for it was the content of Philo or the content of Paul, and not the superficial form, which was decisive.

Christian History after Paul

Now, if we are somewhat in the dark respecting the period of Paul, how much more are we in the dark for the period after Paul reaches Rome in Acts! Our task in acquiring a sense of the organic growth of the movement turns from the narrative history of Acts into a confrontation of the *Sitz im Leben* of the later Epistles of the New Testament.

When one has worked his way through the New Testament scholarship, mastering some of it, controlling some of it, acquainted with some of it, and dimly cognizant of some of it, no matter what his limitations are, he comes to some tentative or permanent, implicit or explicit effort at synthesis. By some of the scholarship he is persuaded, by some not. From some of the scholarship he extracts, often unconsciously, a certain theme or set of themes, even at times against the grain of what he has read. For myself there has always been a certain difference between the focused reading of scholarly studies as part of a particular project and the general reading of scholarship; the former, for example, involves taking notes and recording quotations for specific use; the latter involves reading without taking notes. The latter implies memory, exact or inexact, and impression and impact. To some books one returns, even often; to others, even when he does not return, he is indebted for the push toward revising an antecedent view. But all the reading and the contemplation of what one has read tend to accumulate into some more or less ordered appraisal of the totality; thereafter one's reading results in modifying or in stabilizing the appraisal. The appraisal is always subjective, one man's response to an abundance of materials. Since it is subjective, it is always fraught with the defects of human limitations; one forgets an essay he has read, or remembers it wrong, or remembers it so well that he unconsciously distorts its significance. Yet a viewpoint proceeds to build itself into some more or less coherent whole. The student does this inevitably, not so much to persuade others as to understand the phenomena himself. It is to this that I turn to pursue a theme, the self-determination of early Christianity.[18]

A Construction of Christian History

In my own construction of earliest Christianity for my own understanding, I have found myself turning toward a procedure used in Old Testament scholarship in order to understand the New.

There is one difference we must note between Old Testament and New Testament literature, namely that Old Testament literature spans a period of time which is well over a millennium. The New Testament literature, on the other hand, comprises a period of about a century. The Old Testament literature lends itself to division into rather well-defined periods: the patriarchal age, the settlement period, the monarchy, the pre-Exilic period, the Exilic period, and the post-Exilic. We are able to give rather good dates for these periods. For New Testament literature, we are bereft of such clear chronological divisions. We can speak, as some have done, of the age of Jesus, of the Apostolic age, and of the sub-Apostolic age, but not with a comparable kind of clear, chronological division. Indeed, there is as much inner diversity in the New Testament literature, the product of roughly a century, as in Old Testament, the product of well over a millennium.

In the Higher Criticism of the Old Testament, on the assumption that the P code was the latest stratum and the youngest, and that the Chronicler, Ezra and Nehemiah, represent comparably late writings, scholars such as Wellhausen used the method of beginning with the latest literature, and working back from the latest to the earliest. Thereby, through focusing on what the Hebrew religion had come to be, it seemed possible to trace back to the stages through which it had come. The two developments I have mentioned before, a sense of affirmative inner growth, and a sense of differentiation from Judaism and Jews, seem to me essential to be borne in mind.

Second-Century Factors

If we were to apply this Old Testament method to the New Testament writings, then I suppose we could begin with the Muratorian fragment in 175. I would thus begin with the late time at which the Church has come to such a sense of its differentiation from Judaism that it has progressed very far in the decisive process of converting Christian writings into Christian Scripture. I do not find it surprising, some twenty-five years after the author of II Peter[19] has implied in 3:15–16 that the letters of Paul are the equivalent of Scripture, that we get a list in the Muratorian fragment that is virtually the subsequent canon. Perhaps even prior to II Peter some Christian writings had already become sacred and even authoritative, but antecedently there was necessarily a period in which these writings were only writings. Again, the emphasis in II Peter on the need of attention to the doctrine of the Second Coming implies that the eschatology has become greatly weakened, for otherwise there is no reason for its accentuation. This sentiment occurs in the midst of a contentiousness, for the author has opponents he feels he must stigmatize; indeed, his mention of Paul's letters is for the purpose of denouncing those who "twist them as they do all scripture." We are in the midst of a situation in which the Church has grown in size and age to such propor-

tions that there exist false teachers and heresies, and men of
license, and some who "even deny the Master who bought
them"—an unclear allusion to some Gnostic connection. In
the same general period we can see in the writings of Justin
Martyr,[20] both in his *Apology* and in his *Dialogue with
Trypho the Jew,* good evidence of the advanced degree of
the self-awareness of Christianity that it has finally grown
outside of Judaism, and it is now both independent of it
and also a determined rival. Justin, of course, writes in a
tone and on a level that are singularly in contrast with both
Jude and II Peter, a fact which adds a little substance to
our awareness of the varieties within the Church in the
middle of the second century. Marcion[21] was flourishing at
this time, and he and his disruptive movement represent an
imponderable factor, but one probably of very great importance. Indeed, Marcion's anti-Judaism is a clear indication
of the sense of independence from Judaism achieved in the
Church.

The Pastoral Epistles[22] inform us about a crystallizing
officialdom, even to the point of naming the emergent offices.
The Second and Third Epistles of John[23] alert us to the ways
in which there was an interplay between what some individuals alleged to be heresies, and the resultant need of
some control, this ordinarily to be exercised through what we
may denominate as the authorized persons, as distinct from
authorized doctrine. Among the Apostolic Fathers, First and
Second Clement and the Epistles of Ignatius and Polycarp
also deal in specific ways with the related problems of heresy
and apostasy, and the attendant or concomitant prerogatives
of, or the need for, an officialdom. In this context, one point
of significance in the Didache comes to be apparent: it was
both a guide book for proselytes and a kind of manual of
Church organization; one should notice, too, that it concludes with a vivid statement of the eschatological hope. That

is to say, one moves backward, as it were, from the beginnings of canonization, to the sense of some sanctity in some Christian literature, to a period of stress and strain of divergent opinions and divergent movements, and against this last background the gradual fixing of Church offices takes place. What is curious to me is the relative absence from the second-century literature of clear delineations of proper doctrine; there are many asseverations that doctrine must be proper, but less than full clarity about what constitutes this doctrine. Stated in another way, though faith is conceived of as a matter of doctrine, and indeed, as a transmitted depository, we still fall short of *precise* creed or authoritative dogma. Perhaps this latter could emerge only when the authoritative offices were unassailably defined and made secure. Here we are still prior to the period when, as at Nicea, assembled dignitaries could vote on matters, and have the latent power of the state available to enforce decisions. Orthodoxy and heresy in the early second century are subjective judgments, and as yet not determined factors.

Still moving somewhat backward, the Epistle of Barnabas goes from matters of general instruction and exhortation, into a confrontation of some of the issues between Judaism and Christianity, and the increasing awareness of an independence of Christianity from Judaism; in chapter after chapter Barnabas provides a series of contentions on the basis of which Christianity both declares itself to be the true heir of the ancient Judaism, and also contends that the Jews and the Judaism of the time to have forfeited their rights. That is to say, in the Epistle of Barnabas, the Judaism antecedent to Christianity, on the one hand, and the contemporaneous rivalry with Jewish people, on the other, are still problems of such importance for the Church that they are given urgent attention.

In the First Epistle of John, the more significant problems

are the internal ones, of disruptive heresies and apostasies that threaten the stability or even the existence of the Church. Moreover, I John offers its subtle reinterpretation of the meaning of faith; faith is now kindred to a platform, rather than that sense of complete submission to God which I believe characterizes the word in Paul. I John 5:16 makes a distinction between venial and mortal sin. A preoccupation with sin is also found in the Shepherd of Hermas—the issue of whether or not Christians after baptism are capable of sin, and, next, if they do sin, whether they can be forgiven. There is thus in the Shepherd a reflection of the apparently broad similar problem, found in I John and, earlier, in Hebrews, whether the saved are able to abide in their salvation.[24]

When we turn to the Revelation of John, we encounter some of the enigmatic complexities respecting nascent Christianity and the power of imperial Rome. It is likely that Revelation reflects a bitter reaction to some passing persecution, such as that under Domitian, and a date ± 100 for the writing of the surviving version is also reasonable—no matter how ancient the Jewish source materials may be. The First Epistle of Peter is also a document about persecution, and overtones are found, too, in Hebrews.

The "problem" of Christianity and the state arrays itself in my mind in this way. Early Diaspora Christianity participated in the general situation of Jews in the Diaspora, but as its makeup became increasingly more and more Gentile, subtle aspects of differentiation arose. On the one hand, the previous pagan animosity to Jews was directed against Christians too; on the other hand, Gentile Christianity, increasingly aware of the distinction between Jews and Christians, began to feel a need to express its own relationship to the state in a way quite diverse. Thus, exempt both from the half-shekel Temple tax, and from the later *fiscus Judaicus*, and lacking the sense of the centrality of Judea and Jerusalem in its thinking, Christianity needed to find some replacing set of attitudes. Being largely Gentile, it did not have the same urgency of separation from secular laws that Jews had; yet aspects of the Jewish relationship to the state were advantageous, and hence a potential dilemma existed. A complicating circumstance was a series of local persecutions, as in Rome under Domitian and in Bythinia under Trajan; it is likely that additional incidents unknown to us took place.

Persecution, as in Revelation, bred resentment, which may also have been fed by the anti-Roman sentiment so marked in the Jewish insurrectionist movements, quite apart from whatever such movement Jesus may have been associated with. Yet the advantage of the Jewish situation in the Empire led to a wish in certain ways to appease the government, as a theme in Acts of the Apostles attests; but the eschatological hopes, as in Paul, could well have made the problem of Church and State one of little consequence. The incident in the Gospels ("render unto Caesar"), which I do not take as authentic, seems to grant some propriety of jurisdiction, at least in human affairs, to the State. In no single instance in the literature can the immediate attitude be interpreted as *the* Christian view, but only as a Christian view.[25]

The significant matter here is the obligation faced by Christianity, since it was no longer a Judaism, to fashion its own attitude toward the State. In our working backward, the problem is now an essentially Christian one, no longer the Jewish one.

The Epistle to the Hebrews: Transitions

In the above writings, the key issues are those of a maturing or matured Christianity, confronting the problems of an entity independent of Judaism. The earlier literature does not yet exhibit such full independence. The marked transition seems to me to center in the Epistle to the Hebrews. In it there is no reflection of difficulties on the part of Christians with Jews, but rather with Christianity's understanding its relationship to the ancient Judaism, its parent. It often seems to me that Christian commentators give far too little attention to this recurrent problem. When Hebrews was written, Christianity might have been thought by some of its adherents to be disruptive of, or in opposition to, or out of alignment with, a proud legacy from the ancient Judaism; this is the case because the unfolding tradition held that the Five Books of Moses were sacred to it, and divine in origin, yet some of the contents of these books, namely the laws that begin with Exodus XX, were null and void. The younger tradition inevitably faced problems of reconciling, on the one hand, its sense of continuity with its source and origin, and, on the other, its sense of having created those new, inner items that represent a potential inference of discontinuity. It seems to me that we can discern in early Christianity three different attitudes toward the potential sense of discontinuity. First, Paul's attitude, it would seem to me, affirmed a basic, general overarching continuity, and the discontinuity was limited to the laws. Second, the attitude of Marcion, and of other Gnostics, was that the discontinuity was both general and specific, and, moreover, was total, to the end that it must be asserted that Christianity was never born out of Judiasm, and owed no debt to it. (Indeed why should it, inasmuch as it was demons, and not Moses, who wrote the Five Books of Moses?) The third Christian attitude seems to me to be that of the Epistles to the Hebrews, and is passingly but recurrently found in Luke-Acts, namely that there is what one might call a higher continuity between the ancient Judaism and the new entity; in this higher continuity, the loftiest themes of the ancient Judaism have come unbrokenly to be aggrandized and even apotheosized in the younger movement. Accordingly, Hebrews does not reject the ancient Judaism, but rather discovers it to be both the imperfect foreshadowing of, but nevertheless the worthy preparation for, that perfect realization which emerges in the new. In Hebrews, Moses is not disparaged; on the contrary, he is praised. He is praised even within the contrast that Hebrews draws between Moses as a servant and the Christ as a Son. Hebrews is not concerned with Jews, but rather with the relation of the new "Judaism" to the old.

In working backward as we have done so far, the role of the Christ Jesus, as he appears in the writings that we have hitherto traversed so rapidly, is indirect or else allusive, and he is alluded to as an examplar, rather than described in his essence or in his works. On the other hand, Hebrews presents a rounded exposition of the Christ himself. Thereby, Hebrews shares in that focus on the Christ Jesus which characterizes both the canonical and the apocryphal Gospels. Hebrews, written later than the canonical Gospels, is no less concerned with the Christ than they are, but its manner is significantly different, not only in the quasi-philosophical form which characterizes the writing, but also in the significant distinction that the Gospels *narrate about* Jesus, whereas Hebrews abstains from direct narration and only *hearkens back* to him. In Hebrews 5:7–9, there is an allusion to Jesus' offering of prayers and supplications, possibly related to Mark 14:32–42 and the parallels. Hebrews 2:18 echoes not only the suffering of Jesus, but also the temptation, and Hebrews 10:19–20 possibly echoes Mark 15:38 and the parallels. I do not find any unmistakable allusion to the Synoptic tradition as such in these passages, but these few passages are possibly a sufficient basis on which to make the point that the author of Hebrews seems acquainted, if not with the Synoptic Gospels and John, at least with Gospel traditions.

I ask myself why Hebrews uses so relatively little of the Gospel tradition. Perhaps it is for the very simple reason that its major interest occasioned no need to use much of it, and that this single essay in no way exhausts what the author knew, and, not impossibly, there were other occasions on which the author of Hebrews orally retold a large portion of the Gospel tradition to his audience. Again, and in the same vein, I have long been struck by the circumstance that the Rabbinic Literature in its haggadic elements narrates the same kinds of things that the Synoptic Gospels narrate, but, on the other hand, Philo, who deals with "significance," is devoid of narration and singularly free of parable and pithy utterance. I am cognizant, moreover, of the circumstance that John seems to choose to narrate only a few of the things of the large amount that the Synoptic Gospels narrate; one scholar has put it that John seems to select one single instance of the various types of narrations of the Gospels, thereby reducing the quantity of narration and filling out his Gospel with the long, theosophic soliloquies. Hebrews narrates almost nothing, and John narrates a moderate amount, and the Synoptics narrate a great many things. Is all this mere accident, or is it, in the case of John and Hebrews, design? Is there something in the philosophic cast of mind which tends to reject narration, and instead to deal with symbolic or quasi-philosophical matters? Again, what shall we make of the passage in Hebrews 6:22–73, which first likens the Christ to Melchizedek and then specifies that Melchizedek is without father or mother or genealogy and has neither beginning of days nor end of life? Are these meaningful words, or are they simply a preacher's fortuitous homily and devoid of true significance? If the words are meaningful, in what way shall we reconcile the contention in Hebrews with the Gospel tradition that Jesus had a mother, Mary, and that genealogies could be constructed, as they were in Matthew and in Luke, to trace his ancestry? Can this passage in Hebrews be any less than a rejection of the entire process of genealogical tracing?[26]

I have elsewhere commented that since the canonical Gospels have had almost two thousand years of Christian adulation, it seems to me quite understandable for it to be axiomatic to Christians that the Gospel tradition and the Gospels already possessed, even in early times, the sanctity that they ultimately came to acquire. Suppose, however, that, just as Philo could scorn Jewish literalists, and in his treatises, *Questions and Answers to Genesis and Exodus*, could dismiss the literal narratives in Scripture as unimportant, this so as to go promptly into allegory and there to introduce quasi-philosophical views, is it to be ruled out that the author of Hebrews, and the author of the Pastorals comparably, had no great affection for the type of compositions that the canonical Gospels represent? What are the nuances and overtones of the very many passages in the Pastorals and in I John and in Hebrews about the need to preserve the faith, if not reflections of great diversities within early Christianity, and diversities on points of central concern? Shall we limit the denounced divergency from faith merely to Gnostic Docetism? Or was there some need among Christians to search for a middle ground between Gnostic Docetism on the one hand and anecdotal simplicities on the other hand?

There is a great deal at stake in one's judgment at this point, for it has a direct bearing on the question of why there are multiple Gospels, the four that are canonical and the numerous others that are called apocryphal. Somewhat to oversimplify the issue, let me ask the question in this way: were Gospels composed merely and solely out of a desire to express a meditative piety and to add to the totality of this literary piety? Or did Gospels also have the particular purpose of correcting or rejecting previous efforts to write

Gospels? To my mind the possibility is distinctly open that the succession of Gospels represent an effort in the direction of writing the unassailable Gospel, on the premise that the previous efforts are imperfect and assailable. It seems to me that one function of the Epistle to the Hebrews is to provide the most nearly perfect Gospel, and, therefore, though the author knows aspects of the Gospel tradition, he rules them out of his writing, avoiding direct narration and limiting himself to allusion. The author of Hebrews thereby spares himself certain problems in the Gospels and hence is able to concentrate on significance, and to set forth his theme of perfection.

The Epistle to the Hebrews seems to me to serve in still another way. The focus on Judaism in Paul, in Acts, and in the Gospels is on the Judaism of the synagogue, and the Old Testament passages which are cited do not disturb the synagogal centrality. In Hebrews, on the other hand, there is established a sense of direct continuity between the Tabernacle in the wilderness and the new entity, Christianity. To put this in another way, while, historically, Christianity appears to have arisen in the milieu of the synagogue rather than of the Temple, the effect of Hebrews is to broaden the base of Christianity in the Judaic heritage, through a strong emphasis on the major significance of the Tabernacle material. The Tabernacle, as we know, became the Temple.

When I try to hold in balance the paucity of allusions to the Jesus of history with the abundant material linking the ancient Tabernacle to the new entity, this in the oft-recognized typological manner of Hebrews, then I see in Hebrews a remarkable creativity in the realm of Christian Hellenistic Midrash. It is almost as if the author felt about the Gospel tradition that it comprises facts so well known that he need not repeat them, but can instead dwell on significance. Surely, whatever is meant by primitive Christianity, the Epistle of the Hebrews is far removed from it.

Still one other element seems to me to demand further notice. Beginning at least as early as Philippians, in the kenosis passage, it seems to me that we can see a progressive shift by which Abraham ceases to be the exemplar for the true believer to emulate, and is replaced by the Christ. When Abraham gives way fully to the Christ, have we not moved progressively away from the Jewish setting of early Christianity into its inner Christian setting? We notice the blessing of Abraham by Melchizedek in Hebrews 7:7: "It is beyond dispute that the inferior is blessed by the superior."

I have no clear idea of the date of the composition of Hebrews. Recourse to a handbook such as Moffatt provides a range of suggestions. I would raise here the very old question, could Hebrews have been written after the destruction of the Temple in 70? The view has been advanced that Hebrews could not have been written before 70, this on the premise that the author implies the existence of the Temple cult, and that he would have been sure to have commented on the destruction of the Temple if he wrote after 70; another view argues that the interest of the author is in the Tabernacle in the wilderness rather than in the Temple, so he could have written if after 70. If the issue of a pre-70 or post-70 date has not been settled in scholarly discussions, then I see no possibility of my settling it for myself. I believe that Hebrews comes from some period after 70, for it seems to me that the period before 70 is too early to allow for the growth of the kind of elaborate creative Midrash that it represents. Hebrews is not at all arguing that the Christian system is better than a possibly by now defunct Jewish system, but that it is better than that venerable ancient system, the inauguration of which the Pentateuch describes. The rending of the veil of the Tabernacle, or, as in the Gospels, the rending of the veil in the Temple, seems to me not susceptible of interpretation as an allusion to the destruction of the Temple by the Romans in 70; it is rather an assertion that atonement is available at all times, and not just on the Day of Atonement when the Jewish high priest enters within the holy room closed off by the veil.

I find myself unable to account for the abrupt shift in Hebrews from its essay form into its closing words in epistle form. This shift has yielded many hypotheses about the authorship, as the handbooks disclose, but I am sure that the issue of precise authorship will never be settled. It seems permissible to conclude this: the author was someone from that chain of tradition in the Christian sense which Philo represents in the Jewish sense. More important than who wrote the addendum is the question, why this addendum? I can only guess at the answer, as others have tried to guess. My guess is this, that the epistolary addendum provided an implication of an authorship that was both relatively ancient and authoritative, and that without this addendum, and despite all the significant and striking content of Hebrews, the assertion that the Christ was without father and mother and genealogy would have restricted the book's circulation, even to the point that it might have perished.

I am unable to decide whether Hebrews belongs to the early second century or the end of the first century, and in terms of this book, if it is the second century, it should not command the same interest here as it would if it were definitely first century. If one works on hunch, however, then in my own understanding there is nothing to preclude Hebrews from belonging in the first Christian century. I would be more prone to date it around 95 than around 75.

Christian Creativity

A similar type of midrashic creativity in a Christian form seems to me to be characteristic of Ephesians, which I take not to be by Paul, and by Colossians, which may possibly be from Paul's hand or Paul's period. As is in the case of Hebrews, Ephesians needed an external authority, and Ephesians calls upon Paul, but within a totally epistolary form. In Ephesians the Jewish scene seems to me left so far behind to the point that there is no trace of it at all. On the other hand, though we are in a Gentile setting, we have in Ephesians a clear sense of the differentiation of the new movement from "other Gentiles," as in 4:17–22. I find relatively little in common between Hebrews and Ephesians but this the bond of midrashic style, and I assume that both writings are hymns to the Christ, this in a Christianity which has lost its Jewish setting but which differentiates itself from its Gentile environment; that is, it has progressed very far toward its self-awareness as an independent entity.

While I do not think anything is at stake either in attributing Colossians to Paul or in denying Pauline authorship, again I am drawn to notice the midrashic hymn in Colossians 1:9–29. What strikes me as most significant about these three writings, Hebrews, Ephesians, and Colossians, is the absence of allusion to clearly known history, even when the last verse of Colossians mentions the fetters, and the next-to-last paragraph tells us that a certain Tychicus will convey information orally. Indeed, despite the long allusion to particular peoples in Colossians 4:7–17, there is nevertheless no immediate historic event that seems to have spurred the writing in the way, for example, that the Maccabean revolt spurred the writing of the Book of Daniel. I do not find this indifference to history at all startling, for in a somewhat remote way it seems to me kindred to the comparable absence of the bond to history that characterizes the Rabbinic Literature. That the Christian midrash was growing in depth and dimension would seem to me to be more significant than would have been the need to record specific events in these writings, events which in view of the great event of the Christ made all others somewhat meaningless.

John: Incident and Hymn

It seems to me that the Gospel According to John presents a most admirable harmony of incident and hymn. Indeed, John seems to me to provide the paradox of giving us incident virtually devoid of history, and I do not mean thereby the lack of historicity in the incidents, but rather the contrast between the manner in which Matthew gives us a precise occasion of the birth of Jesus, the last year of the wicked Herod, and Luke, in his prologue, not only announces that he is going to give an orderly account but also begins, in 1:5, with an allusion to Herod. John's *logos* prologue abstains from any allocation of the event of the incarnation to a particular time in history. In the Passion narrative in Matthew in 27:2, the mention of Pilate is accompanied by the identification that he is the "governor." Mark 15:1 lacks such an identification of Pilate, but the setting of the accusations before Pilate, namely that Jesus was perverting the nation in forbidding the Jews to give tribute to Caesar, constitutes a kind of identification of the man. In John we read only that Jesus was led to the praetorium and that there an unidentified Pilate went out to see him. If I were asked to guess whether the author of John could have given possible dates for the birth and death of

Jesus, then I would imagine that he could have, and I imagine that he withholds the information only because he does not consider this kind of data relevant to him.

Most of the arguments that deny John knew the Synoptics rest on the premise that John's failure to use the abundant Synoptic data can only rest on ignorance of it. To my mind a much better explanation is disinterest—a disinterest kindred to that of Hebrews. The origin of the disinterest is in John's desire to write about the significance of the Christ, rather than the details about Jesus.

There is to my mind no solution possible to the question of whether the Synoptic view of a single trip by Jesus to Jerusalem is correct, or the Johannine view of multiple trips, for the multiple trips in the context of John can as easily come out of John's midrashic bent as out of authentic historic recollection. Those Jewish scholars who prefer the account of John about the date of the crucifixion to that in the Synoptics (inasmuch as John has the arrest and trial prior to the beginning of Passover, while the Synoptics allocate these events after the beginning of the Passover), seem to me to miss the essential point: that the identification of the arrest and crucifixion with Passover is more apt to be midrashic and theological than historical. If the exact date and the occasion of the arrest and crucifixion were clearly known in early Christianity, and clearly established, then there would not have been divergency between the Synoptics and John. If perhaps I overstate the unhistorical character of the Johannine Gospel, this in my zeal to emphasize the deepened Christology, let me state that my attitude is not that the data in John ought to be discarded out of hand as unhistorical, for I have no firm opinion here; my point is that it is the deepening Christology that concerns the author of John, and not precise historical data.

Hegemony in the Church

In the present compass, one can select only limited items on which to comment. A key problem in the Gospels is the issue of relatedness versus unrelatedness to the Jewish setting. The sense of self-determination on the part of the Evangelists forces each into an effort to keep in balance the relationship to Judaism and the advanced sense of self-determination of the later age of the authors. Self-determination cannot, in their view, have failed to begin in the age of Jesus. Is the pericope (Mark 1:12 and parallels) that Jesus taught with authority here relevant? Now, so long as Jesus lived, he was the leader of his followers, but after his ascension, how could the issues of Jewishness, of self-determination, and then the leadership of the self-determined, be solved? To my mind it is significant that the twenty-first chapter of John, as I view it, tends to convey the hegemony of the apostles, after the death of Jesus, to the disciple Peter, but Peter, in the previous chapters, has been supplanted in hegemony by the "beloved disciple." If it is correct that the purpose of the twenty-first chapter is to restore leadership to Peter and that it has been added to John and is not truly a part of it, then the original John goes in a direction other than that which both Matthew and Luke have gone, for in both of those Gospels it is Peter who is unquestionably the leader of the disciples. To my mind, therefore, insofar as the Gospels reflect real life situations in the Church, the Gospel According to John is intended to divert us from the direction in which Matthew and Luke have gone respecting hegemony over the Church in the age following Jesus. The beloved disciple himself seems to me to play a very secondary role, limited primarily to the putative authorship and to reducing the ascendancy of Peter. The key, to my mind, is the role of the Paraclete in the Gospel (14:25–26): "These things I have spoken to you, while I am still with you. But the Paraclete, the Holy Spirit, whom the Father will send in my name, he will teach you all things, and bring to your remembrance all that I have said to you." Where Luke and Matthew envisage a purely human leadership of the new self-determining entity, John envisages divine guidance.

It seems to me that what Luke argues for is this: in the age after Jesus, the Hellenistic Church was to be governed by authorized men. In conformity with this view, Jesus in Luke has a multitude of disciples of whom twelve are designated to be apostles. When Judas is no longer one of the apostles, and has in fact died, there are many disciples available and eligible to supplant him. Acts 1:22–26 speaks of putting forth two disciples, Joseph called Barsabbas and Matthias; after the lots are cast, the choice falls on Matthias, and he is enrolled with the eleven apostles. In Luke-Acts, there is a consistent motif of an unbroken continuity between the ancient Judaism and what Acts calls "the way." In Luke-Acts no Christian, whether Jesus or Paul or Peter, was ever unfaithful to the ancestral religion, but, on the contrary, all were undeviatingly faithful. In Luke-Acts the "gospel" is in no sense a discontinuity, but, rather, Law grows naturally into Gospel. The infidelity, as it were, is on the part of Jews, for it was they who caused the recurrent difficulties which such apostles as Stephen and Paul experienced.

In Matthew, on the other hand, the direction of the Church is not entrusted as much to authorized officials as it is to authorized law, and, consistent with this view, Jesus is conceived of as a lawgiver giving his regulations, as did Moses, in a Sermon on a Mount, and his discourses in five sections comparable to the five books of Moses, and preceded by a babyhood strikingly similar to that of Moses in Exodus. Just as the Epistle of James which holds that "faith" is insufficient, Matthew envisages Christian fidelity as involving obedience, not to Moses, but to the higher laws of Jesus.[27] To Peter is entrusted the responsibility of passing on the interpretation of this law[28] (Matthew 16:19).

I am by no means contending that the matter of hegemony is the sole interest of the three Gospels, Matthew, Luke, and John. I am only saying that in these three Gospels we get three different theories of how the maturing institution is to be regulated, whether by law, or by authorized persons, or in a totally different way, by the working of the Holy Spirit. It would be my opinion that at the time each of these Gospels was written the view being advocated was conceived of as the one single way to regulate the Church, and I believe that Luke was arguing against Matthew and that John was arguing against both Matthew and Luke. With the passing of time all three came to be considered equally canonical and equally authoritative, so that the subsequent Church utilized and blended and harmonized a hegemony by law and by persons and still made room for the Holy Spirit—the latter quite a dangerous thing, as we can learn from the Montanist heresy which appears to have flowered toward the end of the second century and to have entailed factors much more complex than mere Church hegemony.

Mark and Gentile Christianity

Moving further back, back to Mark, I have come to an opinion about the Gospel which interprets its content quite differently from the conventional scholarship.[29] A dominant motif in it is to my mind that which declares that the true Christianity is the Dispersion Christianity of Gentiles, and in my view, Mark is both a polemic against Palestinian Jewish

Christianity and Jewish Christians, and also a kind of Magna Charta for Hellenistic, Gentile Christianity. In Mark it is related not only that the Pharisees and Sadducees and Chief Priests are the opponents of Jesus, but also that the disciples are blind, opaque, and faithless, and the chief among them, Peter, three times denies Jesus; indeed it is only the Roman centurion who has the clear sight by which to declare (15:39), "Truly This was the[30] Son of God."

In my view Mark arises not only from the previously oral Gospel tradition, but also, and significantly, from aspects of Paul's theology, not so much with respect to the themes of sin and righteousness and faith, but with respect to the question, who is the elect of God? In Mark, there is a Pauline answer, but quite beyond Paul: not only is the Gentile Church legitimate, it alone is the legitimate Church.[31] Self-determination involved not only the definition of the relationship to Judaism, but also to the earliest form of Christianity, Palestinian Jewish Christianity.[32]

I wrote once about Paul[33] that it seems to me that we have in his case a deviation from the normal which itself became the norm for ensuing Christianity, and what had before Paul seemed the normal came after Paul to be viewed as a deviation. Exactly what non-Pauline Christianity was in Paul's time I confess I have only the vaguest ideas about, and I would be hard put to give a bill of particulars concerning it. The most that I have been able to tell myself is that I would imagine that early Palestinian Jewish Christianity represented a normal Judaism to which were added opinions about Jesus and the significance of his death and resurrection, without substantially otherwise affecting the nature of Judaism. If the cancellation of the laws of Moses and a special mission to Gentiles are innovations by Paul, then perhaps from these innovations we can form some ideas of what there existed antecedent to him and outside his ambit. Such material is sparse, laconic, and fraught with great uncertainty. If Paul does not himself create the Gentile, Hellenistic church, at the minimum he provides it with its rationale and its sense of direction. In a sense, one of the achievements of Mark seems to me to be this, that it tries to relocate the rationale and sense of direction of the Gentile, Dispersion Church back from Paul to the age of Jesus, and from the Dispersion back into Judea.

Respecting Paul and the self-determination of early Christianity, the theme is present that the self-determining Church is a reality, for the breach with Judaism is unmistakable, but also that the breach is subject to ultimate alleviation, as in Romans 10–11. In speaking of the breach, I have elsewhere emphasized that Paul from his own standpoint cannot mistake that a separation has occurred, but he in no way regards himself as the author of it; rather it is the Jews who have caused it. Paul believes that he is preaching and teaching the surest and truest version of an unbroken Judaism. The theme of the ultimate reconciliation tends to fade out in the post-Pauline literature. In Paul the motif of self-determination, while present, is inextricably bound up with tremendously vivid eschatological expectations. However much Pauline thought served as the basis for the developing Hellenistic Church, I do not see that Paul ever envisaged a Church destined to abide throughout the ages. His direct concern is not so much with the Church as an institution as with the aggregate of those prepared for the climactic moment soon to arrive. Moreover, any assessment of self-determination in the Epistles of Paul needs to take cognizance of the intra-Christian conflicts adumbrated in the Corinthian letters, and the parties at Corinth about which we know so little. Would these parties have agreed or disagreed on the matter of self-determination? I do not know.

From Gospels to Jesus?

It has been a standard scholarly endeavor to move, as the title of at least one book would indicate, back from the Gospels to Jesus. It is an ongoing problem, at least to me, that we see the age of Jesus, and his career, through the eyes of the sub-apostolic age.[34] To this recognition, important to me, there needs to be added the mood of that age—that the Old Testament had come to be understood in the light of the already advanced and creative style of midrash. Can we penetrate this midrash and return to Jesus and his age? Let us look at the figure of Abraham. He is not in the midrash the simple character he is in Genesis. His father owned a shop of idols, which Abraham smashed. He underwent not one test, that of Genesis 22, but ten. He was a great missionary; he had been born in astrology, but had abandoned it in favor of the true God. He taught the Egyptian priests mathematics during his sojourn in Egypt, in Genesis 12. And so on.

I find myself regarding the Gospels as midrashic.[35] The apocryphal Gospels I would take to be *midrashim* on the canonical Gospels, or on the Gospel tradition. But the Gospels themselves are the midrash on the career of Jesus; they are not the career, in somewhat the same way that the midrashic Abraham is not the same as the Abraham of Genesis.

The midrash on Abraham, for all its fancies, seems to be marked by certain restraints. It allocates Abraham's birth to Ur, not to Memphis. It embellishes Abraham's sojourn in Haran, but does not allocate it to Athens. Abraham pursues the four eastern kings of Genesis 14 beyond Damascus, not beyond Antioch. It finds a fault in Melchizedek of Salem, but, while identifying him with Shem, it does not obliterate the man, his role, or his place of activity. That is, the midrash largely remains within some definable limits. Nevertheless, the nature of midrashic expansion is such that we should never be able from the aggregate of midrashic expansions alone to re-create securely the scriptural Abraham of Genesis.

It is, of course, appropriate to inquire, about each pericope in the midrashic material on Abraham, what the *Sitz im Leben* and the purpose were. That Abraham taught the Egyptian priests mathematics, according to Josephus, is accompanied by the statement that they in turn taught the Greeks; we have here a piece of apologetics, a reflection of an ancient Mayflower complex. That Abraham taught Isaac Hebrew commends the learning of Hebrew in an age when Hebrew was no longer the native language; for it to be a Jew's possession, it had to be learned.[36] That Genesis was canonical in no way obstructed the creativity of the midrashist.

The clue to the pericopes in the Gospels—not to Jesus— is midrash. And midrash is meditative piety, not history.

But a written Gospel is more than a concatenation of midrashim, for none of the canonical Gospels lacks an inherent unity or an inherent integrity. They are portraits of Jesus. What is more natural than for modern historians to attempt, again and again, to use scholarship so as to paint a new "authentic" portrait of him? If, from the midrash on Abraham, we cannot re-create the Abraham of Genesis, can we from the midrash on Jesus re-create him and his age?

Having viewed literally countless instances of the efforts that have been made, it seems to me that they fall into two categories. The first category seems to me to be a blend of history and piety, and out of such an effort there emerges a great and noble, and usually human Jesus who is largely a reflection of the noble aspirations of the scholar who has made the effort; there is evidence of a struggle to separate history from non-history, but the clue to such works is the understandable veneration of Jesus deeply felt by the authors.[37]

The second category is quite different, for piety totally disappears and only stern "history" remains. It is exemplified in the effort of Professor S. G. F. Brandon in *Jesus and the Zealots*. The book in substance goes far beyond its title. It has already brought some dismay to Christian scholars, to whom Brandon's views have seemed not only wrong but also very distasteful. It is not nearly as important, as I view things, that Brandon emerges with the opinion that the Jesus of history was himself a Zealot, as it is to try to follow the method by which Brandon feels he can move from the Gospels back to Jesus. Two chapters in his book seem to me to merit notice here. One of these is entitled, "The Concept of the Pacific Christ." By the "Pacific Christ" Brandon has in mind the frequent view of Jesus which divests him of any military connection; the Gospels, in Brandon's view, artificially separate Jesus from the normal Jewish events of his day, thus conceiving of him as a pacific character. In this connection Brandon focuses on the Gospel According to Matthew; he finds support for his view of the pacific Christ both in the Beatitudes and also presented dramatically in the account of the arrest of Jesus in Gethsemane. Brandon finds the "Pacific Christ" also in the Gospel According to Luke, where he is present more subtly than in Matthew. But his chapter which most invites attention is "The Markan Gospel." Let me cite Brandon's conclusion respecting Mark: "On analysis, as we have seen, the story is incredible both on historical grounds and because of its intrinsic impossibility." Brandon's view of Mark is, in short, that of a complete falsification of the facts, this falsification having been made tendentiously and deliberately.

We must set in contrast to each other here in the usual process from the Gospels back to Jesus the ordinary scholarly but adulatory view of Jesus, and Brandon's view, which I am sure many Christians will regard as impious.

I am by no means sure that Brandon is right. He has gone far beyond what I had myself felt to be the case respecting tendentiousness in the Gospel According to Mark. Nevertheless, in some sense his views amount to prolonged extensions of more restrained opinions I have had. It is with respect to these extensions that I feel some uncertainty. But if I were to be asked, which view of Jesus seems to be, according to my hunches, the more nearly historical, that of the adulating scholars, or that of Brandon, then I would align myself with Brandon. At the same time, I have an uneasy feeling, even respecting Brandon, that there is no real sense in which one can move from the Gospels back to Jesus.[38]

I am troubled by this personal inability to go beyond the Gospels back to Jesus himself. This is just as much the case respecting the teachings[39] attributed to him in the Gospels as respecting the events of his career. I have tried to express this inability in a variety of ways. I have said that the portrait of Jesus in the Gospels is kindred to an oil painting, and one had best stand at a distance and not move up too close, or one will see only the brush lines and the accumulated oil—not Jesus himself. I have spoken in defense of the Gospels as potentially historical in this sense, that I do not believe that a Gentile Christian, such as the author of Mark, living in the Dispersion, could out of mere imagination have concocted the Jewish scene with such relatively high general reliability. The paradox, then, is that I can neither dismiss the Gospels, especially Mark, as totally unhistorical, nor yet accept all the specific details as reliable history. And I know no unchallengeable way of objectively distinguishing between the history and the non-history. If I know anything, it is Gospels, not Jesus. Moreover, I think I have been fairly consistent in holding that the Gospels are not about the man Jesus, but about the human interval in the eternity of the divine Christ. Jesus the man is nineteenth and twentieth century, and not the first. The question "what manner of man" is asked not so as to elicit an answer about a human, but so as to stress the supernatural character of Jesus. Only in the sense that I deny the Christ myth and its assertion that there never was a man Jesus, am I willing to discuss Jesus. To affirm as I do that there was such a man is different from asserting that I possess precise information about him.

I find this situation to be one of great unsatisfaction to me. How much easier it would be for me if I could be sure about Jesus! How easy it would be for me if I could delineate Jesus as either a prophet or a proto-rabbi or an Essene. Perhaps since I am Jewish and not Christian, it is easier for me to live with the unresolved problem. But my frustration is quite as great as I imagine it is for a Christian student.

I think that I perceive in some of the recent writing about Jesus, even on the part of scholars who are not Fundamentalists, that there is a note of irritation toward earlier New Testament scholars. I find it hard to understand a spirit in some modern scholars which seems to me not a very generous one, in its disparagement of the liberal scholarship of the nineteenth century and the early parts of the twentieth century. Some of this newer writing often seems to me to imply that the Christian scholars of the past were in some way guilty of infidelity to Christianity in coming to honest but negative conclusions, or else that they were in some sense ornery or wicked people, or else that they were simply miserable failures in the chores that they undertook. I do not share in that disparagement. The negative conclusions came out of an uncontrolled desire to be too precise, to be too certain. Had there not existed this extra measure of zeal for certainty, the frustration would not have arisen. The issue as I see it can be put in this way, that we cannot go back beyond the Gospels with any certainty, because the

Gospels at the same time that they reveal Jesus, also conceal him.

I am unable to give an opinion on the question, how much of the ultimate self-determination of Christianity begins in, and finds its impulse in, Jesus or in his age.[40] I cannot agree with views that put him over and against the Judaism of his age, but I cannot agree with the views that disconnect him from the incipient movement. To say that Paul substituted a religion about Jesus for the religion of Jesus, a frequent nineteenth-century verdict, or to say with Bultmann that the preacher became the preachment, can in a sense be true, but still unconsciously dodge the issue. I suppose that my own procedure also dodges the issue, but it has the possible potential merit of doing so consciously. Accordingly, the elusive character of the figure of Jesus deprives us of all but speculative answers to the questions we might raise about Jesus and Christian self-determination. Perhaps it is illegitimate even to attribute to him any semblance of direct relation; such certainly is the import of the normal nineteenth- and twentieth-century form critical view that Jesus founded no Church, and the Gospel passages that imply that he did represent the later Church and not Jesus himself. The question, however, can be asked respecting possible influential impulses. For example, was there something in the authentic teaching of Jesus, as Morton Smith[41] speculates, which is picked up and carried on further by Paul? If we deny this we tend to separate Jesus from subsequent developments; if we assert it we remain constantly in the area of the most speculative interpretation of extant passages, and from the standpoint of the critical scholarship, we proceed without persuasive evidence. Personally, I know no way of dealing with the issue except to include it too in the area of impenetrable uncertainty; it too is an item about Jesus wherein

I feel that I must stop at the Gospels, and abstain from trying to go further.

Controllable History

It seems to me that if we follow the procedure that I have advocated, namely starting with the latest documents and working backward, then we do not impose upon ourselves the insoluble task of discovering the precise history, or precise origin, of this or that element in Christianity, or the precise definition of the terms used by the intuitive ancient thinkers. We deal, rather, with matters after they have come to some fruition and some maturity, and we can see the fruition and maturity in fairly good organic relationship with broader matters. We free ourselves of the need to inquire into the origins, not because they ought not to be inquired into, but because the inquiry into them has yielded such uncertain and contradictory results. Most of all, when we array matters in this way we come to be aware of elements in Christendom which abstain from being surprising. On the other hand, if we start in the customary fashion, we come to be puzzled, for example, that all of a sudden Gnosticism appears. When we work backward through the documents, we discover that Gnosticism has arisen and taken on particular form; this seems to me much more meaningful, for it deals with the known, rather than with the unknown, and the unrecoverable origins of obscure matters.

We can know with certainty and fullness about first-century Christianity only a restricted number of the motifs and preoccupations. Again, for every datum that we know in its full clarity, there are nine that we either know dimly or know nothing about. For every answer we can give, there are nine instances in which we can give no answers. For every relationship that we can see clearly, there are nine relationships that we cannot see at all, or nine that are either hazy or completely invisible.

THE VALUE IN UNCERTAINTY

Is there any virtue in stressing, as I have done, the areas of our uncertainty? In the first instance, it is far better for scholarship to know where it stands than for it to fail to know. It is far better for us to present guesses as guesses than to pass them off as reflections of accurate and unmistakable knowledge. Scholarship seems to me to be at its best when its claims are not extravagant and when they are substantial rather than hazardous.

The Supernatural

In the second instance, when we deal with the internal question of the supernatural, it is perhaps worth pointing out that it is at all times difficult to recapture the past, but it is especially so in the case of highly significant religious movements. There seems an inevitable mystery relating to elements that go into the fashioning of some particular personality, and relating also to the impact which he makes on his environment and which the environment makes on him, and the resultant movement which ensues and which goes through growth and development.

In religious situations, a keen interest in the original personality arises ordinarily only at a time when it is too late for the relevant facts to be set down in pedestrian and unvarnished fashion. There is an inevitable element of the unknown and the unknowable surrounding the great religious personalities and the elementary beginnings of great religious institutions.

It seems to me to be quite consistent with the mysterious

nature of religion that the early phases of particular religions should be shrouded in some darkness. Rationalist that I am, I still feel that that which is essentially religious in religions loses much of its significance when it is all too easily and too readily explainable. All too often there is a tendency in man to explain too much and, indeed, to explain away. To know too much can destroy in man the intuitive creativity which is the element in our being that enables us to fashion or propagate our tremendous religious institutions.

Notes

1. His *Jesus of Nazareth* is not to my liking; see my *We Jews and Jesus*, pp. 91–93. On the other hand, that this book was written in Hebrew gave it a broad circulation among Jews. Before Klausner, Claude G. Montefiore had vexed many Jews for what seemed an excess of adulation of Jesus, and the effect was to make Jews suspicious of this area of study. The effect of Klausner's book among Jews was to make the area study much less forbidding, and, in fact, his book tended to open it up in a way previously unknown. It is likely that, had there not been Klausner, I myself would probably not have had the horizons through which to enter the field.

2. In my *We Jews and Jesus* I have alluded to a tendency among Jews in Western countries in the nineteenth century to "reclaim" Jesus for the Jewish people. Isaac Mayer Wise (1819–1900), founder of the Hebrew Union College, the Union of American Hebrew Congregations, and the Central Conference of American Rabbis, wrote a great deal about early Christianity, much of it in the vein of reclaim-

ing Jesus, this by separating Jesus from subsequent Christianity. Very curiously, in 1865 Wise believed that there had never been a Jesus; in 1869 he embarked on a biography of Jesus in his weekly journal, *The American Israelite*, but did not complete the work. I described Wise and his effort in "Isaac Mayer Wise's 'Jesus Himself' " in *Essays in American Jewish History: To Commemorate the Tenth Anniversary of the Founding of the American Jewish Archives*, pp. 325–58. Wise's work is of no importance for New Testament scholarship, but is highly important in documenting aspects of the shift in modern Judaism from ignoring Jesus (or worse) into admiring him and "re-Judaizing" him.

3. Perhaps a candid word here is susceptible of being as inoffensive as I intend it. I have long been an admirer of Catholic Old Testament scholarship; see my review of Bruce Vawter, *The Conscience of Israel*, *Jewish Social Studies*, XXVI (1964), 179–80. I commended this book especially for those Jews unacquainted with Catholic Old Testament scholarship who wished to see the basis of my contention that "modern biblical scholarship among Catholics need not apologize to the best scholarship of Protestants and Jews." I could not then have spoken in the same way about Catholic New Testament scholarship, but to do so becomes increasingly more possible. If one compares and contrasts Catholic "introductions" of a generation ago, as I have, with Robert and Feuillet, he will discern the reason for my changing attitude. Moreover, I am a charter subscriber to *New Testament Abstracts*, a Catholic publication of fullest scholarly integrity.

4. There is a tremendous problem in nomenclature in connection with Gnostics. If one follows Hans Jonas, then the term "Gnostic" is inapplicable unless it meets certain requirements: a fallen god, a benighted creator and sinister creation, alien soul, cosmic captivity and acosmic salvation; see his "Response," J. Philip Hyatt (ed.), *The Bible in Modern Scholarship*, p. 293. But see also the papers by G. Quispel and R. M. Wilson, ibid. pp. 252–78.

Perhaps one needs to differentiate between full Gnosticism and Gnostic tendencies. In the latter case, however, the word "Gnostic" can tend to be meaningless, and to be only a rough synonym for theosophy, or for speculative mysticism, or for what have you. To complicate the problem, the divisions at Corinth are often interpreted, or over-interpreted, as involving "Gnostic" elements (see James Robinson, "Kerygma and History in the New Testament," ibid. pp. 122ff.), with the implication that Gnostic tendencies are almost as early as earliest Hellenistic Christianity. But does diversity in Christology necessarily involve specifically Gnostic tendencies, or, instead, a kind of Greek speculation less particular than the word "Gnostic" implies?

I know no way out of the forest of confusions except to rely on irritating compounds such as proto-Gnostic, quasi-Gnostic, and the like. Jonas's insistence may be a good corrective against a possible scholarly looseness, but it strikes me as rigid, and perfectionist. See below, note 22.

5. Let us take three issues as example. I have read a spate of efforts to reconcile the difference between John and the Synoptics on the date of the trial and the crucifixion. If reconciliation fails (as to me it seems to), then at the first level, we are faced by the need to choose one and discard the other. But, on a second level, may we not suppose that at the time of the writing of the Gospels the date of the crucifixion was unknown, or else disregarded in favor of a theological, not a historical, identification of Jesus and the paschal lamb? In such a case, cannot both accounts be set aside from the standpoint of accurate history?

Second, did Judas die as in Matthew 27:5, or as in Acts 1:18—or is Judas not at all historical? Divergency can as easily mean that both the divergent accounts are unhistorical as that one is and the other is not.

Again, Luke alone narrates that Herod Antipas was in Jerusalem at the time of the trial and that Pilate sent Jesus to him. If Luke is right and historical, why do the other Gospels abstain from narrating this? If the other Gospels are right in failing to narrate this, can we accept Luke's narration as historical? Or must we set aside Luke's narration, from the historical standpoint, as tendentiousness, with its point being that the Jewish tetrarch abstained from condemning or from finding grave fault in Jesus? But if the Passion narrative is susceptible of such handling by an evangelist, what historical confidence can we have in any of the Gospel forms of it?

6. I think that there is no area in scholarship in which I immersed myself as deeply as in the Synoptic Problem. I studied it in Moffatt, Mac Neile, Bacon, Weiszsäcker, Schmiedel, Hawkins, Wernle, Enslin, Fascher, Bussmann, Grobel, Ropes, and, in recent times, Feine-Behm-Kümmel. The particular opinion I cite seems to my recollection to have been widespread, but especially to have marked Wernle.

7. Schweitzer has come so to be canonized that at times it seems heretical to challenge not only his views on Jesus as an apocalyptist but also the judiciousness of his many omissions from his *Quest of the Historical Jesus*. Weinel and Widgery, *Jesus in the Nineteenth Century and After* (1914) speak (p. 410) of Schweitzer's "scornfully superior manner." It seems to me that Schweitzer's judgments are often unsound, and his "thoroughgoing" eschatology unsubstantial, and his neglect of non-German scholarship astounding. Most amazing to my mind is the way in which, after countless pages of a critique of others, he abstained from all self-criticism.

Nevertheless, his book is a great and useful one, but not in itself superior to the broader study by Luigi Salvatorelli, "From Locke to Reitzenstein: the Historical Investigation of the Origins of Christianity," *Harvard Theological Review*, XXII (1929), 263–7, or to Weinel and Widgery, or to C. C. McCown, *The Search for the Real Jesus* (1940). The last, for all its usefulness, is marred for me by what seems to me to be too abundant crotchets and too frequent snap judgments.

8. The term is, of course, not mine; the sense in which I here use it is possibly different from the original or usual sense. I have in mind that approach, culminating in one type of neo-orthodoxy which scorned "mere historicism" and which, by such means as "dialectical theology" tended to affirm by existentialism what historical scholarship has rendered uncertain or untenable. See Stephen Neill, *The Interpretation of the New Testament 1861–1961*, chap. VI, "Re-Enter Theology," pp. 191–235, but esp. pp. 204–6. Karl

Barth's insistence, cited by Neill (ibid.), that "the histor-
ical-critical method of biblical investigation has its rightful
place" seemed not to persist, and led later to Oscar Cullmann's protest in *The Early Church: Studies in Early Christian History and Theology*, p. 11, that some seminarians
seemed to be dismissing historical and philological study as
consistent with "the law of minimum effort." The point at
issue, so it seems to me, is not so much the irrefutable
contention that the merely historical is only antiquarianism,
but rather that the attacks on the admitted insufficiency
of the merely antiquarian has led to unrestrained assertions
that fly in the face of reliable scholarship; and, moreover,
"existentialism" seemed to sanction capricious, intuitive conclusions in place of sober study. See also Hugh Anderson,
Jesus and Christian Origins, pp. 4–6.

9. The insignificance of the question of writing is stressed by
Dibelius, *Die Formgeschichte des Evangeliums*, pp. 4–5.
Respecting this, in my "Prolegomena to a Commentary on
Mark," *The Journal of Bible and Religion*, XXXI (1963), I
described this adversely as a sort of "tape recorder" theory,
according to which "the writer's heart and mind are supposedly of no import whatsoever, for the writer only recorded, and without change, what he heard or read." I
added, "No man ever picked up a pen without having some
purpose in writing."

10. See, for example, the very admirable work of John Knox,
Chapters in a Life of Paul, and the excellent confrontation
of many of the problems.

11. See the very important work by James Barr, *The Semantics
of Biblical Language*. Barr's reservations (pp. 6–7) are not
so much theological as philological, for he is raising only the
question of the soundness of the philology that often ac-
companies the interpretation of theological terms. I am
fully persuaded of the justice of Barr's contentions.

My own reservations are not so much philological; I am
skeptical that the modern interpreter is justified in the subtle
nuances or overtones which I see him ascribe to terms or
concepts in the ancient authors. The best illustration of
what I object to is Joachim Jeremias's treatment of *Abba*
(*Studien zur neutestamentlichen Theologie und Zeitge-*

schichte, 1966). He argues that the only use of this term for God is that by Jesus. On the one hand, this is largely an argument from silence; on the other hand, the appellation by Jews of God as "father," in Hebrew is so broad that the focusing on the Aramaic instance as determinative is preposterous. But even if one were to grant that only Jesus addressed God as *Abba,* the denotation which Jeremias puts into the term is totally without restraint, or credibility. See the broader, and trenchant criticism of Jeremias in Hugh Anderson, *Jesus and the Christian Tradition,* pp. 114–17.

My reaction to E. Fuchs, *Die Frage nach den historischen Jesus,* is that his conception of *Sprachereignis* is, again, a highly subjective bit of "eisegesis," and is scarcely susceptible of objective demonstration.

12. I must abstain here from entering into the substance of a question which often preoccupies me—that of how Christianity came to be Hellenized. Two facets seem susceptible of separate approach: one, the question of the facts, that is, the quantity and quality of the Hellenization; two, the question of the slowness or rapidity of it. The latter is an old and divisive question. I hold to a rapid Hellenization, against the old Tübingen view, and I believe that a Hellenized Judaism abetted the rapid Hellenization of Christianity.

13. In his *Marcion and the New Testament.*

14. See above, pp. 129–30. I, of course, do not share in Paul's Christology or his soteriology. I find, nevertheless, a tremendous personal relevancy in very much of Paul in that he deals profoundly with matters of human experience and needs and hopes that seem to be of universal importance, and in that sense he speaks both to me and for me. There are some viewpoints which, I must confess, are repugnant to me, such as his attitudes on sex relations.

Paul is very vivid to me. I am not sure that I should have relished being his traveling companion; I rather suppose I would not. But in terms of stimulation, and, indeed, of my own understanding of the human predicament, I find Paul both eloquent and enlightening.

15. The volume by A. M. Hunter, *Paul and His Predecessors,* seems to do as well as can be done in trying to fix some

facets of pre-Pauline thought. Yet I wonder if such thought is not considerably more elusive than Hunter supposes? Moreover, must we not be on guard against confusing non-Pauline thought with pre-Pauline? I am beset by a great haziness in these matters.

16. Here I have in mind William Davies, *St. Paul and Rabbinic Judaism*. Mr. Davies is a most learned man (and a delightful gentleman). In his "Paul and Judaism" in *The Bible in Modern Scholarship*, pp. 178–86, he seems to me to lean over backward to be admirably fair to those whose assessments of Paul and Hellenism differ from his. I cannot escape the conviction, though, that prepossession governs him in the issue of Paul, and Hellenistic and Rabbinic Judaism.

17. See by contrast the prudent and learned essay by Arthur Darby Nock, now republished as *Early Gentile Christianity and Its Hellenistic Background*. It is a book to which I frequently revert. How often Nock contends that some things are only probabilities, others uncertainties, and others unknown! The only real quarrel I would have with him is not so much that he sees a narrow tendency in post-Christian Judaism, but that he does not see a comparable tendency in Christianity (p. 56, n. 2). There I think his usual perspective forsook him.

18. In reality, no single theme is adequately handled in isolation, for other matters inevitably are intertwined. Accordingly, I must touch briefly on other themes as they impinge on the thread I pursue: literature, liturgy, the state, inner diversity, the modification of eschatology, the officialdom, and, indeed, many others. Any single one of these lends itself to an exposition much longer than these four lectures, and most of them have been so explored. I limit myself merely to the suggestion of horizons, without any intention of supposing that I have here dealt adequately with these relevant matters.

The impossibility of properly exploring these matters in a short time is to be seen in the worthy efforts of H. Conzelmann and Martin A. Cohen, *The Bible in Modern Scholarship*, where they attempt to handle first-century history. Cohen's bibliographic citations are most useful; his text, however, seems to me to be marked by some imprudent statements: p. 244, on liturgy; p. 247, on the authority of the

Nasi; p. 248, on Hellenistic Judaism; p. 250, on the *Shekhina* and Philo's *logos*. These appear to be the end products of excessive compression, so that one must bear this omnipresent pitfall in mind.

19. I take it, as do most liberal students, to be a pseudepigraph, the youngest book of the New Testament, and derived from Jude (rather than vice versa). The tone of the invective seems to me to have increased from Jude. The identification of the denounced people is beyond recovery; it is possible that there is some overlap in the persons denounced in Jude and II Peter, but certainly II Peter's denunciation of those who deny the Parousia is not found in Jude.

20. A reading of Justin Martyr scarcely prepares one for II Peter, or II Peter for Justin Martyr, yet they are roughly contemporaneous. Justin's testimony to the Lord's Supper, now distinct from the common, ordinary meal that it appears to be earlier, as in the Didache 9–10 and 14, throws some light on the developing liturgy. The prudence of C. C. Richardson, "Worship in N T Times, Christian," *Interpreter's Dictionary of the Bible*, IV, pp. 883–94, is most admirable, especially pp. 884–5. The origin of Christian liturgy in the synagogue liturgy seems to me to be more a matter of logical inference and inherent probability than something that can be documented. Granted a synagogue liturgical basis, what eludes me is when and how and through what process the necessarily Christological elements entered in. Moreover, how universal can the testimony of the Didache and Justin Martyr be taken to be? My own *hunch* is that in the Hellenistic church the Christological elements entered early, and led to divergency rather soon.

Justin's oblique espousal of Greek philosophy (*Apol.* II, xiii) represents still another important dimension to Christianity in the middle of the second century.

21. The most handy brief but adequate exposition of Marcion that I have encountered is in Hans Lietzmann, *A History of the Early Church*, I (trans. by Bertram Lee Woolf, 1953 rev.), pp. 248–64. I read Harnack over two decades ago, and also Tertullian's five-book attack, but much of the detail has slipped away. Indeed, I recall primarily Harnack's dictum that it was only Marcion in the early Church who

understood Paul—and he misunderstood him. I find especially enlightening, in E. C. Blackman, *Marcion and His Influence* (devoted largely to "correcting" Harnack), the chapter, "Marcion's Paulinism," pp. 105-12.

The extent of Marcionism is difficult to weigh; Harnack makes the effort in the only possible way, namely the large number of second-century writings hostile to him; see Lietzmann, *Early Church*, pp. 261-2.

That the "canon" of Marcion was a spur to the larger and abiding canon is most reasonable; see Morton Enslin, *Christian Beginnings*, pp. 464-5. On the other hand, I have long suspected that the canon would have emerged, as in the Muratorian fragment, without a Marcion.

The opinion of Donald W. Riddle, *Early Christian Life*, that the Pastoral Epistles are later than Marcion, and written to attack him, seems unconvincing to me, especially the latter contention. If, perhaps, I Timothy 6:20 does allude to Marcion's *Antitheses*, then I must venture the opinion that some passages of the Pastoral Epistles (I Timothy 1:3-11, Titus 3:9) seem to me to have some accord with Marcionism. That is to say, a disdain for Marcion and his movement would not necessarily impede the entrance of echoes of Marcionism into the Pastorals.

Mention was made above of the view of John Knox, *Marcion and the New Testament*, that Luke-Acts is a post- and anti-Marcion composition or new recension.

22. If it were possible to identify the "Gnostics" whom the Pastorals attack, then there might be some purpose served in focusing in the anti-Gnosticism in them. In note 21 I expressed my reservations that the Pastorals are anti-Marcion. The attack on would-be "teachers of the law" (I Timothy 1:7) and disputes over the law (Titus 3:9; see also Titus 1:11ff. and I Timothy 6:9) gets its natural clarification, and in the simplest way, by positing a Jewish Christianity (see Feine-Behm-Kümmel, *Introduction to the New Testament*, p. 267). To my mind, this, the simplest of explanations, is in need of modification. I have found it quite impossible to envisage a growing Christianity in which, in the interests of inner consolidation, there was not some legalistic tendency, this in some reaction from the license which a literal

Paulinism would have spurred. If so, such a tendency would not be as much Jewish legalism which received advocacy, but a purely Christian legalist tendency. What better way to denounce it than to spurn it as "Jewish"? Similarly, the phrase "Jewish myths" (Titus 1:4) is to my mind only name-calling, and the efforts of commentators to discover what these Jewish myths were has been a little preposterous; see my "Myths, Genealogies, and Jewish Myths and the Writing of Gospels," *Hebrew Union College Annual*, XXVII, 1956. It would seem to me that in the second century the concerns have become inner, and are no longer an external issue with Jews, and hence the men denounced are not Jews, but Gentiles whom it was convenient to denounce as Jews; a Jew does not Judaize, only a Gentile does. J. C. Beker, "Pastoral Letters," *Interpreter's Dictionary of the Bible*, III, pp. 668–75, puts it well (p. 672): "The essentially Hellenistic character of the Pastorals . . . shows that the fight between Judaism and Christianity is over."

The resolution of genealogies as representing Rabbinic speculations (the commentators have been unable to document these in the Rabbinic Literature!) makes no sense to me. Again, the matter is an internal Christian concern, and again it reflects Christian, not Jewish, efforts to construct genealogies. But genealogies of what, or of whom? The inescapable answer is, genealogies of the Christ, such as are found in Matthew and in Luke, but not in John. Was there once a genealogy at the beginning of Mark? Why does Hebrews 7:3 stress that Melchizedek was without father or mother or genealogy?

The Pastorals, whether pseudepigraphs (I hold with this view) or else rewritings of originally Pauline letters, deal with problems of consolidating a quite chaotic Church; hence the need for bishops, elders, and deacons. What is striking to me is that the bases for eligibility are limited to the possessing of good moral or ethical traits, but not one word is said respecting the manner of selection, or any chain of authority handed on in the act of appointment. The officials are here, as Beker notes, still charismatic, including the teacher. In Acts 6:6 and 13:3 there are semblances of transmitted authority, through the laying on of hands. The laying on of hands is found in I Timothy 4:14 and 5:22, and II Timothy 1:6, but not in a comparable sense of transmitting the authority of an office. Perhaps, as Lietzmann suggests (*Early Church,* p. 146), the charismatic teachers were considered to be above the elected bishops and deacons. In I Clement XL 40ff., it is asserted that the apostles appointed bishops and deacons, and perhaps we have here a kind of "apostolic succession," but the New Testament seems to know little more the vague clues respecting it, and nothing respecting an unbroken chain of properly ordained officials. Cerfaux, in Robert and Feuillet, *Introduction to the New Testament* (Eng. Trans.), p. 516, sees in II Timothy 2:2 evidence that "there is already a definite concern for a succession of authority." I do not see this verse as exhibiting anything more than a tendency.

I do not know exactly when to date the Pastorals, whether the period of 100–125, or, as some would have it, even as late as 150. The correlation of data, as in I Clement, the Pastorals, and II and III John, troubles me, and the only way out that I find is to suppose that these voices spoke from different segments of the Church and without direct relationship to each other.

23. As Enslin, *Christian Beginnings,* p. 359, points out, II John warns against an indiscriminate welcome to traveling teachers, and III John warns against local officials who withhold the cordial welcome of traveling teachers. See also Feine-Behm-Kümmel, *New Testament,* p. 314. I wish I could recall where I read, or heard, that the author of III John laments his having been personally treated by Diotrephes (III John 9) in exactly the way that he himself advocated others be treated in II John 9.

24. A target for denunciation in I John 1:5–2:2 appears to be people who make the claim of not sinning, a matter curiously passed over without comment in Robert and Feuillet, *Introduction to the New Testament,* pp. 671–85, where ample attention is paid to the problems of structure and unity, as well as to the denial that the Christ was Jesus, and its possible clue to Docetism. The possibility of identifying these heretics is a complicated one (as the literature cited in Feine-Behm-Kümmel, *New Testament,* makes clear) and

the juncture of a possible Docetism with licentiousness elusive. I find the paragraph in Caird, "John, Letters of," *Interpreter's Dictionary of the Bible*, II, p. 948, column 2, quite as vague as the Epistle itself. It seems to me that the denunciation arises from a real confrontation with opponents who alleged they were either sinless or incapable of sin, or else who denied that any of *their* actions were susceptible of being termed sin; but I see no way of going beyond an affirmation that the author confronted real people. Yet I have a kind of misgiving about the matter which I find difficult to state, but I must try. First, by the time of I John, two potentially contradictory themes were part of the unfolding tradition, the one theme that the death of the Christ had brought atonement for sin, and, second, those atoned for, as through faith and baptism, were now sinless. Could it be argued that the now sinless were incapable of sin either totally, or at least in the sense that there was no possibility any more for their moral trespasses to be reckoned as sin? Is the author of I John a moralist of such sturdiness that he declines to be taken in by what to him is a specious argument, amounting to this, that now that we have been baptized, there are no moral standards of relevancy to us? Perhaps this is the case; perhaps not. At any rate, I find it necessary to choose between an assertion such as "I am incapable of sin," and "Whatever I do, you can't classify it as sin."

I find still another fascination in the passage, namely that sin is no longer primarily what I think it is in Paul, that is, a state of affairs, or a condition of man, but has become essentially a matter of the single act, either of omission or commission. I find it very hard to hold in balance the contrast between *sin* and *sins*, for I am not sure that the ancient mind separated them as sharply as I tend to do, and as I think many Protestants also do. Perhaps in our day we are prone to set up as antitheses what to ancient minds were only diversities in accentuation.

I John, in having asserted that potential sinfulness of even the saved, proceeds (5:16) to distinguish between forgivable and unforgivable lapses. The absence of this sort of distinction from my inherited Judaism makes the whole topic quite difficult. I find it hard to see the balance which Christians hold between repentance (what man does) and grace (what God does); the key word here is *balance*. Yet Enslin, *Christian Beginnings*, p. 346, is very illuminating to me; so, too, is Frederick C. Grant, *An Introduction to New Testament Thought*, p. 183.

I like the phrase (in S. J. De Vries, "Sin, sinners," *Interpreter's Dictionary of the Bible*, IV, p. 375, respecting the view that "the purest saints are never entirely free from sin and from sins"), that "I John puts this in its characteristic enigmatic way."

25. Some relevant passages outside Revelation include John 19:11; Romans 13:1–7; Titus 3:1; I Timothy 2:2; and I Peter 2:13–17. See Robert M. Grant, *The Sword and the Cross*. Older literature is found cited in Cyril Bosley, "The State Religion of Rome at the Time of the Christ," *The History of Christianity in the Light of Modern Knowledge*, pp. 20–41.

26. See above, note 22.

27. There is a noticeable unwillingness among recent commentators to accept the view of Benjamin W. Bacon (in both *Studies in Matthew* and in *The Making of the New Testament*) that Jesus is portrayed in Matthew as a "new Moses." G. Bornkamm prefers to suppose that Jesus is not giving a new law, but only interprets Moses, and that Jesus is not set in antithesis to Moses in Matthew as he is in John. So, too, Krister Stendahl, *The School of St. Matthew*, is cautious about a Moses "typology" in Matthew. See Hugh Anderson, *Jesus and Christian Tradition*, pp. 222 and 340–41, n. 65.

I confess to being astounded by this unwillingness, in the light of the structure of Matthew and the section 5:17–43. To my mind the unwillingness is explicable only on the basis that "legalism" is so completely distasteful to Christians that there exists among many an inability to recognize it in its very palpable Christian form. Some Christians seem, indeed, to be embarrassed by the passage, 5:11–43; W. D. Davies writes (*The Setting of the Sermon on the Mount*, p. 433) that "Matthew has helped to generate an isolated understanding of his commandments which has often prompted, on the one hand, a shallow moralism, and, on the other, what sometimes appears to be a kerygmatic amoralism, which, in its despair before the utter radicalism of his words, evacuates them of any real significance for the understanding of Jesus himself or the business of living."

To my mind only that kind of exegesis which deliberately chooses to suppose that the statement, "John was a man" means "Mary will be a woman" can work mayhem on the utter clarity of Matthew in general and the Sermon on the Mount in particular. The endless discussions a generation or two ago on "interim ethics" point to the paradox that there is a Christian legalism in Matthew, and that its requirements are stringent almost to the point of an absence of viability; hence, a way out of the difficulty is to assert that the legalism is not really a legalism at all. Indeed, there is no dearth of commentators who can make the Sermon on the Mount and Paul's attitude to the Laws completely synonymous. Virtually all scholarship attributes the form of the Sermon to Matthew, not to Jesus, and those who would deny the "legalism" are hard put to explain why Matthew adopts a legalistic manner. A frequent explanation is that he was a rabbi, a Pharisee, and hence utilized a method familiar to him. The implication often seems to be that the manner of Matthew is, accordingly, negligible, and can be set aside.

28. "Bind" and "loose" are also terms in Rabbinic law, "bind" denoting "prohibit," and "loose" denoting "permit."

29. The recent work by William R. Farmer, *The Synoptic Problem: a Critical Analysis* (see review by F. W. Beare, *Journal of Biblical Literature*, LXXXIV [1965], pp. 295–7) seems to me to have failed to generate the excitement that it might have. The nineteenth-century view of the priority of Mark has seemed to me the most reasonable on the basis of an Ur-Mark; the *tendenz* in Mark seems to me to force a very late date, even second century, for the canonical Gospel. Perhaps it was an Ur-Mark which Papias had in mind as embodying the reminiscences of Peter.

I should comment that the Protestant scholarship has noticed all the phenomena in Mark related to the opaqueness and the infidelity of the disciples. A normal view is that "Mark is hard on the disciples." My own opinion is that Mark goes far beyond being hard on them; he openly repudiates and disowns them.

30. The Greek lacks the definite article, with the consequence
that the Nelson edition RSV renders the relevant words "*a*
son of God," while in the Oxford Annotated, at least in the
early version, the text reads *the*, but a footnote supplies *a*.
The commentaries *ad loc*. supply scholarly support for either
rendering. Frederick C. Grant, *Interpreter's Dictionary of
the Bible*, VII, p. 907 (where the RSV reads *a*, against the
King James *the*) suggests that the Gentile centurion had
in mind "a divine hero. . . . But Mark naturally and properly reads more into it." My comment is that the Roman
centurion is the only human in Mark who discerns who
Jesus was (the demons, of course, discern this).

31. I discuss Mark in three places: *The Genius of Paul*, pp. 164–
76; "Prolegomena to a Commentary on Mark," *The Journal
of Bible and Religion*, XXXI, 4, pp. 294–300; and "Son of
Man," *In the Time of Harvest*, pp. 355–67. The latter paper
was prepared for a symposium on Son of Man at the
Society of Biblical Literature meeting, December, 1959. I
was the third speaker, and the hour had grown so late that
instead of reading the paper, I gave a very brief summary
of it. Like many a paper published in a *Festschrift* dedicated
to a person not in the biblical field, my paper has been
almost entirely unnoticed. From it I would here quote a
passage:

> There is a device used frequently in literature
> wherein author and reader share information not
> shared by a character within the narration. Indeed
> the device has become so conventional in the theater
> as to constitute a cliché. In Noel Coward's play,
> *Cavalcade*, a honeymoon couple stand on the deck
> of a ship planning their future. The scene ends with
> the wife removing her wrap from the nearby life
> preserver, so that we read the word *Titanic*. The
> dramatic impact comes out of the audience's know-
> ing something which the characters do not. The
> movie biographies of Edison and Pasteur have used
> the same kind of device; the audience knows that
> Edison's inventions and Pasteur's researches come to
> succeed, and therefore, they respond, as it were, to

the beginning efforts of the two and to the obstacles the two encounter, with increased sympathy. This same device is present in very many of the Greek tragedies. In *Oedipus Rex,* for example, the plot line was thoroughly familiar to the audience; the drama consisted in their sharing in the emotional vicissitudes of the characters who do not know what the audience does know; and the foreknowledge of the outcome by the audience not only does not decrease the interest but through heightened empathy increases it.

All "disguise" plays and stories use this same device, whether it is Shakespeare, as in *Twelfth Night,* or whether it is a farce such as *Charley's Aunt.* Perhaps preeminently in the drama is Rostand's use in *Cyrano de Bergerac,* wherein Cyrano, unseen to Roxane but visible to the audience, provides Christian with the words with which to woo Roxane, and later, and most pathetically, Roxane relates to Cyrano the great ardor which she ascribes to Christian.

Preeminently among the Gospels, John employs the device unsparingly, even to the point of making sure that it is not missed. In John 2:19 Jesus says, "Destroy this temple and in three days I will raise it up"; 2:21 tells us that "he spoke of the temple of his body." . . .

Mark too employs the device. Indeed, Mark's aim is not to inform his readers of what they do not know, but rather to employ the knowledge that they already have to heighten the emotional impact. They know that Jesus was crucified; they believe that he was resurrected. They hold him to be more than a man, the Son of God. They know that Jews did not share in this belief. They already believe that the crucifixion was neither a surprise nor a defeat, for they believe that the divine Jesus knew in advance what was to happen to him; that is, Jesus is depicted as knowing in advance of the events what the readers of Mark knew after the events from

Christian preaching on Jesus. Mark hence portrays Jesus as going through a pre-ordained schedule of events; accordingly, Jesus three times predicts his crucifixion. He informs his disciples that one of them will betray him; he informs them that they will fall away; he tells Peter that Peter will three times deny him. At Gethsemane Jesus says "The hour has come."

The thesis in Mark's Gospel, the "plot" of which was known to the reader, is that Jesus was abused by Jewish opponents, misunderstood, betrayed, denied, and abandoned by his disciples, but recognized only by the demons and the Roman centurion (and the blind beggar Bartimaeus who "sees" who Jesus is). Mark had need of a title which could simultaneously mystify his characters and still be fully clear to his readers. Had Mark focused on a title such as Christ or King, he could not have portrayed his characters as mystified. But Son of Man served admirably for this purpose in that the characters in the Gospel fail to comprehend the title, but Mark's readers understand it immediately.

32. We know very little about Palestinian Jewish Christianity! We cannot place full reliability in some of the studies (e.g. Schoeps, *Theologie und Geschichte des Juden christentums*). I wrote in *The Genius of Paul*, after a survey of the literature (p. 222), that almost nothing is knowable.

33. *The Genius of Paul*, p. 113.

34. I would classify work such as Krister Stendahl, *The School of St. Matthew*, and H. Conzelmann, *The Theology of St. Luke*, as studies in the sub-apostolic age. Respecting Stendahl, I am not moved from my opinion that one single hand wrote the canonical Matthew, but the assembled material on a possible school of Christian exegetes broadened my horizon. Conzelmann seems to me to have overextended the reasonable possibilities; nevertheless, I learned from him. I cannot agree with P. Carrington, *The Primitive Christian Calendar*, but profited from it. Similarly, C. H. Dodd, *The Apostolic Preachment and Its Developments*, enlightened me.

Perhaps it might be put in this way, that the difficulties in using the Gospels as witnesses to the sub-apostolic age of their composition are almost as great as using them for witnesses to the age of Jesus. Nevertheless, even those studies of the sub-apostolic age which somehow fail to overcome some of my reluctances manage constantly to enlighten me. I find a satisfaction in such studies which I do not find in studies in the age of Jesus.

35. My view is not at all that of the Scandinavians, especially Birger Gerhardsson, *Memory and Manuscript: Oral Tradition and Written Transmission in Rabbinic Judaism and Early Christianity*. The supposition that in early Christianity there was a similarity to the transmission of the Jewish oral tradition is hypothetically possible, though the evidence adduced seems to me flimsy. That such an oral tradition would faithfully reflect *ipsissima verba* of Jesus seems to me less likely. There seems to me, moreover, a considerable difference between whatever reliable transmission of Jesus' words may have existed, on the one hand, and the creativity of the midrashic speculation of him and on his role on the other hand. In general, the Scandinavians, correctly stressing the role of oral transmission, inadequately gauge the alterations in what is transmitted, and they attribute a reliability to oral tradition that seems to me to fly in the face of the demonstrable variety and often unrestrained idiosyncrasies within the totality of our inherited plural versions.

Perhaps an example can clarify my skepticism about Gerhardsson's view. I once attended an Orthodox home service late in the day after a funeral. The officiating rabbi properly insisted on a hiatus between the late afternoon service and the evening service. He used the time to give a pleasant discourse on the origin of the services, hearkening back to the midrashic fancy that the patriarchs had instituted them; the rabbi, however, presented the matter not as a midrashic fancy, but as historical fact. The point is that modern scholars cultivate an acute distinction between the historical and the haggadic; I doubt that the ancient mind did so. To find a historical reliability in the developing midrashic tradition is to my mind to be untrue to the material.

36. See the material assembled on Abraham in my *Philo's Place in Judaism*, pp. 30–95.

37. I admire the effort made by G. Bornkamm, *Jesus of Nazareth*, to maintain scholarly objectivity. While recognizing the effort, I must allege that the book is incredibly subjective and, for all the modesty of its style, high-handed. It teems with instance after instance of arbitrariness. I have asked myself the question, in what way is Bornkamm significantly less capricious than Hugh Schonfeld in *The Passover Plot*? There is a difference, of course, in degree; is there a difference in kind?

38. The call of E. Käsemann (*Essays on New Testament Themes*), in 1953 for a renewed inquiry into the historical Jesus is to be applauded. No generation ought to abstain from challenging the academic procedures and inclusions of an earlier generation. The question is therefore not, *should* a new quest be made, but *how successfully* can it be made? And is the quest truly new? Even while I applaud Käsemann's proposal, I do not feel that the results of the new quest have been substantial or, when based on the Kerygma, methodologically sound.

    Professor John Reumann has invited my attention to Käsemann's withdrawal from the "new quest," in "Sackgassen im Streit um den historischen Jesus," *Exegetische Versuche und Besinnungen*, Vol. 2; I have not personally seen this, though I think it significant.

39. The question of the teachings of Jesus is bound up with the question of Q. I belong to the minority who doubt that there ever was a Q. It is my opinion that Luke utilized Matthew. The normal objection to this view is principally twofold, which Künmmel (op. cit. p. 50) formulates as follows: "What could have moved Luke to break up Matthew's Sermon on the Mount and to embody part of it in his Sermon on the Plain, to distribute part over the various chapters of his Gospel, and to omit part? How is the fact to be explained that Luke not a single time brings the texts common to Matthew . . . to the same place in the Markan plan as Matthew, if he took them over out of Matthew . . . ?"

    Respecting the second question, the answer I would give

is Luke's freedom, as exemplified in his relocating the rejection at Nazareth, his innovation of having Herod Antipas present in Jerusalem, and his moving the death of Judas into Acts. Many other instances can be cited. The use of Matthew by Luke does not imply slavish dependency on Matthew, but only the source of the materials he uses quite freely. That is, Luke uses Matthew for the materials in Matthew, not for Matthew's use of the material. Luke does more than merely polish up Matthew; he substantially rewrites and notably reinterprets. Luke uses Matthew for data, not for slavish conformity to Matthew's presentation.

Respecting the first question, I believe that it has been precisely the Sermon on the Mount which troubled Luke (see my *The Genius of Paul*, pp. 180–86). Luke's view is that Christianity represents an unbroken continuity with the ancient Judaism; the Sermon on the Mount implies something new, something that ruptures the continuity. In place of regulation by law, as Matthew proposes, Luke wants regulation through authorized persons. Accordingly, Luke breaks up the unity of the Sermon on the Mount deliberately, and he deliberately scatters that portion of the material which he retains to utilize.

Beyond the questions raised by Kümmel, this can be said; the hypothesis of a Q would tend to support a view that there were teachings by Jesus that come authentically from him, while the denial of the hypothesis would reduce the quantity, and even the quality, of the authenticity of these teachings. The word studies on Q are not decisive, for if they were, there would not be the scholars who deny Q; accordingly, the affirmation or denial of Q is often a matter of a scholar's disposition, a matter of how instinctively he feels that the Q material goes back to Jesus, or does not. In my attribution of the materials to midrash, I am obviously predisposed against authenticity, and possibly the case I make is no more than my own rationalization for an instinctive judgment. But there are some abiding questions to me. If there was a Q, why does the canonical Mark seem ignorant of it? If there was a Q, was it not of such preciousness that its disappearance is astounding? If there was a Q, would it not have been mentioned directly in early Christianity, rather than emerging from the researches of nineteenth-century scholarship?

Perhaps in connection with the teachings of Jesus, I should append here a bit more of the dissatisfaction which I feel in G. Bornkamm, *Jesus of Nazareth*. I cannot follow the method by which he seems able to separate authentic teachings from inauthentic. His use of *Abba* (p. 128) is as capricious as that of Jeremias, and the views of neither should be taken seriously. Jeremias's *The Problem of the Historical Jesus* (now a pamphlet, published by Fortress Press, Philadelphia) is a good example of cultivated fuzziness.

40. Let me confess a subjectivity. I own that there was a Kerygma. I consider that Kerygma to have been midrashic. The "new quest" for the historical Jesus invests the Kerygma with some historical reliability, or potential for that reliability, both of which seem to me untrue to the midrashic nature of the Kerygma.

41. See his brief, but stimulating, paper, "Jesus' Attitude Towards the Law," *Fourth World Congress of Jewish Studies Papers*, Vol. I, pp. 241–4. I would hope that Smith will some day expand it to the fullness it should have. Smith argues, as I see it, logically rather than historically, and I agree with his logic. But can the case now become adequately documented? And how much historical certainty can emerge?

The basic pattern which has commended itself to me respecting early Christianity has been to think of it along three topics: first, what Christianity inherited and perpetuated from Judaism; second, what in Judaism it rejected; and third, what it innovated.

If only the materials with which the historian works arrayed themselves so neatly, then this logical pattern could readily be filled in! Not only do the materials withhold themselves from this wondrously simple pattern, but within the first century the dynamics of a spreading and increasingly diverse and innerly inconsistent Christendom make the pattern feasible, if at all, only for retrospect from a later century, and not from vision within the first century. For example, we do not see clearly and unmistakably exactly what changes if any were wrought in first-century Christianity by the fall of Jerusalem except insofar as we can infer about them, much as S. G. F. Brandon has done in his *The Fall of Jerusalem and the Christian Church* (1951). Though I largely agree with Brandon, the point here is that the case rests not on documents indubitably contemporary with the events, but rather on inferences made from a somewhat later time. The consequence is that inheritance from Judaism or rejection of Jewish motifs in the first century require us to envisage a Christianity changing and developing, and possibly at 70 going through a drastic inner revision, this of uncertain extent and uncertain depth. Indeed, the effects of 70 may have been different in 150, or in 120, or in 90, from what they were in 75 or 73. The validity of the pattern is the greatest when it is the most removed from specific moments and dates, and when looked at cumulatively.

Select Bibliography

BOOKS

F. M. Abel. Histoire de la Palestine depuis la conquéte
  d'Alexandre jusqu'à l'invasion arabe   1952
I. Abrahams. Studies in Pharisaism and the Gospels[2]   1924
C. Albeck. Untersuchungen über die Redaktion der
  Mischna   1923
D. M. Albertz. Die synoptischen Streitgespräche   1921
H. Anderson. Jesus and Christian Origins   1964
S. Angus. The Mystery Religions and Christianity   1925
———. The Religious Quests of the Graeco-Roman
  World: A Study in the Historical Background of Early
  Christianity   1929
V. Aptowitzer. Parteipolitik der Hasmonäerzeit im rab-
  binische und pseudoepigraphischen Schrifttum   1927

This bibliography is designed to reflect not the full field of
scholarship, but those writings that I have actually read—I
have not listed what I have not read—and that I believe have
exerted some influence on me. Most of these, though not all,
go unmentioned in the text, or are there alluded to only by
mention of the author. I have deliberately omitted the primary
sources, encyclopedias, and periodicals, since I take them to
be the normal possession of scholars.

W. Bächer. Die Agada der Tannaïten   1884–90
————. Die älteste Terminologie der Jüdischen Schriftaus-
legung   1889
B. W. Bacon. The Making of the New Testament   1912
————. Jesus and Paul   1921
————. Studies in Matthew   1930
L. Baeck. The Pharisees (English)   1947
————. Judaism and Christianity (English)   1958
B. Bamberger. Proselytism in the Talmudic Period   1939
S. W. Baron. A Social and Religious History of the Jews[2] 1952
J. Barr. The Semantics of Biblical Language   1961
C. K. Barrett. Luke the Historian in Recent Study   1961
W. Bauer. Rechtglaubigkeit und Ketzerei im ältesten
Christentum   1934
F. W. Beare. The Earliest Records of Jesus   1962
S. Belkin. Philo and the Oral Law   1940
H. I. Bell. Jews and Christians in Egypt   1924
J. Bergmann. Jüdische Apologetik im neutestamentlichen
Zeitalter   1908
A. Bertholet. Die jüdische Religion von der Zeit Ezras
bis zum Zweitalter Christi   1911
E. J. Bickerman. From Ezra to the Last of the Maccabees 1962
C. Bigg. The Origins of Christianity   1909
M. Black. An Aramaic Approach to the Gospels and Acts 1946
————. The Scrolls and Christian Origins   1961
E. C. Blackman. Marcion and His Influence   1948
J. Bloch. On the Apocalyptic in Judaism   1952
A. Bludau. Juden und Judenverfolgungen im alten Alex-
andria   1906
T. Boman. Die Jesusüberlieferung im Lichte der neuern
Volkskunde   1967
J. Bonsirven. Le Judaïsme palestinien (2 vols.)   1934–35
G. Bonrkamm. Jesus of Nazareth (English)   1964
W. Bousset. Jüdisch-christlicher Schulbetrieb in Alexan-
dria und Rom   1915
————. Volksfrömmigkeit und Schriftgelehrsamkeit   1903
————. Die Religion des Judentums im späthellenistischen
Zeitalter[3]   1926
S. G. F. Brandon. The Fall of Jerusalem and the Christian
Church   1951

————. Jesus and the Zealots   1967
W. G. Braude. Jewish Proselytizing in the First Five Cen-
turies of the Common Era: The Age of the Tannaim
and Amoraim   1940
E. Bréhier. Les Idées philosophiques et religieuses de
Philon d'Alexandrie²   1925
————. The Hellenistic and Roman Age (English)   1965
F. F. Bruce. Second Thoughts on the Dead Sea Scrolls   1956
M. Buber. The Prophetic Faith   1949
A. Büchler. The Economic Conditions of Judea after the
Destruction of the Second Temple   1912
R. Bultmann. Der Stil der Paulinischen Predigt und die
kynischstoische Diatribe   1910
————. Geschichte der Synoptischen Tradition   1919
————. Jesus and the Word (English)   1934
————. Urchristentum im Rahem der antiken Religionen   1949
————. Theology of the New Testament (2 vols.,
English)   1951–55
F. C. Burkitt. The Gospel History and Its Transmission   1906
————. The Church and Gnosis   1932
C. F. Burney. The Poetry of Our Lord   1925
D. W. Bussmann. Synoptische Studien   1925–31
H. Cadbury. The Making of Luke-Acts   1927
P. Carrington. The Primitive Christian Calendar   1940
S. J. Case. The Evolution of Early Christianity   1914
————. Social Origins of Christianity   1923
————. Experience with the Supernatural in Early Chris-
tian Times   1929
H. P. Chajes. Markus-Studien   1889
R. H. Charles. The Religious Development Between the
Old and the New Testaments   1914
B. Cohen. Law and Tradition in Judaism   1959
J. R. Cohu. S. Paul in the Light of Modern Research   1912
F. C. Conybeare. Myth, Magic and Morals   1910
————. The Historical Christ   1914
H. Conzelmann. The Theology of St. Luke (English)   1960
J. M. Creed. The Gospel According to St. Luke   1930
F. M. Cross. The Ancient Library of Qumran and Modern
Biblical Studies   1958
O. Cullmann. Peter: Disciple-Apostle-Martyr (English)   1953

————. The Early Church: Studies in Early Christian
History and Theology (English)   1956
F. Cumont. Oriental Religions in Roman Paganism (Eng-
lish)   1911
G. F. Dalman. Jesus-Jeshua (English)   1929
D. Daube. The New Testament and Rabbinic Judaism   1956
W. D. Davies. Paul and Rabbinic Judaism   1955
————. Christian Origins and Judaism   1962
————. The Setting of the Sermon on the Mount   1964
A. Deissman. Light from the Ancient Near East   1910
J. Derenbourg. Essai sur l'histoire et la géographie de la
Palestine d'après les Thalmuds et les autres sources
rabbiniques, I   1867
M. Dibelius. From Tradition to Gospel (English)   1934
C. H. Dodd. History and the Gospel   1938
————. The Apostolic Preaching and Its Developments   1949
————. The Interpretation of the Fourth Gospel   1953
N. Drazin. The History of Jewish Education from 515
B.C.E. to 220 C.E.   1940
C. W. Dugmore. The Influence of the Synagogue on the
Divine Office   1944
J. Drummond. Philo Judaeus; or, the Jewish-Alexandrian
Philosophy in Its Development and Completion (2 vols)   1888
J. Dupont. Gnosis   1949
I. Elbogen. Der jüdische Gottesdienst   1913
L. E. Elliott-Binns. Galilean Christianity   1956
M. S. Enslin. Christian Beginnings   1938
J. N. Epstein. Meboat le-safrut ha-tannaim (ed. by Ed.
Z. Melamed)   1957
W. R. Farmer. Maccabees, Zealots, and Josephus: An In-
quiry into Jewish Nationalism in the Greco-Roman Pe-
riod   1956
————. The Synoptic Problem: A Critical Analysis   1965
A. M. Farrer. St. Matthew and St. Mark   1954
P. Feine, J. Behm, and W. G. Kümmel. Introduction to
the New Testament (English)   1966
L. Feldman. Recent Research on Josephus and Philo   1964
P. Fiebig. Das Vaterunser   1927
A. Finkel. The Pharisees and the Teacher of Nazareth   1964
L. Finkelstein. The Pharisees (2 vols.)   1940

F. J. Foakes-Jackson. The Rise of Gentile Christianity   1927
F. J. Foakes-Jackson and K. Lake (eds.) The Beginnings
of Christianity (5 vols.)   1920–33
J. Freudenthal. Hellenistische Studien I   1875
G. Friedlander. Hellenism and Christianity   1912
M. Friedländer. Der vorchristliche jüdische Gnosticismus   1898
——. Die religiösen Bewegungen innerhalb des Juden-
tums im Zeitalter Jesu   1905
P. Gardner-Smith. Saint John and the Synoptic Gospels   1938
F. Gavin. The Jewish Antecedents of the Christian Sacra-
ments   1928
B. Gerhardsson. Memory and Manuscript: Oral Tradi-
tion and Written Transmission in Rabbinic Judaism and
Early Christianity   1961
M. S. Ginsburg. Rome et la Judée   1928
M. Goguel. Jésus de Nazareth, Mythe ou histoire?   1925
——. Jésus et les origines du christianisme (3 vols.)   1932–47
E. R. Goodenough. The Jurisprudence of the Jewish
Courts in Egypt   1929
——. By Light, Light: the Mystic Gospel of Hellenistic
Judaism   1935
——. The Politics of Philo Judaeus: Practice and The-
ory   1938
——. An Introduction to Philo Judaeus   1940
——. Jewish Symbols in the Greco-Roman Period   1953ff
E. J. Goodspeed. The Meaning of Ephesians   1933
F. C. Grant. An Introduction to New Testament Thought   1950
R. M. Grant. Gnosticism and Early Christianity   1959
R. M. Grant and D. N. Freedman. The Secret Sayings of
Thomas   1960
C. Guignebert. Jesus (English)   1947
——. The Jewish World in the Time of Jesus (English)   1939
H. Guttmann. Die Darstellung der jüdischen Religion bei
Flavius Josephus   1928
M. Hadas. Aristeas to Philocrates   1951
J. R. Harris. Testimonies (2 vols.)   1920
J. C. Hawkins. Horae Synopticae   1899
I. Heineman. Philons griechische und jüdische Bildung   1932
J. Heinemann. Ha-tefila bi-tekufat ha-tannaim veha-
amorim   1964

W. Heitmüller. Im Namen Jesu   1903
M. Hengel. Die Zeloten: Untersuchungen zur jüdischen
  Freiheitsbewegung in der Zeit von Herodes I bis 70   1961
S. B. Hoenig. The Great Sanhedrin   1953
G. Hölscher. Der Sadduzäismus, eine kritische Unter-
  suchung zur späteren jüdischen Religionsgeschichte   1906
F. J. Hort. Judaistic Christianity   1894
W. F. Howard. The Fourth Gospel in Recent Criticism
  and Interpretation   1931
A. M. Hunter. Paul and His Predecessors   1940
W. Jaeger. Early Christianity and Greek Paideia   1961
J. Jeremias. The Parables of Jesus (English)   1955
———. Abba: Studien zur neutestamentlichen Theologie
  und Zeitgeschichte   1966
S. Johnson. The Theology of the Gospels   1966
H. Jonas. The Gnostic Religion   1958
A. Jülicher. Die Gleichnisrede Jesu²   1902
J. uster. Les juifs dans l'empire romain (2 vols.)   1914
E. Käsemann. Essays on New Testament Themes   1954
G. Kittel. Die Probleme des palästinischen Spätjudentums
  und das Christentum   1926
J. Klausner. Die messianischen Vorstellungen des jüdis-
  chen Volkes im Zeitalter der Tannaïten   1904
———. Historia Yisreelit (Vol. II–IV)   1924
———. Jesus of Nazareth (English)   1926
———. From Jesus to Paul (English)   1943
J. Knox. Marcion and the New Testament   1942
———. Chapters in a Life of Paul   1950
W. L. Knox. St. Paul and the Church at Jerusalem   1925
———. St. Paul and the Church of the Gentiles   1939
S. Krauss. Griechische und lateinische Lehnwörter im
  Talmud, Midrasch, und Targum   1898
P. Krieger. Philo und Josephus als Apologeten das Juden-
  tums   1906
J. Z. Lauterbach. Rabbinic Essays   1951
H. Lewy. Sobria Ebrietas: Untersuchung zur Geschichte
  der antiken Mystik   1929
M. Lidzbarski. Ginza: Der Schatz oder das grosse Buch
  der Mandäer übersetzt und erklärt   1925
S. Lieberman. Greek in Jewish Palestine   1942

———. Hellenism in Jewish Palestine 1950
H. Lietzmann. Der Menschensohn 1896
———. Messe und Herrenmahl 1926
———. Petrus und Paulus in Rom[2] 1927
———. Der Prozess Jesu 1931
———. A History of the Early Church (Vol. I, English) 1953
R. H. Lightfoot. History and Interpretation in the Gospels 1935
———. Locality and Doctrine in the Gospels 1938
E. Lohmeyer. Galiläa und Jerusalem 1936
A. Loisy. Les mystères païens et le mystère chrétien[2] 1930
———. La naissance de christianisme 1933
J. Mann. The Bible as Read and Preached in the Old Synagogue 1940
H. Mantel. Studies in the History of the Sanhedrin 1961
R. Marcus. Law in the Apocrypha 1927
A. Marmorstein. Studies in Jewish Theology 1950
C. C. McCown. The Search for the Real Jesus 1940
A. C. McGiffert. History of Christianity in the Apostolic Age[2] 1899
———. The God of the Early Christians 1924
J. L. McKenzie. The Power and the Wisdom: An Interpretation of the New Testament 1965
E. Meyer. Ursprung und Anfänge des Christentums (3 vols.) 1921–23
N. Micklem (ed.). Christian Worship 1938
J. Moffatt. Introduction to the Literature of the New Testament 1922
C. G. Montefiore. Rabbinic Literature and Gospel Teachings 1930
G. F. Moore. Judaism in the First Centuries of the Christian Era (3 vols.) 1924–32
S. Mowinckel. He That Cometh (English) 1956
J. Munck. Paulus und die Heilsgeschichte 1954
S. Neill. The Interpretation of the New Testament, 1861–1961 1964
M. P. Nilsson. A History of Greek Religion 1925
A. D. Nock. Early Gentile Christianity and Its Hellenistic Background 1944
E. Norden. Agnostos Theos 1913

W. O. E. Oesterley.   The Jewish Background of the Christian Liturgy   1925
R. Otto. The Kingdom of God and the Son of Man (English)   1943
J. Pascher. He Basilike Hodos: der Konigsweg zu Wiedergeburt und Vergottung bei Philon von Alexandreia.   1931
F. Perles. Bousset's Religion des judentums in neutestamentlichen zeitalter kritisch undersucht   1903
S. Perowne.   The Later Herods   1958
M. Radin.   The Jews Among the Greeks and Romans   1915
S. Rappaport.   Agada und Exegese bei Flavius Josephus   1930
R. Reitzenstein. Poimandres. Studien zur griechischägyptischen und frühchristlichen Literatur   1904
――――. Die hellenistischen Mysterienreligionen nach ihren Grundgedanken und Wirkungen[2]   1920
――――. Die Vorgeschichte der christlichen Taufe   1929
R. Harris.   Testimonies (2 vols.)   1916–20
D. W. Riddle.   Jesus and the Pharisees: A Study in Christian Tradition   1928
――――. Early Christian Life as Reflected in Its Literature   1936
H. Riesenfeld.   The Gospel Tradition and Its Beginnings   1961
J. M. Robinson.   The New Quest for the Historical Jesus   1959
M. Rostovtzeff.   The Social and Economic History of the Roman Empire   1926
――――. Dura-Europos and Its Art   1938
W. Sanday.   The Life of Christ in Recent Research   1908
S. Sandmel. A Jewish Understanding of the New Testament   1956
――――. Philo's Place in Judaism   1956
――――. The Genius of Paul   1958
――――. We Jews and Jesus   1965
――――. Herod: Profile of a Tyrant   1967
A. Schalit. Roman Administration in Palestine [in Hebrew]   1937
K. L. Schmidt. Die Stellung der Evangelien in der allegemeinen Literaturgeschichte   1923
H. J. Schoeps. Theologie und Geschichte des Juden christentums   1949
――――. Urgemeinde, Judenchristentum, Gnosis   1956

————. Paulus: die Theologie des Apostels im Lichte der jüdischen Religionsgeschichte 1959

G. G. Scholem. Jewish Gnosticism, Merkabah Mysticism, and Talmudic Tradition 1960

————. Major Trends in Jewish Mysticism[3] 1954

A. Schweitzer. The Quest of the Historical Jesus (English 1906

————. Paul and His Interpreters: A Critical History (English) 1912

————. The Mysticism of Paul the Apostle (English) 1931

E. F. Scott. The Gospel and Its Tributaries 1930

M. Shroyer. Alexandrian Jewish Literalists 1936

C. Siegfried. Philo von Alexandria als Ausleger des alten Testaments. 1875

A. H. Silver. The History of Messianic Speculation in Israel 1927

D. J. Silver (ed.). In the Time of Harvest: Essays in Honor of Abba Hillel Silver on the Occasion of his 70th Birthday 1963

M. Simon. Versus Israel 1948

R. Stahl. Les mandéens et les origines chrétiennes 1930

W. H. Stearns. Fragments from Graeco-Jewish Writers 1908

K. Stendahl. The School of St. Matthew 1954

K. Stendhal (ed.). The Scrolls and the New Testament 1957

H. L. Strack. Jesus, die Haeretiker und die Christen nach den ältesten jüdischen Angaben 1910

B. H. Streeter. The Four Gospels 1926

V. Taylor. The Formation of the Gospel Tradition 1933

————. The Names of Jesus 1959

V. [A.] Tcherikover. Hellenistic Civilization and the Jews 1914

H. St. J. Thackeray. Josephus: The Man and the Historian (with a Preface by George Foot Moore and Introduction by Samuel Sandmel) 1967

C. C. Torrey. The Aramaic of the Gospels 1942

P. Volz. Eschatologie der jüdischen Gemeinde 1934

B. Z. Wacholder. Nicolaus of Damascus 1962

H. Weinel and A. G. Widgery. Jesus in the 19th Century and After 1914

J. Weiss. The History of Primitive Christianity (English) 1947

P. Wendland. Die hellenistisch-römische Kultur in ihrer
    Beziehung zu Judentum und Christentum[2]   1912
E. Werner. The Sacred Bridge   1959
M. Werner. The Foundations of Christian Dogma   1957
P. Wernle. Die Synoptische Frage   1899
H. R. Willoughby. Pagan Regeneration: A Study of Mys-
    tery Imitations in the Graeco-Roman World   1929
P. Winter. On the Trial of Jesus   1961
H. A. Wolfson. Philo: Foundations of Religious Philos-
    ophy in Judaism, Christianity and Islam (2 vols.)   1947
W. Wrede. Das Messiasgeheimnis[2]   1913
S. Zeitlin. The Sadducees and the Pharisees   1937
————. A History of the Second Jewish Commonwealth:
    The Rise and Fall of the Judaean State: II, 37 B.C.E. to
    66 C.E.   1967

Articles

ABBREVIATIONS

IDB. Interpreter's Bible Dictionary
JBL. Journal of Biblical Literature
JBR. Journal of Bible and Religion
JE. Jewish Encyclopedia
ZNW. Zeitschrift für N. T. Wissenschaft

J. C. Beker, "Pastoral Letters," *IDB*, III.
H. D. Betz, "Orthodoxy and Heresy in Primitive Christianity," *Interpretation*, XIX (1965).
E. J. Bickerman, "The Historical Foundations of Postbiblical Judaism," in L. Finkelstein (ed.), *The Jews: Their History, Culture, and Religion*, I.
M. Black, "Pharisees," *IDB*, III.
C. Bosley, "The State Religion of Rome at the Time of the Christ," *The History of Christianity in the Light of Modern Knowledge*.
T. A. Burkill, "Sanhedrin" *IDB*, IV.

G. B. Caird, "John, Letters of," *IDB*, II.

L. Cerfaux, "The Pastoral Epistles," in A. Robert and A. Feuillet (eds.), *Introduction to the New Testament* (English).

K. Clark, "Worship in the Jerusalem Temple after A.D. 70," *New Testament Studies*, VI (1959–60).

M. A. Cohen, "The First Century as Jewish History," in J. Philip Hyatt (ed.), *The Bible in Modern Scholarship*.

H. Conzelmann, "The First Century as Christian History," in J. Philip Hyatt (ed.), *The Bible in Modern Scholarship*.

A. Cronbach, "Worship in NT Times, Jewish," *IDB*, IV.

D. Daube, "Rabbinic Methods of Interpretation and Hellenistic Rhetoric," *Hebrew Union College Annual*, XXII (1949).

W. D. Davies, "Law in the N T," *IDB*, III.

———, "Paul and Judaism," in J. Philip Hyatt (ed.), *The Bible in Modern Scholarship*.

S. J. De Vries, "Sin, sinners," *IDB*, IV.

J. D. Eisenstein, "Shema," *JE*, XI.

M. S. Enslin, "Paul and Gamaliel," *Journal of Religion*, VII (1927).

F. V. Filson, "Judaizing," *IDB*, II.

V. P. Furbish, "The Jesus-Paul Debate: From Baur to Bultmann," *Bulletin of the John Rylands Library*, March 1965.

T. H. Gaster, "Demon," *IDB*, I.

———, "Samaritans," *IDB*, IV.

J. Goldin, "The Period of the Talmud," in L. Finkelstein (ed.), *The Jews*.

E. R. Goodenough, "Philo Judaeus," *IDB*, III.

R. M. Grant, "The Study of Early Christianity," in Paul Ramsey (ed.), *Religion*, 1965.

K. Grayston, "Sermon on the Mount," *IDB*, IV.

J. Gutmann, "The 'Second Commandment' and the Image in Judaism," *Hebrew Union College Annual*, XXXII (1961).

A. Guttmann, "The End of the Jewish Sacrificial Cult," *Hebrew Union College Annual*, XXXVIII (1967).

E. G. Hirsch, "High Priest," *JE*, VI.

H. Jonas, "Response [on Gnosticism]," in J. Phillip Hyatt (ed.), *The Bible in Modern Scholarship*.

J. Kaster, "Education," *IDB*, II.

P. Katz, "The O T Canon in Palestine and Alexandria," *ZNW*, 1956.

W. L. Knox, "Abraham and the Quest for God," *Harvard Theological Review*, XXVIII (1935).

K. Kuiper, "Le poète juif Ezéchiel," *Revue des Etudes Juives* (Old Series), 1903.

J. Z. Lauterbach, "The Sadducees and Pharisees: A Study of Their Respective Attitudes towards the Law," *Studies in Jewish Literature Issued in Honor of Prof. Kaufmann Kohler, 1913*.

R. Marcus, "Recent Literature on Philo (1924–1934)," in S. W. Baron and A. Marx (eds.), *Jewish Studies in Memory of George A. Kohut*, 1935.

——, "A Selected Bibliography (1920–1945) of the Jews in the Hellenistic-Roman Period," *Proceedings of the American Academy for Jewish Research*, XVI (1947).

G. F. Moore, "Christian Writers on Judaism," *Harvard Theological Review*, XIV (1921).

J. Ouellette, "Le deuxième commandement et le rôle de l'image dans la symbolique religieuse de l'ancient testament essai d'interprétation," *Revue Biblique*, LXXIV (1967).

P. Parker, "Rabbi," *IDB*, IV.

R. H. Pfeiffer, "Canon," *IDB*, I.

G. Quispel, "Gnosticism and the New Testament," in J. Philip Hyatt (ed.), *The Bible in Modern Scholarship*.

C. C. Richardson, "Worship in N T Times, Christian," *IDB*, IV.

E. Rivkin, "Ben Sira and the Nonexistence of the Synagogue: A Study in Historical Method," in Daniel Jeremy Silver (ed.), *In the Time of Harvest: Essays in Honor of Abba Hillel Silver on the Occasion of his 70th Birthday*.

J. M. Robinson, "Kerygma and History in the New Testament," in J. Philip Hyatt (ed.), *The Bible in Modern Scholarship*.

S. Safrai, "Ha-ᶜir ha- yehudit b'-eretz yisrael bi-teḥufat ha-mishna veha-talmud," *Ha-ᶜir veha- qehila*, 1968.

L. Salvatorelli, "From Locke to Reitzenstein: the Historical Investigation of the Origins of Christianity," *Harvard Theological Review*, XXII (1929).

S. Sandmel, "Abraham's Knowledge of the Existence of God," *Harvard Theological Review*, XLIV (1951).

——, "Myths, Genealogies, and Jewish Myths and the Writing of Gospels," *Hebrew Union College Annual*, XXVII (1956).

——, "Isaac Mayer Wise's 'Jesus Himself,' " *Essays in American Jewish History: To Commemorate the Tenth Anniversary of the Founding of the American Jewish Archives.*

——, "Judaism, Jesus, and Paul: Some Problems of Method in Scholarly Research," *Vanderbilt Studies in the Humanities,* I (1951).

——, "Parallelomania," *JBL,* LXXXI (March 1962).

——, "Prolegomena to a Commentary on Mark," *JBR,* XXXI (1963).

——, "Son of Man," in Daniel Jeremy Silver (ed.), *In the Time of Harvest: Essays in Honor of Abba Hillel Silver on the Occasion of his 70th Birthday.*

——, "Understanding and Misunderstanding: Prepossession versus Malice," *Dialog, A Journal of Theology,* August 1967.

——, "The Jewish Scholar and Early Christianity," *Jewish Quarterly Review,* 75th anniversary volume (1967).

——, "The Confrontation of Greek and Jewish Ethics: Philo, De Decalogo," *CCAR Journal,* January 1968.

M. Smith, "Jesus' Attitudes Toward the Law," *Fourth World Congress of Jewish Studies Papers,* I.

I. Sonne, "Synagogue," *IDB,* IV.

V. [A.] Tcherikover, "General Observations," *Sefer Zikkaron le-Johanan Lewy* (Hebrew).

E. E. Urbach, "The Laws of Idolatry in the Light of Historical Facts in the Third Century," *Eretz Israel,* V (1958).

——, "Class-Status and Leadership in the World of the Palestinian Sages," *Israel Academy of Sciences and Humanities,* II (1966).

——, "Ha-mesorot 'al torat ha-sod bi-tequfat ha-tannaim," *Mehqarim be-qabala uve-toldot ha-datot mugashim le-Gershom Shalom,* 1968.

R. M. Wilson, "Response [on Gnosticism]," in J. Philip Hyatt (ed.), *The Bible in Modern Scholarship.*

S. Zeitlin, "The Crucifixion of Jesus Re-Examined," *JQR,* XXXVIII, 1947–48.

Index of Subjects

Index of Names